SPECIAL
DELIVERY

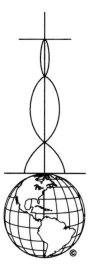

**Learn to Overcome, Grow Stronger and Break
The Repetitive Cycles that Hold You Back In Life.**

James A. Harrison

Special Delivery
Learn to Overcome, Grow Stronger and Break
The Repetitive Cycles that Hold You Back In Life.

Printed in the United States of America

Published By:
Balanced Life Publications, LLC
PO Box 166
Aberdeen, Ms. 39730

ISBN 978-0-9821575-0-3

Book Design by www.KarrieRoss.com
Cover background image from istockphoto.com

Dedication

It is my prayer that within this book you will find encouragement and strength through the very simple things in life that we take for granted so easily each and every day. Everywhere we look we see problems, people at war, our economy in crisis, broken families, loss of direction, natural disasters, lack of joy, dishonesty, envy and greed!

Where does this list stop? I can tell you where it begins and ends. It all begins in our hearts as a child and it will end upon the instruction of God to His only begotten Son, Jesus Christ in His return!!

What has happened to our society? Is it that we have become too tolerant of wrong for what is right? How easy is it to lose our perspective in life? Have you ever thought you did not miss anything in your path but found out at a later date you were mistaken? Were you willing to bet your life on it but later had to swallow your pride? Wouldn't it be sad to have all the ingredients but miss the <u>one</u> key ingredient causing your recipe in life to come up short?

There comes a point that everyone needs to slow down and just breathe to maintain our balance in life. I pray that whoever reads this book is touched in some way to spark a fire we seem to have lost in order to find new strength for our children's future.

How can we honestly expect heat without fuel for the fire? Even if we have fuel it is not worth anything if we don't understand the importance of God's direction through Jesus Christ!!

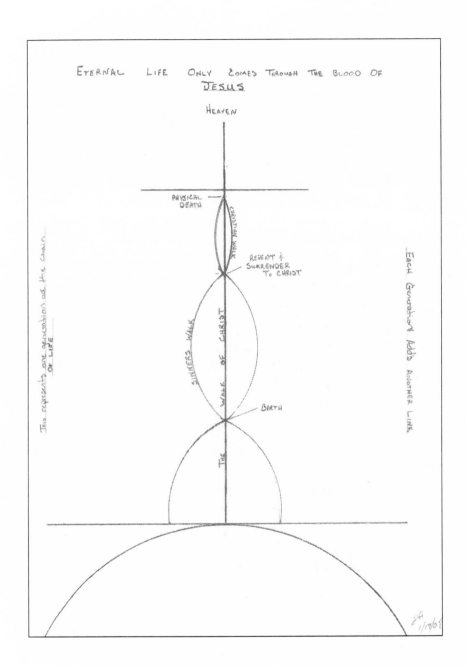

The Symbol

hen you look upon this symbol picture the one body on top of the world under the cross. There are three parts to the body that represent our human walk of life from the beginning in the book of Genesis to the end in the book of Revelation. The straight line of the cross is the walk of Jesus Christ that never swayed in this world of sin. While the other three parts of the body represent different periods of time under God that are the walks of life in the flesh of man.

The legs are the period of time at birth prior to Noah in representing how far away from the Lord we drifted before the great flood cleared the way once again. Within the body the path became closer as we matured with Moses as he was given the instruction of God to follow and obey while the Lord guided their path. But still the walk of life never reached the line that the Lord instructed to follow. So, the Lord sent His only begotten Son to clear the way home due to our sway in our walk of life. At this point in the head of the body the Lord Jesus taught us first hand how to bring our life closer to the Lord in our walk of life with the Holy Spirit guiding our path. But still our walk never can be as straight and pure in this world of sin causing us to struggle in our balance of life. There is only one way to balance in this world under God at the cross with Jesus Christ teaching us how to be one body of believers without separation.

This symbol and now trademark of Balanced Life Publications has a very interesting lesson behind it. The lesson being,

"Even if you have little or nothing
then you still have everything over the world
with Jesus Christ in our life."

In the design of this symbol there were three main items used due to limited resources at hand. All I had in material items were a Tupperware bowl, a ruler, and a lid from an instant coffee container. But there is something far greater that brought it all together in the creativity that God gives to each of us when we open our eyes and ears to hear the message within the wind.

Diamond In The Rough

I once overheard a story of a man that owned some beautiful land with running brooks and streams throughout his property. He decided to leave his land in search of other treasures in diamonds. He went on to sell his property with high hopes and ambitions of finding the diamonds he was looking for. The new owners of the land were enjoying the streams one afternoon and stumbled upon a large beautiful stone. They took it home and placed it on their mantle. Later, at some point, they were informed the stone was a diamond in the rough. This diamond went on record to be one of the largest diamonds in history.

How ironic is it that the original land owner, who sold his property in search of diamonds, left the very piece of land he lived on in search for something he did not see or even search for before he left? Isn't this the story of our life? We had it but could not even see it. Instead of taking the time to understand and putting forth the hard work and dedication it takes to achieve our goals we look in every place except for the one we already have within our reach.

Once we discover our
diamond in the rough, it takes time
and daily polishing to make
it shine!

Seasons

Seasons come and seasons go
Within each season we can relate
To our lives when we open our eyes
And begin to feel the real reason why
Winter brings comfort
Spring brings life
Summer brings joy
And Fall brings peace.
There is a purpose within each season
That we often fail to recall
When you study the Word of God
You will discover the true reason
For the season and hear God's call
It is within the wind of each season
That you will begin to hear God's whisper
And feel the Lord guiding us to our future.

The season has come to repent and regain our unity in where we stand in Christ. It is time to appreciate what the Lord has given us within each season of change and within our homes. In (Ecclesiastes 3) Solomon wrote **"For everything there is a season and a time"**.

Introduction

Throughout our life we are faced with many hurdles and sometimes even walls. Does this mean we are to give up? Absolutely not!!! When we face obstacles in life there is a reason and even a purpose behind each of them but we often fail to truly understand or recognize this, so we continue facing the same hurdles over and over.

How do we break this cycle of events or emotions that we seem to face so often? How do we pick ourselves up when we have been knocked down? How do we overcome the hurt or emptiness that we may be feeling inside? How do we grow stronger in our walk each day?

To overcome, grow stronger or break that repetitive cycle we must dissect our circumstances on an individual basis and learn how to turn our negative circumstance into a positive learning experience. Once we learn to do this we can overcome any obstacle that we ever face or that we might face in the future by always knowing where to stand.

There is a reason and a purpose in everything in life. Some things we can explain and others we can't. When we don't seem to have the answers or we can't seem to pick ourselves up this is when we must completely surrender in believing and having faith to overcome our challenges. Our problem is that we are by birth weak and we are always looking for physical answers and looking for that easy way out by thinking we hold or have all the answers. In my life one of the hardest bridges to cross was learning how to stand on the edge, let it go and realize that we are not the ones in control! What we have in us is the ability to learn and retain, but what we receive is just passed through us. Think about it, where would we be without ever having books or being taught? Don't neglect the Holy Bible, where it all began.

Before we begin this journey and discover how to overcome negative circumstances, no matter how big or small, it is important to insure the person leading the discussion has credible experiences and qualifications. It is equally important to make sure their topics and circumstances are in relation to your beliefs and goals in life. With this said, I feel <u>unworthy</u> but <u>overqualified!</u> ***It is not our place to judge upon what someone might have done but to understand what someone might have learned.*** How can we expect to learn something when we are totally focused on the problem?

How many of us fall into this category of only seeing the bad in people verses finding the good in them? It is easy for us to fall into this because it is what our surroundings focus on. How many of us give up on something without really giving an all out effort to understand and repair? Would you agree that everything is repairable when we believe? To believe in something we have to have faith. In (Mark 9) Jesus said, **"Anything is possible if a person believes"**.

We must remember and understand that the process to repair and rebuild is discovered by what and why something first failed. It is very important that we understand there is a reason and even a purpose for why something went wrong. Our problem, by majority, is that we had rather throw it away and move on to something new. We become lazy and impatient rather than searching for the truth.

Everyone has an experience in their life which can inspire and possibly help someone else. The experiences can be of negative and/or positive circumstances. All of us can relate to some sort of negative experience in our life, rather big or small. Unfortunately, some of us seem to have more than our share. Why is that? Is it because some of us lost our direction? Is it because some of us know when and where to stand while others don't? Is it because some of us are weak in some areas but strong in others? There is a reason why something works or fails but that doesn't mean the things that fail can't be repaired. It takes time and dedication to overcome failure. Someone once said, "Failure is just an event, never a person". There is a relation between failure from sin verses failure from an experiment and both require totally different methods to solve. They are similar in the process or formula in learning what and why something went wrong but totally different in the way to correct the problem. This is not to say the road to personal recovery is pain free because it requires personal sacrifice, true acceptance and sincere repentance to gain the true purpose in life. In other words, expect pain if you ever plan to gain. The relationship between the two processes is vital to discover the root of infection leading back to the success of the experiment or road to recovery.

Our country, the United States of America, has allowed an infection to grow out of control and this is something man cannot correct without understanding and repentance from the heart with God! By allowing our doors to be open and neglecting who holds the single key through His Father that was placed at our door for a reason, has allowed this all to happen. All of this begins in our homes on an individual basis and then will spread like wildfire over time to our nation in finding direction with new strength!

It is very easy to lose our direction when we follow what society continues to show and this is where we must stop ourselves to regroup with the Word of God to understand the overall picture of life. Once this process starts we will not only see a difference but even feel a difference!

To better understand this book, imagine it like a family reunion that you continue to miss after several years of excuses and this time you must attend. Sometimes you may not like to hang out at a family reunion and relive where you have been in your life when you have so many other things going on. This is where we begin to lose touch within the unity of the family. Once you finally make that step and join in you can smell the sweet aroma of all the best dishes someone could bring to the table, while everyone sits around to sample the one that has never failed to be so good!

There is no need for fine china or crystal glasses with all the family and friends because by everyone knowing the roots of your foundation and there is no "Stained Glass Masquerade" to cover the real you, this allows conversation and sincere joy from the heart in recalling your childhood memories while enjoying that <u>one</u> dish that fills every void in your heart and soul.

The most memorable, touching and filling meals in life are not eaten off of fine china; instead they are eaten off of paper plates that aren't quiet as fancy as all the rest! These are the meals with your family and friends that weigh in above all the rest! Like the buffet at the reunion, when you go back to the table for seconds or thirds you're always going to find something more.

I know this book might not be perfectly written, due to my own lack of education, but I can assure you of one thing, if you will open your heart and listen to what is being said then you will feel something not of man but from the wisdom of God. The Holy Bible is like that perfect dish at the family reunion. It gives us a thirst and hunger for more and we will continue to go back to it, craving all we can get.

This book is the paper plate that has been used and dropped a few times. The author has stains and marks for where he has been. The one thing that a paper plate has that fine china doesn't is that it can be dropped over and over and still serve it's purpose, feeding the people in need. It has the right product to hold it together. When this book began to come together my life was a spiritual struggle. Now, with the understanding I have searched for my entire life, I can tell you without a doubt that anyone can overcome anything in life with faith and the belief in God through Jesus Christ! There comes a point when we all must let go of the flesh of our humanistic selves to feel the spirit of God whispering upon our hearts. With God we have every-thing we ever need and without God our time is limited in life, never understanding how to be truly free!!

I don't know about you but I enjoy every meal ever given to me, especially on those paper plates. There is a time for fine china and a time for paper plates when we understand how to keep our perspective in life!

Table of Contents

CHAPTER 1

Personal Repentance

I would like to share with you what has been passed on to me and how I've overcome hardships by learning proper balance in my life, and possibly help someone going through stress or heartaches of their own. There is no doubt in my heart that there is a purpose for what we experience and go through in life. For there is NO WAY that I would be alive today if there wasn't a reason and a purpose for me not to overcome my personal experiences physically, mentally and spiritually.

The strength and wisdom I have received did not come from degrees, a solid home or teachers but from one book, the Holy Bible, and from God in divine understanding and providing me with everything to make this all possible. I want to thank everyone who has ever believed in me and who has never stopped praying for me but I owe my life to the Lord for the wisdom and strength which He has given me to overcome every obstacle in my life and most of all for the opportunity to live again through His son, Jesus Christ.

Being that I have been blessed with a little time on my hands I have completely analyzed my life and I can see where He did not ever leave me but I lost my direction and left Him. I was guided properly as a child but then I became lost in the wilderness of this world, hurting and searching. Ever since my home was broken up as a young child, I have had a burning desire to retrieve the love that was lost. My burning desire to regain love caused me to search in all the wrong places. Therefore making wrong decisions and trying to buy love through worldly possessions. I knew the feeling but I just didn't know how to retrieve it. I searched for every material thing that my parents or others had shown me prior to my fall.

Being a young child, having the right foundation early in life, I found myself still vulnerable to the world due to not having the maturity and strength to stand alone against everything that came my way. When my foundation was broken at home it led me to trying to achieve happiness in what so many of us today fall subject to. When I saw someone happy with all of their material things I went searching for them only to discover how short lived they were compared to what I once had as a child, my genuine feeling of love.

When my foundation of love was lost or taken from me as a child it was like taking a good tootsie roll pop from a kid's mouth, just when he is getting a good taste of it. This will make anyone mad and it created my desire to get it back. Don't fool yourself and think it wouldn't make you angry too. Just try taking candy from a child after they have already received a taste of it and see how upsetting it will be to the both of you. The child will do whatever is necessary to gain his candy back and you will probably give in to stop the crying.

When the love was taken from me as a child, I made up my mind to do everything I could to get it back! Making sure no one would ever take it from me again. I got my tootsie roll pop back but not quite as I had planned. The problem was, without proper guidance, a solid foundation and understanding I did not know how, due to immaturity. This is in direct relation to the parable of the lost sheep in (Luke 15) of the Holy Bible. Jesus tells us of a shepherd with over one hundred sheep. What would he do if one of them gets lost along the way? Would the shepherd think "What will I do, forget it and move on?" Knowing that he still has ninety nine other sheep and it doesn't really matter. Shouldn't he stay with the herd and send a group of men after it? Think about the meaning of Christianity and its purpose. Wouldn't you look for or even send someone after your lost child? Or do you just write them off because you have enough to deal with already? How do you think the other brothers and sisters in the family should feel upon the success of finding the lost one? Would they be angry, sad or full of sincere joy? As Christians, they should rejoice when reunited. My personal problem was that I lost my herd on the trail and I grew up wild in the wilderness. As I matured in life I turned from my ways and began looking for my way back. I felt lonely and scared at times. There were even times when I didn't know where I was going to sleep. This did not make me quit trying though because I knew that I wanted that feeling of security and love all over again!

Think about a time in your life when you might have been lost. How did you feel? What about a time of losing a child in the grocery store. What would you have done to get them back? Let's think about it another way. How hard would you swim of you felt that you were drowning? Would you not grab a hold of anything within reach and try to stay afloat? How do you save someone in a panic? Sometimes you have to take extreme measures to calm them and maybe even save their life. This is where I failed on numerous occasions by putting my arms around a worldly float instead of the solid one, being Jesus Christ. My intentions were always good but because my foundation lacked understanding during a large period of my life, I often slipped and eventually fell. There could not have been any better timing for the fall because of the age I was and now knowing that it was in God's perfect timing, not mans. I always knew there would be a day, either in this life or the next that I would have to answer for my sins and pay for my wrong-doings. There is no way that everything would have happened as it did without there being not only a needed lesson to be received but also one to be revealed.

Have you ever read the story of the donkey speaking in Balaam in the book of Numbers in the Holy Bible? Although I deserved to be kicked and beaten for my sins, unlike the donkey, never underestimate where the message will or might come from. The Lord plainly tells us that He will take something unworthy and make it have worth to serve His purpose. I am guilty...but forgiven! I thank God for the foundation I received as a child because this is what pulled me through every storm I have had to face and I owe this to my mother and to my grandparents. By having received the Lord early in life, it was like having a rope tied to my float. Every time my float began to sink, the rope, which was Christ's hand, would reach down to pull me back up. Each time that I surfaced I knew to look for love but failed to know where to look and to be patient. Because of my hurt I would grab hold of the nearest thing floating, only to sink all over again. I could always hear the call to swim, through the love of Christ, but I just couldn't stop my panic of drowning. I had no solid home and didn't know how to truly begin.

Throughout my life I have experienced many trials and tribulations. My life can be seen in three major stages with a few years separating each one. The second stage of learning to look within myself is when my life really began all over again. The first intervention came after an uneventful life when I was running wild without any guidance or direction. I felt like I couldn't take it anymore. I was ready to give up, being basically homeless, jobless, with minimum education and with a majority of my family even turning from me. There were only two people who never gave up on me. They were my grandparents on my mother's side of the family. When I had nowhere else to go they offered me a place to stay, a home. One night when I was living on my own, with tears falling like rain, I put a rifle to my mouth and cried out with a broken heart in prayer to the Lord asking Him for help and to help me to get through this pain I carried. At that moment I laid the rifle down. The very next morning my strength began with wisdom and motivation like I could never explain until now. I became focused, bought a planner, created a game plan and within two weeks I had a job forming a verbal partnership bringing new products to the table for an existing company that was struggling to survive.

Every since that dark lonely night, with the brightest stars above me, my life in business and marketing became unstoppable, I thought. I began paying attention to detail with a vibrant thirst, gaining a hunger to learn like I never had before and had the determination to make everything better in my life and in anyone else's that I possibly could. This is where my lack of understanding and maturity became dangerous. There were large amounts of money to be made and it was all in my grasps.

The second intervention came a few years later when I had to learn how to stand on my own and quit letting individuals abuse me emotionally. I learned to look within myself and pay more attention to the objectives and intentions of the people that I surrounded myself with. Accepting people for who they really were and realizing that a person has to be willing to receive help before they can be helped, was a hard lesson learned. Most people have no problem receiving material things but when it comes to welcoming advice, you had better be cautious. During this period of my life I filled my emotional void with bought friends. When I finally stood up for myself and broke my false ties with a certain few all of the others drifted away as well.

It was shortly after this point when I received the third intervention in my life. The Lord quickly intervened and blessed me with the love of my life! He brought us together on a blind date and the Lord's plan began from this point in restoring my home to eventually help others. We all travel the wrong roads at times but when your heart is sincere you will persevere. The Lord blessed us both by fulfilling what we had yearned for in our hearts with a partner giving love and compassion. ***I will always say that she is my angel that led me back home.*** Like the rest of us, she had her faults as well and has never claimed otherwise. Nor has she ever thought of herself as being better than anyone else. She has a sincere and genuine heart that had been walked on just as mine had.

Here is the good part of where God brought us together, after thirty years of searching for each other. The last place that I can recall feeling that sincere love and comfort of a solid home was at a cabin my parents had purchased on Pickwick Lake located on the Tennessee River prior to their divorce. Behind our cabin was a beautiful creek that ran right through the back yard. You could hear it in the cabin at night with the windows opened. To this day I can still hear the sprinkles of water hitting the rocks. When my parents divorced, I was about nine years old, my heart was shattered and since then I have found myself being pulled back to Pickwick Lake for that comforting feeling that I once lost. The desire that I had was so strong that I fell guilty of doing whatever it took to get back there once again. Little did I ever know this is where I would regain the love I had once lost as a child.

I will never forget on a cold winter day my wife and I sat in my vehicle below the Pickwick Dam enjoying a good old fashioned milkshake while overlooking the calm waters of the Tennessee River and sharing conversation. This day came only after knowing her for a week or so and then these words were placed on my heart to share with her, "You have something to give to me that I lost so long ago." Little did I know that what I was saying was so true, I really never understood the meaning of what I had said until now. This is when I began to learn the true meaning of what love really is and where it all derives from.

At this point in my life things began to change and gain purpose! It was time to turn what I had been wasting into something and to overcome where I had been. This love we shared gave me a burning desire to change my past and build it into something that would last. Now knowing that I not only had a home but finally my children could receive their needs. Little did I know how Jesus began to work in my heart, giving me the drive that wouldn't stop! Within this third stage of my life came the fall and the Lord getting my attention. By humbling me once again and my heart being broken He gave me a true understanding with purpose for my future ahead. This is where I am now, learning who is truly in control, how to let it go and learning how to use my gifts the way God wants me to and not for my own recognition. To God's glory, not man's!!!

There is a difference when something is based on human desires instead of when we allow God to bring things together in His timing and not in ours. So many times we fail due to not involving or putting the Lord first in our lives. We can see signs of this in every direction we turn but the problem is that we want to think we are the ones in control. We are constantly trying to take God out of the picture and rely only on what we can actually see. This is our human weakness. When you study the Holy Bible you will find that this is nothing new and history keeps repeating itself. **How can we expect to have a relationship without a true understanding? Without any understanding there is NO relationship!**

Many individuals think, like me at one point, that we can just take one part of the puzzle and start on our own. How many times have you had to tear your puzzle of life apart only to start all over again? Or what about struggling to put your own puzzle of life together? This is exactly what I have done throughout my life by grabbing hold of the false things of this world instead of recognizing the Lord in my life and the foundation in which He gives us in the rock of Jesus Christ.

Throughout my life I have encountered many unfortunate hurdles, which have fortunately, by the grace of God, given me much needed wisdom with each lesson. Not only how they affected me mentally and physically but also how our choices will and can affect others. It is one thing to suffer pain on an individual basis but even far worse when it spreads to others!!

Before sharing with you what I have learned I want to share with you my personal desires which have been, and I pray to always be, my goals in life. I would be lying if I said that I never swayed on my standards or that I didn't lose control at one point in my life but one thing to always remember is that when someone is put into the fire his roots will prevail.

Many people look at success as having materialistic things and this is where we all fall short from time to time. I define success as learning from my mistakes or wrong doings, always striving to improve, laughing often, sharing with others and respecting our time in life. I believe it is a blessing to be loved, to have children, to have a family, to have our freedom, being able to help others and most of all having a relationship with God through Jesus Christ our Savior.

When you read my descriptions of success and blessings ask yourself if you agree with me or not? We all can add more but do you agree with the principal beliefs? If so, let me pass on to you what has been passed on to me. To possibly open your eyes in a way that mine has now been opened. To overcome the many obstacles in my life I have to attribute my passion and desire to the love of Christ for achieving the success and blessings that I previously described. The blessings have never stopped through all of the trials and heartaches I have had to overcome because I never gave up on the one thing in life that I knew was right in my belief and faith. In fact, the closer I come to my understanding the more I begin to recognize the Lord's presence throughout my life and even in the darkest of times when I thought I was all alone.

This may come to shock many but I can honestly sit here where I am today, in a prison camp, and tell you that I am at peace, internally, more than I have ever been before. ***There is great joy in recognizing where you are spiritually and how to overcome where you have been no matter where you are in life.*** This is not to say that I don't hurt for what I have done or caused and especially being separated from my family. I know the person that I am on the inside, never intentionally meaning to hurt anyone, but like many others from time to time I failed to think about the affects of my wrong decisions. Sometimes out of desperation we make wrong decisions trying to overcome our issues in life and this is like building on sifting sand without analyzing the foundation on which it stands. The Lord warns us of this but I failed to truly understand the meaning of it all, until now.

It is very easy to get wrapped up in our own world and not realize how we may affect other people without intention when making our decisions. Once you begin to roll down a hill it is very difficult to stop the momentum when people around you are pushing and steadily depending only on you. The fact of the matter is that there is no excuse or justification in making wrong choices when we know what we are doing is wrong. Because wrong is wrong and right is right. It is that simple and anything else is just an excuse! Some choices need a clear understanding before we move forward and this is often where many individuals come up short. It is very easy to be impatient rather than understanding the purpose of time.

I will always have regret for the poor choices I have made in my life but I will never carry shame for the way in which I have handled them. Individuals need to remember that it takes time to heal and walk again once you have been wounded. There is a difference between a wound and a scratch. Both take different amounts of time to heal.

I thank God for sending His son, Jesus Christ, to wash our sins away allowing me to live again and for the time I have spent in this camp being able to study His word to fully discover my purpose in life.

When we make wrong decisions in life it is important to remember that it is how we handle them that determines who we are. I ask you, "What type of person are you? Are you someone who gives up easily when knocked down or are you a fighter when it comes to survival?" I will be the first to tell you that I am a fighter and God is in my corner!

Behind every fighter or survivor in life you will find a spirit that made them rise and overcome any fall they ever may have faced. The spirit which has carried me through every fight in my life is the Holy Spirit. The day I opened my heart and accepted our Messiah, Jesus Christ, as my savior was a day when I was just a young child before my childhood home was ever broken. As I grew up I climbed through the ropes and into the ring of this world without direction. Jesus was in my corner and the Holy Spirit was telling me not to make the choices I did. I never understood this until now. Every time I fell He picked me right back up and put be back together for another lesson learned. Some of my fights and challenges were near fatal. Many people around me never expected me to survive but little did I know there was a reason for me to experience all that I did. There finally came a point when I just had to completely surrender all and because Christ never left my corner, He was able to throw in the blood stained towel for me to live another day! I had to realize that I couldn't stand in the ring of this world on my own anymore and finally tapped out. Sometimes it takes getting knocked slap out before we can regain sight once again. It is sad when we don't know our position and we feel that we are a heavyweight champ like Muhammad Ali but in all actuality we are nothing more than a water boy. *No matter what your circumstance may be, never quit and always remember that as long as you have breath, there is hope and the ability to overcome anything as long as you have Jesus in your corner. WITH GOD IN OUR LIVES ALL THINGS ARE POSSIBLE!!! Never give up or surrender to the material things of this earth or man but surrender to Christ and everything else will begin to come back together in time!*

The lord has blessed me with vision, creativity, an eye for detail and the ability to do anything that I set my mind to, within my limits. In previous years I did not fully understand these blessings and I even abused them on multiple occasions. Now that I have an understanding of where our blessings truly derive from, it breaks my heart to know that I not only hurt man but I hurt God our Father. I always acknowledged my talents as blessings from the Lord but I did not use them always in true productive ways. If you try to do something good but it starts out originally in sin, how can you expect it to ever be worthy of His praise? You cannot get back on the right foundation without some kind of sacrifice. This is exactly why I am here, to be realigned, learn to appreciate my time and to understand the word of God.

In (Isaiah 57) God says to clear away the rocks and stones and rebuild the road. He restores the crushed spirit of the humble and revives the courage of those with repentant hearts. God continues to say that He will not fight against you forever and will not always be angry. He will comfort those who mourn and bring praise to their lips. This, sums up everything more than I could ever say. All praise to God Almighty!

Now that I look back I can see my purpose of having to experience the challenges and face everything that I have had to face.

I want to break my father's chain of defiance of sin and teach my children and anyone else who will listen to what I have learned before anyone else suffers as I have in my past. Looking back now I can only humbly smile and kick myself in the rear for not seeing the picture or even trying to interpret the writing on the wall.

In developing and marketing I have always said that they are like building a home. Some individuals can see it before they ever begin, some can't see it until the walls are up and others can't see it until it is completely finished or even lived in. I prided myself in this vision but now I am humbled because I fell subject to being the person who couldn't see the real picture until it was almost too late. How many times must we hit snooze before finally waking up? Believe me, I have hit it one time too many. Now I can finally see the whole picture with the writing on the wall and I am SOLD!

The verse taken from **(Isaiah 55)** says, **"For just as the heavens are higher than the earth, so my ways are higher than your ways and my thoughts higher than your thoughts"**. Throughout my life I have tried to fit God into my mold, attempting to make his plans conform to mine. This is where I was a fool by not striving to fit into His plans. Have you ever felt guilty of this or can you relate with this in someone else's life? Have you ever witnessed someone who continues to have a cycle of events in their life but they won't listen?

The vision and creativity that the Lord gave to me lead me to designing and developing things in my own unique natural way. I was inspired by God to see the natural beauty of this earth and to make the most of whatever I had but I failed to understand proper steps in time to reach what He revealed to me. The drive I had was so intense to get away from where I was and make things better in life that it got out of control. I took pride in every foundation I developed but a house won't stand on wood and concrete alone. It is destined to fall if it isn't built on a firm foundation of God.

Trying to overcome my obstacles and hopefully making things right, was my plan. Some people are able to do this while others stumble and fall. The Lord had another plan for me that I always felt in my heart but neglected to try to understand. This is the funny part, in the past I would tell my wife that I wished I could just go sit in a room somewhere, with everyone leaving me alone, to see what I could creatively come up with. I just never meant for it to be under such restrictions. Another funny part is that I am still pushed for time to meet my daily schedule and when 'count-time' is called it is like being disrupted by a phone call. But there is one major difference now…I understand my position!!

For several years now I have always felt that I could possibly write a book. There are chapter titles written from over ten years ago and even short writing's that I've written and published in local papers. The Lord has given me nibbles of the bait but I never locked in and took it home voluntarily until now. *For the record, if you hear the Lord's call I would strongly advise you to listen because one way or another He will have the final word!*

We can compare life to a mathematical equation. The formula was originally given to Moses and after numerous attempts to solve or follow; we never fully understood the answer. In the original formula, being the Old Covenant, if there was even one negative then the whole thing was wrong. After years of trying to guide us and show us the answer the Lord sent His only begotten Son to ultimately teach and fulfill the law completing the formula, giving us everlasting life. The formula given to Moses cannot be fulfilled by man because we are all born with a sinful nature. This formula and chain of events was broken by Christ and He gives us the answer to the ultimate reward.

Do not repeat what I have done by nibbling on the hook. Grab the bait and travel the sea. God doesn't want us to have slack in our line. The true fisherman, in Heaven above, will release the drag in proper timing and bless us according to His will. So swim freely with the unbreakable line of Christ and build on the right foundation of love, honor and respect for God. *Don't walk over or neglect your own personal diamond in the rough. Everyone has their own unique shine once they have been refined. If you hold steady in your refining process, He will give you the ultimate shine.*

Before going any further, I want to clarify something very important. Please do not take or receive what has been written as any form of arrogance. I don't want to be perceived as such. I have always felt a message has been placed on my heart but I never understood it until now. There is no way I would know what to do, nor how to overcome the things I have without God revealing it to me.

I pray that each individual who reads this book will open their hearts and ears to read the "Voice of Truth" in the Holy Bible to hear the same message that "I can see clearly now that the rain is gone" singing "Empty Me" of my pride in now being "Broken and Beautiful". The rain that is gone is the fog of this world distorting our picture and purpose in life. Along with these song titles mentioned, I pray you will not only listen to them but most of all, read the Word of God, not only for yourselves but for our children's future. Sing songs of praise like "Lord God Almighty" saying Holy, Holy, Holy......

* * *

A Sinner's Prayer

Dear Lord our Father in Heaven,

I come to you as a child at heart asking for forgiveness from my sins in my life. I know that I have done wrong in many ways for which I am ashamed and deserve all blame. Please Lord forgive me for I am a sinner and I ask for another chance to prove myself from the heart in turning from my wrong ways to improve my future through the blood of Jesus in my heart and my new life to now start. I took you for granted Lord and neglected your Word in how to properly follow your guidance in understanding the purpose of obedience and self-discipline to truly succeed. I have committed many sins in my life that I regret and I no longer want to be the man I was. But to be only the person you want me to be. My life is no longer my life, it belongs to you!! I know in my heart through my belief in your Son, Jesus Christ, and feeling your Holy Spirit in my soul, you are teaching me the true meaning of being ONE!

Previously, I had one foot in your door and the other one still outside not wanting to take that step. I now understand what it takes to let it go and feel your love really begin to flow. Thank you Lord for everything you have given me and provided me in my life. I ask for you to lift me from this darkness so that I can live in your light. I am limited and restricted without you Lord, guiding my path and opening doors for me. I know without a doubt there are no limits to how high I can climb, with you in my life. So, please Lord, forgive my past ignorance and wrong thoughts, for I seek your eternal deliverance from this physical place, knowing and feeling your love in your mercy and grace.

Thank you Lord for everything in life, I pray for strength and wisdom going forward. I turn my load that I bare over to you and I pray that you will continue to show me the way each and every day, for you are just and fair in all ways. Please provide the guidance and I will provide the work in order to change my life into who you want me to be, learning the art of being free!

I thank you once again for your forgiveness in love and I forgive those who have ever hurt me as I have them. In Jesus name I pray, Amen.

CHAPTER 2

Snap Shot

*D*o you ever feel like you are losing control, someone is constantly pulling at you, you can't keep up, or your personal world just seems to be getting more demanding? What about ever feeling like you have no reason to continue, the odds are always stacked against you, your relationships never change or you just feel like there is something missing? Well, let me go ahead and hit the nail on the head. "This is just part of life, due to our human nature." Life is a constant struggle without the proper understanding, and can ever be more mentally testing today in trying to balance our time with how fast everything else is moving around us.

The demands of today have not changed from yesterday. What has changed is our mindset in trying to keep up. Cars keep getting faster, boats keep getting bigger, computer's change before they are even out of the box, buildings keep getting more luxurious, fashion changes constantly, and many individuals fall into this constantly looking for change. When we allow our culture control our thinking, it becomes very challenging and even dangerous. The two things that have not changed since the beginning of time are our directions and essentials to live. It is very easy to fall into the culture of this world and lose our perspective in life without proper knowledge or respect for what has been given by our creator, along with our founding fathers. When this happens we possibly can suffer many heartaches, and even death. One of the hardest things to ever do in life is learning how to balance what we have been given. To balance, we first must evaluate and accept what we have. Then study the directions or objectives to walk, and always keep our focus on where we stand. The most important factor in change is to know our foundation.

To balance life it is important to prepare for the winds ahead, and if prepared in where you stand then it doesn't matter if you fall. What matters is how you pick yourself up, and begin to walk all over again. Due to our society chasing constant change, and removing God out of our lives, it becomes very difficult, if not impossible to ever know where we stand. Life is short enough on its own, much less when we are chasing the wind. In order to balance within the wind of this world, it helps to know what we are dealing with in our surroundings, and ultimately know our foundation. Our American culture continues to expand in such way's that the original formula to life is being neglected, and even forgotten.

When you look at our current economic situation, and all the negative things that are continuing to happen, there is no doubt that we can see the results of getting away from what we have been given. This is not to say there are not some who do understand, but the ones that continue to stand out are the vast numbers who don't! There used to be a meaning behind every individuals name at birth, and now not only is there little meaning left behind their names, there seems to be a growing disregard for even life. When individuals neglect the Word of God and fail to teach the principles of life, don't expect things to get better but even worse! By taking love and respect out of life there is very little, if any reason, to even care. It is imperative that we teach our children to love one another, and respect what they have been given. By losing touch with our foundation and getting lost in our daily task, it helps to return to the roots or beginning to maintain strength in our balance.

Life is a beautiful thing from birth to this earth. Our country offers us a breath-taking environment when we open our eyes and begin to see. There is no creation that compares to what God has created, but often we need to go back to the beginning in understanding time.

Have you ever found yourself searching for an answer and then later realized that it was right in front of you the whole time? What about a time of asking someone a question, only to discover the answer before they even have a chance to speak? We all can relate to this at times, but for those times we can't find the answers, we often tend to search everywhere but in the right place to begin with.

It is in our human nature to look for short cuts rather than understanding and having faith in the Word of God. Just look at Sarah, Abraham's wife in the book of Genesis. In (Genesis 16) you will find consequences within Abraham's family that can be related directly to individuals today. When you look at the emotional consequences of Sarah, Hagar, and Abraham you can see directly the results of taking shortcuts rather than being patient for God to fulfill his promise. Our life is a daily battle of remembering that we are not the artists of this picture in life. Everyone wants the picture now, rather than giving the artist time to develop it! How many people do you see wandering or searching for a picture with no meaning? Some individuals are able to paint a picture by what they have been shown here in this world, but there is a major life and death difference between what's being taught here verses what is taught in the Word of God. Just look at the difference between the individuals who try to force something to happen in art verses those who discover the depth of love in the picture of life. When God guides, the artist does not stop with just one individual and the depth goes beyond what we can even see. What is art without meaning or purpose? When you remove passion within love from art, you will find no meaning or purpose in the end!

Our life can be compared to a puzzle and the picture we reflect can be taken from what has been given and even influenced our lives since birth. The puzzle can be complicated when we don't listen to our proper teachers and the true directions that guide each individual piece. Often, the problem in the picture can be determined by where we place our puzzle. Have you ever tried to assemble a puzzle on something not level or unstable? Did it not cause more work in attempting to hold it all together? Or, how long did it stand before the fall?

Before assembling a puzzle, it is very important to prepare for growth. As the puzzle begins to grow or take life, the stronger the footing will need to be. There comes a point in all growth, that we must evaluate our footing to maintain proper strength. There is only one way to have a footing that will last forever, and that is to stand with Christ under the cross, and follow what has already been given!

Our personal picture of life, which reflects on our puzzle, is compiled and formed piece by piece in the choices we make affecting our words and actions towards others. How many of you can recall a fork in your road of life? Do you ever recall a time of looking back and saying, "If I only would have taken the other path?" Everyone, on most occasions, can relate to this at some point in our life, believe me! Some individuals accept their decisions and consequences and move on, while others get stuck and dwell on the "what ifs." Ask yourself, "What are you really accomplishing when you dwell on the past?" If we only dwell on the past, we are not only hurting ourself, but we could possibly be robbing others of their joy in knowing how to move forward!

Can you imagine Adam and Eve's conversation after choosing the path they took? They had everything beyond what we can ever imagine, and it still wasn't enough. Can you relate to this feeling? When is enough, enough? When Eve was deceived into eating from the tree of knowledge of good and evil, she probably thought, "I'm not going to travel this road alone!" So, she convinced Adam into traveling with her by Adam falling weak in not standing on what God had instructed. From this very point our human nature became infected with the knowledge of evil. Causing us to think the grass is always greener on the other side of the fence.

Have you ever heard these words spoken, "I have what you want and here's a short cut to get there?" Everywhere you look, that is the message being shown. But we need to beware of the short cuts in life, because you never know where they may take you, or even cause you to come up short! Rather than following your wants, follow your needs.

Many individuals fail to acknowledge or ever neglect the effort that it takes to improve our own grass. It is easy to become lazy and only focus on what we must do in overlooking the importance of daily nutrition! But this is where we need to understand what it takes to improve our own yard in life. To make our life better we must follow true direction, take proper care, and understand the purpose of time. This is the root of it all, being the choices we make daily in our environment and what leads us to where we are today.

Individuals have often asked this question, "Why did the Lord place that one tree in the middle of the garden, and then instruct to not go near or eat of the fruit?" This is where we are taught the true meaning of love from the very beginning. How can we expect true love in return if we are directing it? True love can only be achieved through free will in the freedom of choice. Think about it. If someone instructs you to love them or someone else, is that love? When you don't consider the other party's feelings, how can this be showing love? True love comes only through sacrifice and putting your feelings behind another. The Lord truly revealed this to us in the sacrifice of His Son, Jesus Christ teaching us how to love in life!

In the Holy Bible, the Lord's characteristics are revealed in love and justice. This is taught throughout the entire Word of God with individuals following His Will, and with the fall of others who took matters into their own hands, against His instruction. This is where it helps to recall the meaning of love with justice. Everyone has the opportunity to turn their life around through the love of the Lord within his grace. Just look at the life of Lot, Abraham's nephew, or King Manasseh in the Holy Bible, with many others, to show God's mercy and how He brings about positive circumstances from wrong decisions. The Lord showed mercy and discipline throughout the Old

Testament and then ultimately taught through love in the physical presence with Jesus Christ.

When we evaluate our surroundings, we can see some individuals love to the point of excusing wrong actions, while others are right the opposite by forgetting love and only showing discipline. How many times have you seen someone give a child something to keep them quiet? When they give like this every time the child lashes out, what do you think this is teaching that child? Giving should be a reward earned and not always to pacify the real issue at hand! What about a time that you may have possibly witnessed someone only showing discipline without any compassion? Or, what about those who discipline and then give something in return besides love to make up for the hurt? All of this is very difficult to keep in balance, but vital to a child's life and their children's to come. The Lord teaches us to discipline through love and in love throughout the Holy Bible. There is a balance in this to constantly work on in every relationship and to maintain the maturity within growth giving strength in our homes.

Love without justice leaves people in their sins because it is not aiming or guiding them to reach better standards. And justice with only discipline shows no heart, leading individuals to have no care about themselves, much less others! When you read the Holy Bible from the Old Testament through the New Testament you will find a relationship between our Father in Heaven and us that parallels the feelings we show to our children. Imagine this. If you and your child were building something together and you spent many hours' everyday and even years constructing the same project. And then one day the unfortunate happens! The child loses their parent due to sudden death and they are left to complete the task all alone! Wouldn't you want your child to fulfill or carry on what you both were working on? If you could see your child sitting on the floor at the foot of the project in tears, would you whisper in their ear to pick them up from their hurt and guide them to complete the task you both began if you were able?

How proud would you feel if everyday your child went to work following your teaching on the project, especially if they continuously acknowledged you whispering from their heart saying, "I love you."

This relates directly to what God, our father, wants from each of us. The difference is he does whisper through the Holy Spirit guiding our way and He provided us with a full set of blueprints to follow in the Holy Bible. The Lord knew that we would never grow up and mature properly if He continued to do all the work for us. Can you relate this to your feelings of love for your children? There is much more to life than just what we see in this physical world. Don't let your children be miss lead without the guidance to know how to continue and where to look for the answers they vitally need. There comes a point when our children need to work for what they receive in order to succeed. When we study the history in the Holy Bible, we find a repetitive cycle of events in the rise and fall of individuals, families, cities and even nations when they lose focus from the primary source in the Word of God, our creator! There is proof in past and the present, of the strength in following the single source of instruction giving us peace in the Spirit of God!

This can be compared to the wide variety of colors in a paint store that we use everyday. All colors come from a primary source, but we have fallen so far away from our original focus that the true formula, through Jesus Christ, is being distorted and even lost! Just try walking into any paint store and ordering a specific color. You will be overwhelmed with all the choices and possibly get sidetracked from your original choice unless you know without a doubt what you are looking for or may need! It is not that simple any more to pick a specific color! Everyone has a different taste and continues to create their own shade. Some have even gone as far as thinking that their shade is the true color, neglecting where it came from, and not ever remembering the formula or path they took to reach their shade of color!

This same process is happening in the Christian bookstore, and the original formula given in the Holy Bible continues to expand into new areas. Going in a bookstore to purchase a Holy Bible is like walking in that paint store for a specific color. If you don't know what you are looking for then you could get something you don't need! The choices are unlimited and some have even begun to move more away from the primary source.

The most important part to any piece of art is not the colors that are used. But the message within the expression it portrays! There are times when we need to evaluate our current expression to insure the proper message being shown. As long as we always know where we stand, then what's being taught or pushed upon us in temptations will have less influence on our decisions and on our children's future!

You can see our beautiful country continuously drifting further and further away from where our primary foundation began. It helps to overcome any issue by studying history and learning how to break the cycle of negative events. The longer someone neglects to face an issue at hand, then the worse it will become for our children in the future. When we open our eyes to the actions of this world, it is obvious to see the affects of our inner struggles and how they are spreading to other countries. You can see it in the value of our American dollar or even on the cover of *Time Magazine* for the man of the year in 2007. There's nothing wrong with a little friendly competition but no one likes to lose the title!

When we look at our country, the United States of America, we can see an infection in every direction. Americans are falling away from God with all the different directions being shown and this is even beginning to distort our principle foundation from where we built this nation! We need to uplift each other, rather than tear down! This country was built to be united and not live in fear! It is sad when we have to worry about our children or family members going to school, shopping in the malls, and even trying to travel. Everywhere you turn, someone is being hurt or even losing loved ones from someone else who failed to properly care! We have a beautiful country that offers so much, and we need to be proud of what the Lord has given us by not neglecting our American heritage! It is time to "WAKE UP" and appreciate life through the love of Jesus Christ and respect each person for who they are rather than tear them apart!

All the keys to life and even success have already been given! The single key to all success is right within reach but many fail to listen! They continue to search every other book, every other speaker, and fail to acknowledge the wisdom in the Word of God giving us true success in life. Why is it that we can't seem to drop our pride and admit the truth? Instead, we search every speaker and even self-help books looking for the answers to discover our purpose. Where do you think the real secret lies? Here's the secret! It plainly lies within the Holy Bible through the life of Christ, but it was never meant to be a secret! Our keys to success have already been given in the directions and principles of God and personally taught through the ultimate teacher, Jesus Christ!

It is in our human nature to make things more complicated than they really are. How many times have you set out for a specific issue and got totally sidetracked from the issue at hand? We are easily distracted in today's society, and to overcome this weakness, we must learn how to focus on each specific issue one at a time! This is a daily task and can be difficult considering the fast moving pace of this world. This focus is vital though to maintain ourselves not only mentally and physically but most of all, spiritually!

We all can accept change as long as we are strong and content in where we stand in case of a fall. But far too often though we lose our footing because we lost or neglect our perspective in life! It is easy to accept or want something before we may be ready, and this is where we can hurt not only ourselves but also other individuals by not properly thinking everything through.

For someone to say that this country was not built on Christian faith is being blind to the facts! Christianity teaches love, peace, joy, equal rights, freedom, and justice! This is just a fraction of what Jesus taught and the Lord gives! Why do we continue to refrain or acknowledge this truth and not give the recognition to who it is due? Everywhere we turn someone is trying to remove God out of the picture of life. You can see this in our schools, our government, our homes, and now even with our leaders too worried about losing support for standing on the foundation of God. Here's the kicker though, "Many individuals who want to remove God still want to claim or stand on His principles taught and given in the Holy Bible!" For there is no more loyalty ever shown than by Abraham and ultimately by God in giving His Son for our eternal life! How can someone stand strong on someone's principles from their character if they can't ever acknowledge the one that gives them? In today's world, many individuals are not looking at the overall picture of life and only seeing the picture before them causing us to lose focus of our direction within the body and not understanding the principles within the foundation to maintain strength in being united as one! And even worse, by some being mislead or overlooking history, they can't find their direction towards the overall glorious picture in the end!

It is time to overcome our differences and understand our distractions in life to rebuild what we have lost in our direction with a purpose in serving other's in need! Sometimes in life we must start at the bottom floor to pick ourselves back up again! But this time not falling to where we went wrong the last time by understanding how to grow strong! In order to do this, we must evaluate our roots and foundation before we can ever begin to move forward! Like any sport ever played, it helps to know the game and your opponent before you begin to play! If we don't know the objective or we don't know who to follow, then how can we ever know how to pick ourselves back up after a fall and especially in today's time?

Game of Life

Life is a game that can be compared to chess.

Analyze each move and know your surroundings.

Protect your family and guard your heart.

Don't make the same mistake twice and take your time
before you move.

To insure your objective and not to hurt others,

Move graciously with love and enjoy the time you have to play.

Instructing others for the day that you must step aside and let
someone else begin carrying on our true King's way! (Amen)

CHAPTER 3

Appreciation and Understanding

*L*ife is a beautiful thing when we stop and learn to appreciate what we have been given. The sad part is how it often takes a hard lesson before we really begin to see. There are two things in this world that often get neglected and abused. These two things are our appreciation of life and our understanding in our freedom.

Have you ever had the breath knocked out of you or been choked? What would you have done to regain your breath? Can you even imagine how good that first breath felt when you received it? What about a time of being restricted or even grounded as a child? Did you like the feeling? How did you feel once you were able to regain your freedom? Have you ever been in a hospital and unable to walk or even see? How did you feel to walk again, or regain your vision? Can you even imagine what it would be like to be blind or deaf to the sounds of nature? Can you imagine being a child and growing up with no love or affection? What about a child that everyone picks on? Or, being a child who is left all alone? Can you even imagine how scared you would be? Imagine being a parent and being told, "Your child is terminally ill, or they weren't going to make it." Can you even begin to imagine the pain?

It is so easy to take what we have for granted, until it has been taken from us. When you really open your eyes, you can find appreciation for the very simple things in life that are the most important. There is nothing more important in this world than sharing in life and the ability to be free! When you see someone in need, in pain, or even being handicapped, how do you treat these individuals? Have you ever thought about someone who is paralyzed and how they felt when they watched someone neglect what they have in the freedom to walk or run? Recently, we witnessed a great couple who once was on top of the world and even faster than a speeding bullet. The life story of Christopher Reeves and his wife is a true superman story along with a true love story in loyalty from his wife Dana. Have you ever thought about how you would be if you were faced with a major issue like Dana Reeves? It is far too easy to neglect what we have been given in our life and how fast it can be taken away!

Before ever moving forward to improve any circumstance or issue in life, it is imperative to have appreciation, understanding, and to give thanks to the Lord for what we have no matter our stage in life. Let's start with the basics. Do you appreciate the shoes on your feet, the wheelchair which you sit in, the Seeing Eye dog that leads your way, the air which you feel in the wind, or even the communication with the ones you love? No matter where you are in life, or what you have or may not have, there is someone that would love to be where you are and have what you have in the basics of life. Don't take what you have for granted because it can be taken from you before you can even blink your eye! The simple things are the most important and everything else is just a luxury.

It is vital in understanding in any game or sector in life that we always have appreciation for the goals! How can we honestly be an athlete or a fan without proper respect, self-discipline, order, unity, direction and even knowing our purpose in your Field of Dreams? Each individual has a roll in every part of life from big to small and you can compare it to any particular sport. Think about it! The coach is to uplift and teach. The spectator is to support win or lose. Some players master the game and learn how to help others succeed. While other players sit on the bench to relieve others in a time of need. The water boy provides nourishment and the referee keeps the players in line. One without the other leaves a void in the game and another factor to always keep in mind is our appreciation for time!

The object is to learn how to move with appreciation for what we have been given. Communication within any game is crucial to the life and performance of players and to the life of the team. What would you expect if you were thrown in a game without knowing the goals to achieve, nor the rules to follow? There comes a point in every game that we must have rest and allow someone else to do their part. It is within this process and appreciation that we can learn how to live each day with God providing the way!

Imagine life like this: God is our creator and ultimate coach in life. Jesus was and is the all-star who came in to save the game. Rather than being an all-star who had all the moves, He ultimately taught us how to live the game. The ball field is earth and we all are the players. Some will make the team, some will sit back and just observe! While others become arrogant in the fact and neglecting the true purpose in life! Too often, we get stuck in our own game only looking at the picture, which we see. Can you ever begin to imagine God's view from the best seat in the house? When you look at life as a game, you can view this place as a breeding and training ground to see who makes the ultimate winning team. Our homes, our work-place, and even our homeland can be broken down into individual games. Each one should strive to always keep respect and grow with-in itself to reach others. Competition is good and fun when played out of appreciation, respect, and sportsmanship between opponents! Meaning to support and help the ones in need even if they are our opponent in life! Every player, whether on top or on bottom, requires the same necessities to survive and there is always room to improve any sector in life!

Now let's take our appreciation for a game in life to another level in thinking of it as the earth as one house, and with the people as one body. Can you see the ultimate game would be to unify the body into one team, honoring the true coach? Isn't the objective of any game to win eternal rewards? By looking at life compared to a sport, it helps to clarify our position and understand our rules to reach our goals! Now, let's look at our history in the first game of life and then where it is today. The first game ever to be played began with two players and two different teams. The player's names were Adam and Eve. The coaches of the two different teams are God, the Master and Creator, and Satan, the envious opponent.

The two teams are called good and evil! The coach of the evil team, Satan, once followed God the Master, but filled with envy he forgot his position under the true coach God the Father. So, he thought he could overtake God in trying to turn the players against Him. (Just out of curiosity, have you ever seen this characteristic in individuals today?) Back to the game, in the first game there were no play-offs, no try-outs, or no proving themselves to be worthy to play. The players Adam and Eve went straight to the eternal game in the Garden of Eden. There they were loved and taught by God but later recruited by Satan. This created our game that we now live in and evicted the players to a new field. Now having to believe and have faith they must go through agonizing hardships to return to the eternal rewards in life.

Due to Satan's envy and jealousy, it blinded him into recalling that God not only knows all the plays from the beginning, but to the end! So upon the infection of evil, God cast Satan to earth for the physical game of life to begin. A spiritual war broke out on earth between good and evil. The major difference in the teams are one tempts going after the players while the other stands strong and lets the players come to Him. God, the Almighty coach, represents perfection and His team number is seven! The other team's number is the number six, for always coming so close to winning but <u>always fails</u> at the final moment! The other team lead by Satan is full of jealousy and pride which transfers to extreme anger. As this progresses on, it then transfers to rage! The other team, lead by Satan, wants what God has so bad that Satan and his players are willing to try anything even death to win. By Satan, being evicted from the eternal game and losing other battles his rage has become so vibrant that he puts up one hell of a fight! Bringing death and destruction to everything he infects. The devious side of Satan misleads others to follow his team, <u>without them ever having knowledge of whose team they are really on!</u> They are deceived and blind to the facts in life!!!

Over the course of history there have been numerous spiritual battles that still continue today. There have also been major wars that took place and the first war was prior to Noah until God stepped in and knocked Satan out! This war can represent the first of the three number sixes representing Satan. After this, Satan's rage ever grew and then the second war came throughout the Old Testament. Over a long period of time Satan began to grow again, while God coached the players who failed to follow. Just before Satan was seeing victory, God came in the form of man to save the game. This war was won once again, just when Satan was so close, he thought, to victory. You can relate this second war to the second number six in the sign of the beast! After this second loss, Satan's rage grew in now knowing that Jesus Christ has broken the chain of death. Never before or never again has there been anyone completely sinless as Christ that will provide the way home! Now that Satan's reign has been broken in this spiritual game of life, his rage has become fierce and even in the wide open with no regard to life! The third number six, or war, is yet to come with the vengeance of Satan and the wrath of God winning this game of life! Upon the team members who are faithful and all believing in Christ to our Almighty coach, God, they will re-enter the ultimate ball field in Heaven being filled with love!!!

The vital thing we all should remember is that it is not about human competition. It is about doing the best we can with what we have been given and serving the Lord in everything we do. When we work hard and serve the Lord, we will move forward and have eternal life upon accepting and receiving Christ as our Savior. This is how we receive our eternal goals in life! Sometimes we must go through very tough times to get to the other side and achieve our goals! But never do we have a reason to complain because there is always someone that would like to have what we have in health, in life, and even in our freedom given through Jesus Christ!!!

Hopefully you understand the seriousness to this analogy, as I now do, before it is too late! Because don't forget that in every game there is a time clock and in this one no one here on earth knows when that time will be called or let's say, the horn will be blown! As long as our hearts are prepared, there is no need or room for worry!

In every sector of life, we have instruction to follow to understand how to live.

The Lord pointed out a very important rule right out of the gate, after proving himself to the people of Israel. In the book of (Exodus 16), the Lord instructed Moses on how to pick up food for just one day and this was a test. The vital rule to follow and teach to our children was taught right here from God through Moses. This rule is "Self-Discipline". Our true coach, being God, knew our weakness of not being able to handle large amounts of anything without proper discipline. When we don't have discipline, then we will often waste or neglect what we have been given. Think about it! If you were not taught proper responsibility and discipline, how would you react if you were hungry? There's nothing wrong with having a refrigerator or pantry full, but if you can't discipline yourself to only consume what you need, then you could overeat and suffer consequences. Or if you don't teach respect for the dollar, than how can you expect your children to react when money is put in front of them when they are in need?

By the Lord teaching us a very important rule and lesson in the very beginning, He went on to give us the Holy Bible to teach from and follow for future questions. In instructing the people of Israel to only receive enough for the day, teaches us discipline in attaining moderation of consumption, and always to focus on one day at a time! Once we learn this, the Lord may possibly bless us with more, but if we don't have discipline or guidelines then we can consume and waste more than we need. This is a crucial lesson to teach to our children and apply to ourselves. Not only will it give us respect for what we have, but save something for another day ahead.

So in order to live and grow, it is imperative that we understand the purpose of self-discipline! Once you learn your position, it is our choice to decide which level we choose to play based upon our talents given. For if a coach held back a player, would he be a coach? A true coach, like God our Father, gave us this life to live how we choose, and there are consequences when we don't follow the rules! The object is to always balance our time and maintain our faith even in troubled times! A quitter can never be a winner! And if we want our life to improve, it starts solely with ourselves! Then as we improve our life we will begin to see others who will improve theirs. This is why God in the Old Testament gave us the commandment, **"Do unto others as you shall have them do unto you."** Then in the New Testament, Jesus physically taught us directly to **"love thy neighbor as thyself"** and this is how we all can grow positively in life!

When we treat and give respect to others, as we want to be treated, this teaches true respect and even sportsmanship within any game! There is nothing wrong with helping another player or individual up after they have been knocked down, and this is taught in love as a Christian. As we live our life or play a game, we should respect the others for whom they are! It is not about human competition, but about being the best we can be, for who we are on an individual basis. Lose or fail at something then learn from it and try again! If you succeed just learn from it by helping others in how to improve! When we only live for ourselves, then before we know it we could fall behind and eventually be left all alone!

In order to help yourself grow, ask yourself "Why I live, and who do or what do I work for?" Is it to grow healthy, and live a happy life loving others? Is it to improve a relationship, to be a better parent, maybe a better employer, to be a better employee, to be a better friend, or how about just being a better person? It helps in life when we call time out and examine the picture around us being shown, and to prepare for tomorrow, to examine ourselves for strength in order to maintain our balance in life. Our life can be very uplifting being filled with joy, but can also scar us for life if we don't follow the rules. Fortunately, all scars can tell a story when you don't try to hide them and learn from them! As any physician would advise in a repeated injury, if we continue the same path, we can expect the wound to never heal! So, in life we must examine our history to insure our future, for our children.

There is no doubt we can live this life and achieve many rewards from big to small. But when you look at the rewards within this physical world, what do you see as rewards? Do you think of rewards as money, material items, or personal achievements affecting your pride? If so, this is where the other team can recruit you without even recognizing whom you are working for. The material goals of this world can never touch what we can receive in love, honor, respect, and ultimately to the eternal reward in heaven above! This is the part that will always hurt me, of how I hold these values to such high regards, but I dropped my standards due to feeling I had no other choice within my pressures and this was bad wrong! Making wrong decisions does not mean we are kicked off of the team, but we may be suspended or placed in time out until we learn our lesson. The important part to always remember as a player or an individual is to never give up, and learn how to over come! There is always room on any team to return and play like never before, once we are prepared. Then the goal is to do your best to rebuild our strength and one day we may regain our honor. Unfortunately, there will always be a scar but this should never stop you from trying! A scar only tells a story of how to overcome our falls.

When we look at rewards and achievements, we should try to focus on our relationships with others. The most crucial relationship is with Jesus Christ and then every other relationship should fall into place if everyone follows the Word of God. There are no greater rewards that we can receive in this physical life than times when we help others in need and possibly improve something in life for our children's future. In addition to these rewards we receive love. There is no more gratification within the heart than watching someone you have helped in the right way to reach their goals and achieve the true understanding of loving another as thyself.

For this being said, my treasures in the heart are far beyond what this world can ever offer. When individuals often ask me, "Why do you keep on?" I can't even begin to understand why someone would give up. And as you read just two of the letters from my children you will see why I never will give up or lose faith! I love my children beyond words and it is my duty to do everything I can not only for my children but for the sake of their future in making things better in their life ahead. For if something is better for my children then it is better for yours! And if it's better for your children, then it's better for mine! That's how this life should work and it is all in honoring our Father in Heaven and treating others as we want to be treated. I share these two letters with you to only reveal the importance of God in our family and how our children seek our instruction in wanting to learn about our relationship with God. I pray that these letters may touch you as they touch me and they encourage you, in some way, to stay close with your children to help them in understanding the purpose within the Word of God. I owe it all to the Lord for what He has given in love, sacrifice, and even discipline to give us our direction in life!

Hey Dad,

I miss you like crazy! I cannot wait till you get to come home. It will be a wonderful day! We go back to school in 3 more days. It will be Jan. 8, 2008 when we get back! I love you so much. I love it when I see my father is talking about "God". You have changed so dramatically. You are an awesome father. You have a great personality. I can't wait to get to hang around with you on vacations. Doesn't that sound fun! You mean so much to me. Well, I have run out of words. All I say to y father is

Love always
Your only daughter
Karlee!

Hey Dad,

That catfish was nothing I've caught 2x that before. I was thinking about that high priest in the Bible that you were telling me about and wandering where exactly in the Bible is that. I'd like to read about it. "Happy New Years" Thanks for my stocking stuffer. I had a really good Christmas next years will be twice as good I can't wait because then I'll be getting a car. Ha-ha, I'm ready to spend Christmas with you. A car wouldn't hurt either though. I'm still craving a big steak. I love you and I'll hopefully see you soon I love you.

> *Talk to you later bye.*
>
> *Colby*

Before we ever begin to think of our own purpose in life, we should ask ourselves, "Who do I live for, and where am I in my goals in life?" These two questions are vital to always keep us in check and most of all maintain our focus in our daily direction to reach our goals.

After you answer the questions above ask these questions to follow, "What type of person am I? Am I a loyal and dedicated individual? Do I accept my responsibilities and face my challenges as a time to grow? Can another individual depend on you when they may lose their balance and fall? Are you a player or individual who wants all the attention? Or are you a team player who accepts their position and is always looking to improve not only your game but also help someone else?

These are very important questions in realizing the type of person we are and most of all to help us see where we may need to improve. If we just drift through life and neglect our purpose in what we have, then we should prepare to have struggles, lack of respect, and worse case scenario, possibly never making the team. Don't fool yourself into thinking that once you are on the team your work is done. This is where we need to understand the purpose behind the Christian team. Our purpose is given in the Holy Bible, the ultimate playbook, and the eternal goal is real!

In the book of (Exodus 19), we are taught great lessons on delegation and how to properly appreciate what we have. The Lord told Moses that, **"The whole world belongs to me,"** and this doesn't mean just parts or the part we worked for is ours. It means the whole world belongs to the Lord and He is the One who provides us with the ability and wisdom to accomplish or have what we do!

So let's look at this another way. When someone provides us with an opportunity or something like a roof over our head, clothing, a car, or anything else, how do you think it makes them feel if we don't appreciate it and take care of it? Now take it a step further in the things our physical parents have provided. Who really provided them? The Lord said, **"The whole world belongs to me!"** Based on the Word of God not only are we disrespecting our parents as a child when we neglect what they provide, we are in addition disrespecting the Lord for giving us the ability to attain our goals and the passing of wisdom which He gives to make it all possible! It is our responsibility to take care of what we have been given and appreciate everything we have! When we don't do this, then we are neglecting and abusing what our Father gives!"

As we move forward, I pray that you open your eyes and ears to hear the message that I have always felt but never understood until now! It is far too easy to neglect what we have and where we are in life without God guiding our direction! It has been my experience that if we don't understand our roots in our foundation, what we have right in our hands, and who we are, then it makes it very difficult to ever find new strength and stand once we have stumbled or even have fallen. Just think, how our world would be if everyone showed appreciation for what they have been given. Never forget that no matter how bad our circumstance may be, it can always be worse. And to improve, or find strength each day we find this in appreciation for what we have been given in every loving way! You will find that you will have a positive outlook on life no matter how bad it can be by the way you address it and look at it will make it better! Not only for yourself or others around you, but most of all for our children's future!!!

Game of Music

How can a team play music where the players play totally different tunes? A team is to be one instrument but of different cords. The closer the cords, the closer in tune. The key to every team is to play in harmony together and not against. When the players align their hearts for the game, they then align their souls and begin to feel the spirit within the music of the game.

The objective of each player is to complement the other players for who they are and for and for how they play. When a team plays for the love of the game, they will play music like you have never heard before. There is nothing more moving to the soul than the soft stroke of the heart. Many players never learn the art of playing music due to one constantly plays too hard or they try to play their own tune.

The game of life is in love for every move. Each move is in the speech and touch of each player's heart. So when you begin to play, learn how to react in tune. It's all in the art of the heart in how you play and who knows our heart but Christ!

CHAPTER 4

Following Established Guidelines

*I*n order to ever stand strong in the winds of this world and to maintain our balance, it is vital to always know our foundation! How can we honestly expect to have strength if we don't even know where we stand? If our foundation is weak, then we should prepare to have struggles or even fall when we don't understand what it means to properly stand!

One of the most difficult characteristics to develop is balance of our understanding in faith and knowing how to let it go! When we learn how to let go of our wants, and of what we know in this physical world to allow God to guide our lives, then we can overcome any obstacle that we may face in giving us peace. This can be applied to every relationship in life because without faith and trust, what do we have?

Think about it! How strong is the line you walk? Does it waiver from side to side? Does it sag in the middle? It is easy to stretch a tight line, but the ingredients which fabricate our line are vital. If there is a kink in our line, then we will have a weak spot! And if we don't nourish our line properly it could become dry and even break! The line which we place our life on is vital to maintain and not allow it to sway in the winds of this world!

Often we can find our walk in life short lived because we neglect to think about how to properly connect the future players, being our children, and the lines they walk. The Lord gave us the rock to fasten to in Jesus Christ, but due to our human nature it can become very easy to take it for granted. Just look at how Eli in (Samuel 2) suffered due to his poor parental teaching and to realize the importance of correcting our children to the Rock for their future life. Think about it! Our children connect their lifelines to ours in how we teach and show in our relationships, principles and worship. So how our own personal lifeline is stretched in time can be vital to our children and others in life ahead! It helps to examine our life daily for strength and for our future connections. The last thing any loving individual or parent should ever want is to see someone to fail due to their negligence of teaching or not giving needed time! Why do you think the Lord did what He did in teaching, guiding, and even sacrificing His life for ours today? The Lord wants what any loving parent desires in being honored, committed, and giving appreciation for whatever we have!

Unfortunately, it is very easy in our human nature to neglect others when we get wrapped up in ourselves. This is what the Lord teaches throughout the entire Holy Bible in our instructions to maintain our perspective, and when we allow our emotions to control our actions then we should prepare ourselves for possible troubles in return! This is better revealed in (Joshua 6, 7, and 8) in the Holy Bible. This is a very important lesson to apply to our lives and to teach to our children in how to allow God to open the doors for us to do the work! Upon crossing the Jordan River, the people or children of Israel were given strict instructions to follow, and before they were to move forward into battle, the Lord had them to stop to keep their focus on God who is in control.

I can't even imagine the emotional high they must have felt! Can you even begin to imagine a forty-year trip, let alone a walk, and their witnessing something as great as the waters being separated to create a path for you to cross? In addition, imagine being suited up for battle and prepared to fight for your life after you crossed the river. Can you even begin to imagine the confidence and spiritual power that you would feel in your emotions? Having to tell the ones you love that no matter what happens, always seek God, and remember what we do is not for ourselves, but for our children's future!

Now, let's think of it another way. Imagine taking a long trip with your children to some place you all have dreamed of going. Have you ever experienced this emotion between yourself and others? Did your children complain along the way? Better yet, did they ask how much longer before we get there? Here's a real test, how our children act once they finally arrive at the destination? Do they run wild or help carry the luggage in their respect and love for each other?

The Lord gives us a great lesson in Joshua that is vital to teaching not only ourselves but also our children in controlling our emotions to maintain our perspective in reaching our goals. Joshua was instructed to stop and build a memorial before going forward after crossing the river to maintain order under God. This lesson teaches each of us the importance of keeping our balance and focus in life on God to prepare for our future steps. When we just jump into things allowing our emotions to guide our actions we can and will lose touch in how to live or even survive! This is like a child being so excited once they arrive to that destination and no sooner than the car stops they jump out to run across the parking lot! If we aren't careful, they could jump out in front of a car in their excitement and never see what is coming!

This analogy does not compare in the levels of emotion Joshua must have experienced, but the principle of maintaining our focus and balance in our daily walk of life does apply. Everyone can recall actions in our emotions from childhood to adulthood when we really open our eyes to what the Lord teaches us in examining ourselves! This is a vital lesson to always keep in thought to not get hit in the traffic of this world and to maintain our balance! So before we react when some one pulls out in front of us, we should think about our actions.

And most of all, before we jump into anything, we should take time to study our steps before we move forward on the line we are trying to balance to possibly save a fall. Because if we neglect our connection of who gives and connects our lifeline, then can we honestly expect others to follow or have balance or even connect? The most important connection in life is in our relationships, first with God, and then to others, to maintain our strength and balance in life. This is what the Lord reveals throughout the entire Holy Bible.

It is easy to place one foot on something we physically see and speculate the other foot in the unknown. But to believe in something takes both feet in one direction in accepting whatever comes in our path for better or for worse! Many individuals never even attempt to pick up either foot, even when standing on solid ground, and this is where many will suffer in never looking beyond what we can see in this world. And the same goes for the others who only place one foot in and never learn how to properly believe in having faith with God through Jesus Christ!

Balancing on something physical is one thing but learning to balance on something spiritual is another! When we only place half our heart into something, how can we honestly expect the full joy of love spiritually and even physically? If we can't stand by placing both feet on solid ground in our belief, then benefits are limited and could even be short lived in our future. This can be very difficult at first and even periodically throughout life when faced with opposition, but there comes a point we must learn how to always believe! The lesson of Joshua in stopping to give honor and allowing God to provide the way is vital to stay in tune with life not only physically, but most of all spiritually! Our society today is playing many different tunes, and even from different instruments causing us to lose the harmony of God! The Lord taught the importance of unity to Joshua when conquering the city of Jericho, and this still applies to our lives today! They had strict instructions, but were very simple to follow to maintain order within the body giving direction, and even providing the way to enter the city!

Think about it! In that analogy of the trip earlier with our children, after a long ride, can you see the importance of maintaining their attention to always feel your presence and then giving them explicit but simple directions to follow to maintain a sense of order? How much safer do our children feel with order than with no discipline? Can you see how disciplining our children show we care? Unfortunately, no one likes restrictions but they are vital to sustain life. If we allow children to run wild with no guidelines to follow and with no respect for life, then prepare for a life full of heartache and even pains! Can you see the comfort and security in knowing that God will always be there for you, even as we mature throughout the Holy Bible?

This can be applied to every aspect in life from our homes, to our adult lives, to our business, and even to our nation! By not main-taining proper guidelines, then our human nature of sin can penetrate whatever we may be attempting to maintain. You can personally witness this today in the removing of God and His Word from our lives everywhere we look! Guidelines are necessary to maintain order. And the Lord has repeatedly taught this in His mercy and grace when individuals returned to Him in repentance to find new strength to live again! For instance, just look at how our financial market is suffering due to lack of discipline and softer guidelines in lending. This is just one example of many in what happens when we don't maintain our discipline and perspective! The Lord plainly reveals in the book of Joshua that we can't become tolerant of sin, and not expect consequences to follow! Fortunately, by the grace of God He gave us the way to overcome our past sins to rebuild our lives, but this doesn't mean we still won't suffer from our lax or wrong decisions in life! But He gives us the instructions and rock to build upon out of love for every individual in life to rebuild what we lost in applying what we have learned!

Where many individuals get tripped up in all the death within the Old Testament is where it helps to look at it from another perspective. The Lord looks at us as one body in wanting us to unite! And when we are infected with sin, then how can we be worthy to join Him in the eternal body of Christ? For instance, what happens if you are hurt or sick? Can you see the importance of getting rid of your infection to regain your health? Your single body is part of the overall body and this is where the blood of Christ saves each of us in God's love for each believer in Him! Jesus provides us the path but we are still accountable for our actions and we will also suffer consequences when we don't follow God's instruction.

You can see how the people of Israel in (Joshua 7) were defeated in the city of Ai by acting on their emotions and taking matters into their own hands. The first lesson in Jericho is a beautiful lesson for our children and as adults to always apply to our lives. It consisted of staying focused having order and then discipline to have unity with a purpose to reach our goals. But once this was accomplished, the people of Israel became caught up in the emotion achieving their goals and failed to recall who provides the way in opening and closing the doors in life causing loss of direction once again.

By not stopping to examine themselves and taking matters into their own hands, they were heartbroken all over again! This cycle of events is continuous in history when we open our eyes and ears to the world. Everyone at times has felt the excitement of emotions but if we don't understand how to control them with God in focus then if we are not careful we can lose our perspective. Imagine it this way to help understand what the Lord is teaching us in learning control and how to survive. You are racing on a track and if you just hold your throttle wide open, what happens in the turns? It is all in the respect of power in how we learn to control what we have with God giving us our direction to follow. We must learn to slow down in the curves of this world to maintain our traction in life! There are even times we must shut our engines down to insure proper health and to maintain our perspective going forward. One other thing to remember is "Just because someone may have a fast car that looks good, doesn't always mean they will win the race!" It is all in the respect and discipline in using what we have been given that will determine the life of our race!

When we look at our society as a race, we can see all different types of directions or tracks being followed. The most important part of any race is the overall unity in achieving the same goal in peace and love with a common direction! Everywhere we look we can see someone trying to drive against the existing path that has already been established, and this is where we must learn to turn the other cheek but never lose our direction in life for our children's future! Always remember, when one door closes, another door will open if we allow ourselves to move forward!

The Lord revealed another beautiful lesson in raising children and receiving rewards once the people of Israel took a pit stop to evaluate what went wrong in their defeat of Ai. Once they returned to themselves in realizing what went wrong, and repented of their sin they were granted permission to move again! The first battle of Jericho was a test run to teach us how to follow and then teaching us to learn from our mistakes in focusing on the Lord to reach our goals in life! The Lord plainly teaches us to earn our rewards in serving within His will to overcome our obstacles in our path and this is a vital lesson to apply to our lives!

The Lord teaches us in the book of Joshua great lessons in raising our children, just as He is raising His! Think about it! How do you see children in showing appreciation for something given over something earned? The sad part of our human nature is how easy we can neglect what we have right in our grasp and we often overlook these answers in our lives by never going to the depths needed. When we search the Word of God and apply it to our heart and soul daily we will maintain a much healthier life in keeping balance for what we already have going forward. This is a valuable lesson to teach our children in personal maintenance to enjoy the fruits of life!

As mentioned earlier, one of the hardest parts in life is letting go to trust fully in what has been already given in the Holy Bible and even sacrificed for our lives today! In our steps of life, it helps to gain strength by knowing that even if we fall, someone else can continue the works or objectives of what we have carried forward! Often we get stuck in only seeing our personal picture and neglecting the future picture being developed around us. It can be very easy to get sidetracked in life with everything that is continuously being taught and shown. Our society continues to show more actions based on negative emotions rather than positive emotions. The test we all face daily is maintaining our positive outlook over all the negative circumstances we see. The Lord provides everything we need, and it is up to each of us to follow his instructions in maintaining our faith to receive our eternal rewards!

Have you ever considered how the Lord prepared this place for us and then gave written instructions to follow? Could you say this is like building a home or business and then turning it over to your child for them to carry on? Can you see the relation in how we should prepare our children and teach them in the instruction given by God can be vital to the life of the home or business? As Jesus taught, isn't everything that is truly successful built on solid ground with hard work, principles, and even sacrifice? Think about it! How do you prepare your children for their life ahead? Do you instruct them with proper discipline or do you overlook them to just figure it out on their own? There is no better way to learn than hands on from someone you love, and it helps to prepare our children for the cold days they may face ahead. Our Father in Heaven gave us everything we need and even taught hands on of how to grow! Not only did He give us life in the blood of Christ, He gave us a beautiful book of instruction on how to have comfort and peace in this world! All our Father is instructing is to always honor Him over any other person, place or thing and treat others as we want to be treated in life. Why is this so difficult for people to understand and accept what God gives, along with what we can receive in the Holy Spirit of God?

When you really think about it, can you relate this characteristic to your own children in respecting you and never wanting them to forget you? The Lord tells us how we were created in His image but the negative side of our human nature derived from the fruit of deception in the Garden of Eden! Often people don't realize how dangerous deception of evil can blind us to the Truth of God and before you know it, we can be consumed with sin casting us far away!

Here is a picture to develop in your mind to possibly understand the book of Genesis to the book of Matthew in the Holy Bible. Can you see where the Lord gave us this ground in earth and then sat back observing how we used it? Look at the chaos prior to Noah and then to the faith of Abraham in the very beginning. Based on the word of God, we were turned completely loose in this world prior to Noah to see how we would live and mature, and after failing to have respect; the Lord washed it all away! And then after this period of Noah, life was based on a verbal oath with Abraham that reached many generations. Over time the verbal oath became neglected and then the Lord hovered over his child instructing them the proper way to live with Moses guiding the way! Not only did He tell them how to act, He took the verbal oath to a written book of instruction in the Holy Bible, and after years of disobedience and lack of following the instructions, the Lord sent His only begotten Son to teach and show us how to live in love having no bounds.

These stages are like a parent and their child here on earth. The child first tells their parent, "don't worry!" "I heard you and I'd mind you if you just let me go play." Over time of continued disobedience the parent changes the verbal direction and begins to discipline them with proper instructions. Have you ever been, or disciplined your child, and then been left explicit orders to follow, possibly written on the refrigerator, to regain respect?

Here's where it gets good, "After that child regained their rights back in proper behavior, how long was is it before they began to disobey once again?" There comes a point when your child continues to disobey in life without understanding verbal instructions that as a parent you must attend personally to guide and teach how to maintain love in life! This requires a lot of patience over a period of time to develop your child in how to understand how love works.

Once you as a parent, teach your child properly and have given them written instructions to follow, then it is time to step back to observe how they apply your word. There must come a point where every loving parent must wean their child to properly mature on their own! If we continuously do everything for them, then how will they ever learn how to appreciate what has been given and learn how to live on their own?

Here's the beautiful thing about God, our Father, even though all the defiance and disrespect over time, He never has left our side! This is taught throughout the Old Testament in revealing His love and mercy for His child when you study the Word of God, He never left us and He won't leave us now! Often we fail to recognize this in not understanding our human nature and picture of time! There is a major factor to always recall in life, "No matter our age, we are all still children of God in this physical world! A person will age in this physical state, but our life is always young at heart, feeling memories of joy in our soul! Our hearts yearn to be loved just as we did when we were a child. Think about it! A 130 year old individual is how old in eternal life? Have you ever spent time with the older generation in a nursing home or experienced a loved one who was blessed with a long life here on this earth? Did you ever feel their spirit of love in laughter in recalling their childhood days?

Even though they may have physical limitations, it doesn't mean their heart is any different from that of a child. Where our elders become hurt is in the cycle of love not being returned even possibly neglected. It can become very easy to neglect others in this life when they may add more to our workload and this is where we need to recall the overall message within the Word of God of our responsibilities in life! A little time shown in love to a child and even to a mature adult will go a long way!

As our bodies begin to mature the Lord still looks at us as a young child in training. Due to our human nature, we forget or can neglect the true understanding of staying in tune with a humble heart. Throughout the Old Testament we are taught by action and given every ingredient in instruction to follow the Will of God. After generations of never fully understanding the importance of keeping the Lord in the center of our life, from a child to an adult, the Lord Jesus came to reveal the glory of God and teach each of us how to have faith no matter what we face.

Due to our infection of the fruit from the Garden of Eden our minds have been downloaded with viruses beyond our human control. The purity of Christ broke the chain of death in providing us the way back home. Jesus lived and taught to the level that God wanted throughout the Old Testament but due to our weakness we never saw the picture. There have been many prophets and even judges but no one ever fulfilled the covenant except for the Son of God. Throughout the Old Testament the Word of God reveals and points to the coming of Christ. Many individuals recognize Jesus as a prophet but not as the Messiah! Many people get hung up mentally in not understanding the purpose behind the Word of God in giving unity and direction leading to Jesus in the Old Testament. It helps to look at the Old Testament as a young child with discipline under the roof of their parent, and then the New Testament moved from physical discipline to mental training in maturity!

The Lord teaches us to control our actions and also our mental thinking to maintain our balance in life. Can you see the picture of raising a child in discipline in being taught with understanding in love and as it was time to mature they were taught how to control their mental process in the negativity in this world? Because if we are not careful, our wrong thoughts can lead to wrong actions or even cause us to become stuck in the middle of never understanding the light of Jesus Christ!

Think about it! How many times a day does your thought process become hindered due to something negative in your mind? If everything you ever thought was revealed, how would the ones you love and care for feel? This stage of thinking is how we recognize and overcome the overall objectives of the evil team. In our spiritual recognition we can begin to overcome our negative thought process and begin to uplift others rather than tear someone down! This stage of life is taught in the New Testament by Jesus Christ, but due to our human nature of deception in sin from the fruit in the Garden of Eden, many never see how to be spiritually free! Remember, the other team of evil wants to break our unity in love to destroy our relationship in life and when we carry sin in our life we are in a spiritual prison without recognition! So before you act on your emotions as Moses and the people of Israel in their first attempt to conquer Ai (in Joshua) control your thoughts to maintain your perspective. This is the most difficult part of our spiritual maturity, but once you realize the joys received in this process, you will learn the art of being free!

Here is a picture to create in your mind that may help you in maintaining your spiritual connection. By the Lord our God sending His Son to earth to teach control of our mental thoughts reveals the meaning of two being one. Often due to our human nature of the flesh, we see separation and this is where we get hung up in our spiritual process. The Lord wants each individual to keep in tune with life, through Him, our Creator. Jesus is the pure connection and direct link! Like the Lord teaches in the book of Genesis, our bodies may be separate but our spirits can be joined into one! This was never possible prior to the life of Christ because of our interference in the seed of sin. Due to Jesus being the Son of Man there was complete purity within Him by not allowing the winds of sin to sway His foundation for He knew the end results were only temporary where God's love is everlasting!

Think about it like this, the Spirit of the Lord is like a radio frequency. It originates in Heaven and is broadcasted to earth. The Lord Jesus, Prince of Peace, is our direct connection through the Holy Spirit that never lost His frequency in the distortion of this world. Jesus taught us how to tune in mentally but due to our constant negative static of sin in the flesh we struggle to maintain our frequency! The red light that lights up when in tune with our station can represent the blood of Christ. Upon receiving the Lord Jesus, our lives begin to hear the music like we have never heard. There is no music ever played like the music of love that moves through the heart and soul. The only way to stay in tune spiritually is to maintain a humbled heart as a child under God! Can you remember being a child and watching your parent with deep love in admiration? That is how God wants us to look upon Him!

Due to our human nature of sin, our line of walk is what separates us from God. The walk of Jesus was straight and pure. While ours can jump from side to side and connect temporarily in maintaining our focus! As our walk matures, the connection can become clearer in learning to control our mental frequency. This is not something that can be achieved in force, works, but only or with a humble heart. Our hearts must stay as humble as a child's to hear and see the overall picture which the Lord creates. There is a connection that exists due to God our creator providing all the ingredients we need to obtain eternal life in heaven above. Everything we ever need has already been given and even sacrificed for the eternal lifeline through Jesus Christ!

The Lord Jesus teaches us how to pull up our cross and follow Him. This means in order to receive the proper connection we must let go of what we know and our desires to maintain our balance in life. In other words, leave your old self behind and begin a new! There is a great example of this in the formation of our country. Let's switch gears briefly to look at the relation of Christianity in forming this beautiful country of the United States of America.

It is imperative to always understand how the Lord looks upon His creation of earth; the world is one body of life separated by sin. The flesh of man formed our individual nations, our country, then our state, then our city, then our home, and then our individual life. Can you see that we are the one who forms the separation in life? Our Creator looks at one body to many parts. Everyone on earth has the ability to reach our Father in heaven through Jesus Christ and it is up to each of us to let go of what we know physically in this life for the next. This does not mean to not enjoy what we have, but appreciate what has been given to maintain our focus in where we stand. What we experience in love and joy here is only a foretaste of what is to come in Heaven! And during this time here, we are to never forget who we are!!!

The United States of America was discovered and formed from personal sacrifice of blood, sweat, and many tears for our independence of today. Upon the formation of the Declaration of Independence our ancestors went to war for the sake of freedom and equal rights creating something new in leaving the old behind for the new! There is much to be appreciated from where we began and this is the main principle, which our Father in Heaven taught repeatedly in the Holy

Bible in teaching us to never forget who gives and takes away when we lose our perspective in life!

Throughout the entire Word of God, the Lord reveals struggles of nations when they don't follow the Lord's Will and what to expect when they begin to remove themselves from keeping the Lord at the center of their focus. There is great <u>power</u> with God in our lives, but when we allow the pressure from our society to control our own well being with God, then we are setting ourselves up for hard times ahead! The Lord teaches us that **"Greater is He within us than he that is in this world,"** and if we allow ourselves to become tolerant of sin, then our foundation can become weak!

Prior to the formation of this country, our ancestors left Great Britain in search of religious freedom and wanting to maintain our English culture. If you really think about what all our founding ancestors went through compared to today; we should really honor and admire the commitment which they carried and gave! Can you even imagine climbing in a ship with no A/C, no special seating, no video, no GPS of where you are headed, and only a mental picture in your belief of where you are going? It can be uncomfortable walking into a strange room with different people, much less sailing the unknown only being guided by the stars! But do you think the stars are what really guided them? Absolutely not!! It was their faith and belief in Christianity with Jesus Christ!

On a lighter note, here is a funny thought or really a reality check! Can you imagine someone walking on a loaded plane and informing all the passengers, "That due to a technology breakdown and no fuel, everyone must unload, and if you must travel, the only method is by ship with no modern conveniences? By the way, overlook the dirt or dust as you board, and we wish you a safe voyage to your destination!" Personally, it would be good for many individuals to do this to maintain their appreciation for what has been given! But I would pity the souls who had to listen to all the complaints of disgruntled passengers!!! It is good for the soul to look at history to keep our life in check, and how good we have it today compared to yesterday! The only thing that has changed in history of this world is our technology, luxuries, and our way of life. Our human characteristics are no different when you study the Holy Bible to our current time of today! At some point it helps to recognize history to learn what went wrong, to keep our perspective and break a cycle of events to grow strength once again! When we begin to think that we are different or above something, is when we become vulnerable and could possibly lose something we have gained! In this attitude, we can begin to recognize someone losing touch with life and even neglecting our Creator. It is vital in all sectors of life to always remember where we have been, our purpose and our direction in unity with God to always maintain a strong foundation!!!

There is no doubt that our ancestors understood the true meaning of (Matthew 16), in denying himself and following the Word of God! They left something they knew for something in which they believed and they plainly displayed their faith when they set sail from their port. You could compare our ancestors setting sail to walking that tight rope of faith with belief for what they knew in their hearts. Our ancestors not only did this for themselves, but for the generations of our children to follow. And did you know that many of our ancestors physically carried a cross when discovering this land representing their Christian faith in sacrificing their lives for ours today? When you study our American heritage you will find that many different types of people came together as one to reach a common goal. There were farmers, sailors, business owners, and even teachers who joined together in contributing to our independence of today. In addition many cultures from all backgrounds played major rolls in helping us achieve our freedom in with the American Revolution separating ourselves from Great Britain.

Individuals like Friedrich von Steuber came from Germany, Theddeus Koscusko was from Poland and Bernardo de Galvez, the Spanish governor of Louisiana all assisted each of our ancestors in our fight for freedom. James Armistead was an African American who served along with five thousand or more other African Americans and he played a major roll as a spy for the Americans.

Women played a big roll that also helped us win the war. They helped to provide for the wounded soldiers and others in need. In addition, many women like Deborah Sampson dressed as soldiers and fought in the war to help reach our freedom of today. One female, Molly Pitcher, brought water to American soldiers when fighting and one day when her husband, John, was injured in battle she took her husbands place in the battle against the British soldiers. With this being said, can you feel the honor we should give in love for what we have today?

There was another man who was a Jewish American, Haym Soloman, who also played an important roll in the American army. During that period, the American army had little money and many soldiers did not even have adequate shoes to protect their feet! Heym Soloman had worked hard and become successful in business giving most of his money to help the American army in buying them food, guns, shoes and even clothes to survive.

The winter months were very tough during the American Revolution. In the winter of 1777, George Washington and his army were stationed at Valley Forge, Pennsylvania. There was a man there by the name of Albiquce Waldo who was a doctor at Valley Forge. He wrote these words in his diary about the soldiers and the hard winter.

December 12

...we were ordered to march over the river –It snows – I'm sick – eat nothing...cold and uncomfortable.

December 14

...The army...now begins to grow sickly...Yet they still show spirit...not be expected from so young There comes a bowl of beef soup – full of burnt leaves and dirt...There comes a soldier, his bare feet are seen thro his worn out shoes....his shirt hanging in string....I am sick, my feet lame, my legs are sore...

December 18

I have pretty well recovered. How much better should I feel were I assured my family was in health?

When you read this brief recording of Mr. Waldo's diary there are two key things to notice. One is his recognition of the spirit on December 14, and the other of his strength gained from love for his family in concern of their health. There is power in the Spirit when we unite for a single purpose with direction. You will find motivation in love that will help cure any type of pain or illness. The Lord reveals this message throughout the entire Holy Bible and it is up to us to maintain our faith no matter how deep the snow may get or how hard the winds may blow!

By studying our history and recalling our past struggles we can see that not one particular culture single handedly won the American Revolution but Christianity played a major roll in the formation of America with individuals knowing the true meaning of pulling up their cross to follow Jesus Christ! When we maintain faith, our confidence, our beliefs, and strength with God, we can overcome any obstacle! Due to our human nature, we can become weak or even broken when we allow our environment or past sins to control our thoughts! And this again is what the other team of evil wants in destroying our unity in love for the body of Christ! In order to maintain our spiritual connection we must stay in tune with God in our lives and keep ourselves humble to the Lord in giving Him all the glory!

This is even revealed in the Declaration of Independence by placing God, our Creator, and Supreme Judge, to guard the front door of our beautiful country in to insure our focus on Him! The document was originated to separate ourselves from Great Britain to give us freedom of religion in equal rights for all mankind!

Thomas Jefferson, John Adams and every other gentleman who assisted in the writing of the Declaration of Independence put aside their personal beliefs in order to not misguide the meaning of freedom of religion. But they never intended to have God removed from our American foundation! Any and every individual living in this country has the right to believe how they choose based on every individual's freewill and because this is the core principle in the meaning of love. Love is free and not to be directed!

Our founders acknowledged and realized the importance of having guidelines to follow as the Lord taught throughout the Holy bible. When we allow our emotions to grow out of control, in relation to the story of Joshua, then there is little order and discipline without God in our focus in knowing who is in control! The critical part in America is maintaining our strength in proper maturity and always keeping God, our Creator and Supreme Judge, in our perspective. Our founding fathers knew this importance to maintain life!

George Washington not only fought and served our nation he never lost his spirit even in lost battles! The last battle the Americans won was in Yorktown, Virginia and the British army surrendered to George Washington upon his surprise appearance at their Christmas celebration. Talk about a Christmas surprise! So, the next time your family is together for Christmas, there are two important factors to recall. First and foremost is the birth and life of Jesus Christ. And secondly, the teaching of Christ in how it inspired our freedom to live as we choose in our American culture today! General Washington once said these words, **"It is impossible to rightly govern the world without God and the Bible."**

John Adams who played a major roll in our country also said, ***"We have no government armed with power capable of contending with human passions unbridled by morality and religion. Our constitution was made only for moral and religious people. It is wholly inadequate to the government of any other."***

One of the interesting things about history is the age of our past leaders. Even though their physical conditions may have aged, their spirits were still young and strong at heart! Due to our human nature, it can be very easy to lie down and allow someone else to do the job. But when a negative cycle of events continues is when someone must rise for the occasion to carry on and strengthen what has been given!

Throughout history within the Holy Bible and to our countries founders we can see that age never stopped them from serving. There is a point to step down when you become ineffective and allow someone else to step up! As long as we all have life, we should always keep the Spirit of God alive for the generations to come in our children's future! Because there is one thing that exist beyond our comprehension with God in that eternal day in Heaven above!!!

Just look at Benjamin Franklin and all his contributions to the generations of Americans. Not only did he help (spark) the Declaration of Independence, he took issues into his own hands with the Parliament of Great Britain. He was seventy years old at the time of his influence in helping our country gain our independence. Who do you think he was serving, his life or the children of our country?

Based upon the Word of God in the Holy Bible, our ancestors displayed and even made personal sacrifices in founding our home in America. By reading the history and actual quotes from our founders, you can see their love and dedication for the purpose of unity within the body of the United States of America!

When you think of a sport or game, one of the most important factors is knowing its purpose and most of all how to grow within the guidelines already in place. If we neglect the history and purpose in being united then we should prepare for struggles to come! The longer anyone continues to overlook the facts and not face the Truth, then how can we honestly expect things to improve if we don't understand discipline, our priorities, our human weakness, and most of all, our foundation? Just because we may fall behind or lose a game is never a reason to give up! Why do you think the Lord instructed us to honor thy Father and they Mother? Think about it! How does it make you feel when you witness children disrespecting their elders, and you continuously see others neglecting what they may have in life? If your children were to disrespect you and give no appreciation within their life, then can you see some struggles and even heartaches? Here's something else to think about. Can you see the importance of teaching and showing appreciation daily for what we have in life? Don't forget our actions and emotions guide our children's future!

For it is one thing to say something, but much more important to follow it through! If you speak it, do it! But if you are not going to do it, then don't speak it!

The Lord's commandments are full of wisdom beyond our vision. The lessons of Moses noted in the first four books of the Holy bible are vital to teaching whom to honor, the importance of patience, and the reasons for discipline. In reading the Old Testament, the picture of Christ coming into the world is evident, due to all the continued generations of defiance from the Lord's children and the level of maturity God is seeking!

Think about it! "When your children act out, how do you react to them?" Do you try to pacify them or do you teach respect in love with proper discipline? If we don't teach respect for what has been given in life, then how can we expect it in return? It is very easy when we have children to let them exist in our life, but the crucial part is that we all need to stay close to our children's life. This is why the Lord gave us the ultimate book of instruction in teaching us how to stay close to Him and properly mature in life. And our ancestors did the same in placing God at the center of attention in the Declaration of Independence, to never be forgotten! There is a time to hold hands in staying close, but what matters is the time of when we must let go that we all understand freedom with Jesus Christ in serving others need is how we truly succeed!!!

When you speak to your children or others, touch them from your heart out of love for what has been given and for the children we still are! The difference is only in our physical state and maturity of the heart. It is easy to neglect the time that it may take to peel back the layers or shell that may cover our heart, but this is the only way to always remember who we are and to stay in touch with life. Think about it! Inside every onion is a seed, and as it matures in time additional layers added. It takes time to peel back the layers of maturity to still reach the innocent heart that we all carry. Either team in good or evil can guide this seed. So it is vital to examine and maintain our seed with love, appreciation, and most of all with the light of Jesus Christ pointing out what we may need to address. The moment we neglect our thoughts, our sins, and especially the blood of Christ, then we better prepare for some needed maintenance to overcome some bad layers that may have formed over our heart. Sometimes the layers that guard our heart could be painful to pull back but if we can't face our fears and handle the Truth, then how can we ever improve or grow stronger in life?

When we spend quality time with our children and others in whom we love, this will teach beyond our imagination the importance of maintaining balance in life! Answers are very easy to give quickly, but the most important answers are given and shown in time! Giving time to someone in sharing teaches our children and shows our heart to others in appreciation for what we have in life!

The answers are within God's grace and in proper discipline, that we learn how to respect this beautiful place! In the Lord's hands you will find the Spirit to all mankind. The Lord gives us strength to overcome our obstacles and how to maintain our foundation in life. Fortunately in God's mercy and grace, whatever we must encounter in life He will never leave us as long as we maintain our faith in our homes with the Lord in standing strong!

The object in life is to learn from our history and begin to move from the heart being guided by God in His Word from the Holy Bible through the Spirit of Jesus Christ! This is where we learn and maintain the art of life in balancing from the heart in everything we ever start! If we are not careful in the winds of sin of our world, our focus from our foundation could be lost! Then our children will struggle in not knowing how to move forward with strength in every step of life! The most important part of anything is the foundation to always know where we stand! Because it is very easy to let our flag get wrapped up around our own individual pole in life and neglect the true meaning behind the colors for which it stands!

So, when you see a soul or flag beginning to fall, do your best to come behind the other who may need rest and pick it up for the love of us all. Each time the flag is raised, it should always fly higher than before. We are to build on the Lord's foundation from each generation with God guarding our door. And when we do this in our nation, this will not only teach us how to raise that lost soul, or flag, in the air, but give us appreciation within the Lord's beautiful creation! (To God all glory, Amen)

* * *

A Flag in the Wind

Have you ever stopped to ever watch a flag blowing in the wind?

It moves so graciously in the freedom

To no end.

As you watch the flag you will begin to see

The importance of its foundation,

And the strength from where it stands

Allowing it to be free!

As the flag moves in each direction,

Blowing in the wind.

Begin to feel the freedom within its grace

And this is when you will begin to appreciate

Our freedom in this beautiful place!

There are times the flag may rest,

And other times it will stand strong!

But all that really matters within the freedom of the wind

Is that the flag's foundation

Holds to the end!

It is in this appreciation, we will find

No other country in all of mankind!

CHAPTER 5

Love and Inspiration

*I*n most games ever played in life there is a common interest among all players and fans. Whether you sit in the stands or participate in the game with the common interest of love in your heart, you will be a better player in having more understanding and appreciation for the game. Have you ever felt or witnessed a time of feeling the passion within the spirit of life? There is great joy in feeling the Holy Spirit within the game. Unfortunately, in some areas you may witness the evil spirit of the opposite team upon the players losing respect for the game. When this happens, certain players allow their human emotions to lose sight of the goal by allowing their feelings to control their actions. In every circumstance you may face, it is vital to show your loyalty to the game you play and give honor to who it is due.

Have you ever been at a point in your life personally or ever in your business where you could not see how you could go on any longer? Or, have you ever been at a point in an illness or injury where you could not see how you would overcome? This is a very common wall we all face from time to time. Unfortunately some of us may face these walls or obstacles more frequently than others. One of the most important things in life is how to see beyond our circumstance or issue at hand when we feel trapped or there is no hope to carry on. This is exactly what happens when we allow ourselves to get wrapped up in the darkness of this world and lose sight of the light in Jesus Christ!

Often during these times of the darkness, we become desperate to overcome our issues and even do things we regret in trying to survive or even possibly make things right. This is where we often don't understand, neglect, or allow ourselves to be misguided by the deception of Satan. Again, this was taught to us directly from the Word of God in (Joshua 7) the Holy Bible. If you recall in (Joshua 6), we are taught how to listen and follow God rather than the flesh of man. In (Joshua 7), the Israelites did not listen and follow their previous instruction in acting upon the deception of Satan misguiding their human emotions, rather than allowing God to open the doors to carry them through.

Have you ever made a decision based on pressure or acted upon something and later regretted it? Would you agree that this is what took place in the lesson of the Israelites when they suffered from their misguided deception in not seeking God for guidance and taking it upon themselves to conquer the city of Ai in (Joshua 7)? It is so easy to lose sight in how the Lord was teaching through the people of Israel when we don't look at them as a single body in unison with a single direction and purpose. When we allow our flesh to guide our direction, then we are only setting ourselves up for obstacles in our path. This occurs in every step of our lives from our relationships, to our churches, to our workplace, and even in our leadership. There comes a point in our life when we are faced with decisions to not listen to our fleshly immediate desires but look beyond to the future in following our heart for what we know is right by God and not of man! There is a very important message taught in the Holy Bible, and was given plainly in the book of Joshua, for us to apply to our lives in how to stay focused and content.

In life we all seek goals or certain desires to attain and the Lord teaches us that He will open the doors based upon our maturity in His timing, not ours. This is where the power of deception comes into play by Satan, planting some seed of misguidance in taking what we feel in our direction with God, to remove our daily focus in life and cause us to feel pressured to attain it now! Our job is to stay humble daily and focused in our work while doing the best we can with what we have. This parallels the lesson in Joshua of his instruction to conquer Jericho. Because in the deception of Satan, he wants to narrow our focus on a particular goal to remove our overall vision of what is taking place around us. By staying focused on God daily in under-standing what He is teaching, we then stay content with whatever position we hold in life. The Lord plainly instructs us to stay focused on the eternal goals and not to lose sight in our immediate goals! Due to His knowing our human weakness of how the deception of Satan would point us in our desires, and when this takes place, then if we are not planted with God in our foundation, not only do we lose sight of our surroundings, but we become discouraged if we don't achieve our goals! The Lord never discourages, but uplifts our lives daily when we learn to allow Him to bring things together! He never wants us to lose touch in life by forgetting who guides and who deceives! For when we focus on tomorrow, we lose sight of today!!!

Think about it! Have you ever made a decision where you felt one thing in your heart and soul, but allowed something else to influence your decision, like your immediate desires? When this took place, did you ever experience the same cycle of events at a later date and say "I wish I would have listened and followed my intuition that was right to start with?" Often individuals become stuck in their circumstances in life due to never wanting to face the Truth or the hassles to overcome to see the light. This happens, in large majority, by individuals not recognizing who wants us, spiritually, to be held back, and who spiritually will teach you how to not only grow, and also be set free! Without this recognition, you will see relationships stagnant, unhappy, and even unhealthy! And when this occurs in our relation-ships, it not only hurts the couple involved, but even their environment for their children, to their family, and spreading to others. Who enjoys being around someone who is unhappy, always talking about others, or living a negative life? What is that old saying, "Misery loves company?" Well, here is another saying taught by Jesus Christ, "Love enjoys life!"

Everyone goes through negative issues in life at some point, either from heartache or lack of direction in not knowing which way to go. It is very easy to lose sight in the darkness and not understand how to listen to our hearts and make the steps needed to overcome our circumstance. But this is where the roots of love come into play, by learning to listen in time and follow our hearts in belief of Jesus Christ to find our direction in life! In (Mark 4), Jesus taught us a vital lesson of the farmer scattering seed amongst thorns and due to our society, the very lesson He taught is taking place today. Within this lesson, we learn the importance of the roots in our foundation as a child to grow and produce positive fruit in life to help others. But far too often we allow that bird, or Satan, to rob us of our step in faith, or remove that positive seed, that we hear in that gentle whisper amongst our heart and soul! The same thing happens in our relationships by allowing the thorns of our society to remove our attention from the ones we love, or the foundation of our homes in recognizing the importance of listening to our surroundings. When this takes place, we become blind to the facts and even deaf to the message being given. Often when distracted by the thorns in this world, we overlook the importance of time needed within love. For example: A young child reached out from his heart to his parent only wanting that brief moment of genuine time with attention and the parent never recognizes what is taking place due to their own distractions tearing their life apart without their own recognition. Can you see this problem causing children to rebel or search for something they need? It is easy to recognize the rebellion of a child, but we often fail to realize the roots of the rebellion, only wanting that sincere time needed in love, without distractions of the thorns in society!

You can see this same event taking place even in our workplace and you can witness employees with broken spirits when they are never, or rarely, given that time by their superiors. In both of these circumstances, the child and the adult employee were robbed by that bird amongst the thorns. There are far more rewards in love shown than anything else in this world! And the beautiful thing about these rewards as Jesus taught is they don't cost a thing except our quality time!

This is so vital to properly teach to our children for it will reflect in their actions as an adult in their homes and even business. The rewards of love go far beyond our comprehension, and when our children don't understand how love works, then they will grow up searching for something they don't know how to find. By learning who gives love, through the life of Jesus Christ, we teach our children how to serve and do the best they can with their God given talents. You can see and feel a difference in the works of individuals who seek to please God rather than man! Think about it! If we seek to please God in our works in everything we do, then should this possibly please man? No one in this world is perfect, and we all have different tastes, but what matters are our roots of love shinning through in everything we do! No matter what we do in life, there is always something else that can be done. But there comes a point we must accept what we have and improve our lives daily to grow!

It is so easy to neglect our roots of love when we get caught up in society or in the spirit of this world causing us to not see what is taking place in the cracks of our foundation! It is imperative to teach where love begins and how it will never end! For this will insure the longevity of our foundation and even give us strength in this beautiful nation! Due to our human nature of sin, it is very easy to neglect the purpose and direction given in God's mercy and grace through the love of Jesus Christ. When this begins to happen in certain individual's lives, we can witness a hardening of the heart, causing separation and lack of unity within the overall body. For there is only one way to clean our home of the heart and soul and that is by applying the light of Jesus Christ to improve our future! Without recognizing Jesus and being able to proclaim His name, we allow our doors to the heart to be freely traveled by the evil spirits of sin! Many people never will understand this or even believe it, but it is so true in how we are guided in this world.

We witness individuals neglecting the Truth and allowing their hearts to be hardened from lack of love in the Word of God. They begin to search in all different directions. Then this spreads from the individual with the hardened heart to others in their environment. The Lord plainly revealed this in the life of one man to point out the dangers of a hardened heart. Rather than pointing it out in multiple people, the Lord placed this lesson in the life of Pharaoh in the book of (Exodus 9), to put it in plain view of how we can be affected personally and even affecting the life of others.

Not only were we taught the warning signs of a hardened heart, the Lord taught us, through the life of Pharaoh, the dangers of compromise and what to expect if we don't listen to God's instruction. Life is so gratifying when we drop our pride and learn how to serve in the love of Jesus Christ to build or rebuild the strength in our homes. It is tough at first due to no one likes to admit they are wrong or they have lost focus, but the end results are always glorious when we regain our perspective with God in our lives! By getting caught up on our own life and neglecting the time of expressing love in our relationships, we can affect others beyond our recognition or even control. It is so vital to be sincere in love and teach our children in our words and actions of how to not only act in love, but also how to give love in return. Often children love and treat others as they have been loved in their life. As a child, we expect and need love from our parents with understanding, and it is vital to teach how love comes through our freewill to share with others without being directed. Love is something we feel in the air, in the presence, and even in the tough of life. And love never stops growing in maturity unless we neglect the love we have in our blessings of God, through Jesus Christ!

This is where so many children have been pushed away from the church and the Word of God in the Holy Bible. Not only has this occurred in children, but even in adults who were seeking for answers. It is imperative to never forget our freewill and how our human nature works. Love and faith develop in time with understanding in how to share with others, not only the lessons in the Word of God, but how to help someone achieve the answers they may seek. Think about it! If someone told you that you must do something when you don't properly understand, then what do you expect to take place? Can you see walls being put up, or even rebellion taking place? Or let's take this a little further with the individual seeking guidance and the teacher talking negatively, verses positively. How would you see this possibly affecting the person wanting to grow or improve something in life?

The Lord plainly teaches us how to uplift others but never did He force His will upon us! The Lord gave us the instruction, the directions and the consequences of what or will happen if we don't listen and apply His Word to our steps in life. Jesus Christ not only taught us love, but also gives us love through our freewill to follow God to reach our eternal goals. Think about it! How does love grow and build in a relationship? Can you see and feel a difference when you give your love in life attention daily? What do you do daily to nourish your relationship mentally, physically and most all spiritually to keep it alive and healthy? Now, look beyond our physical relationships in this world and look at the Lord through the love of Jesus Christ that surrounds us day and night. There is no difference in the needed time and acknowledgement to God, as there is in any successful relationship here in this temporary life! For every single day we learn to serve in love, we will find that there is no limit to the growth and strength we can achieve. This is no different than anything else in life, for what we put into it; we can expect it in return!

This process of growth is amazing at how love within life will spread to others in touching the heart and storing treasures in our soul! With the strength and direction we gain with God in our foundation, it will build beyond our recognition and open our eyes to see like never before! Not only do we gain direction with God, but also in Spirit we will discover that place of peace within our heart opening our ears to hear the harmony in nature. All of this takes place when we earn the art of keeping focus on God, through Jesus Christ, and learning to balance our emotions to maintain our perspective in life!

No matter how high we may climb, or how low we may feel, the Lord is always there when we learn to listen!

Whether on the water, next to a running creek, on a mountain, in the middle of a field, or staring at the stars on a dark night, you can feel the love on your heart when you allow God the time to come in! If you are blessed with someone whom you love, then take this time together to look beyond your picture in life and this will teach you how to unite! A family, or couple, that learns to take time together and pray together will stay together. There is no excuse to overlook what we have been given in this world and no excuse to not appreciate every breath we take! Once we begin to neglect what God has given in love for each of us, then we should prepare for discipline to come! When we neglect love, then our relationships suffer, but if we give time daily in love from the heart, our love will only grow, revealing new levels beyond our imagination!

Take walks in the park with those you love and always strengthen the love in your heart, because we never know when we must part! By sharing daily time together our love will grow, touching others and last forever! God wants our focus on Him. He will touch each of us in our hearts as we touch them. If we allow our attention to move from God, then this is when we will lose our direction. This is never God's intention! Stay close to God and He will stay close to you! Think about it! When you spend time and share your feelings with others, doesn't there appear to be a better relationship and understanding? When we allow walls in our relationships, then other hearts can be broken and cause us to miss the true joys in life! It is crucial to spend time with the ones with whom we love and teach the true meaning of love in freewill to allow others to be touched in their lives and even touch others in theirs!

In the book of (1 Corinthians 13), Paul wrote some beautiful words on the meaning of love and this is often overlooked in life. It is important to teach and give our children every part of love that Paul instructs to insure they love others as they have been loved! As you read the noted scripture below, give it time to sink in to feel the true meaning of love!

Love is patient and kind. Love is not jealous or boastful or proud or rude. It does not demand its own way. It is not irritable and it keeps no record of being wronged. It does not rejoice about injustice but rejoices wherever the truth wins out. <u>Love never gives up, never loses faith, is always hopeful and endures through every circumstance.</u> (NLT)

Within these words above, the word love is used in place of charity in different versions of the Holy Bible. And due to our society abusing charity for personal gain or recognition, it is vital to understand that true charity comes from the heart for the love of God without restriction! The Lord plainly tells us in (Matthew 6), how to give gifts and how to insure our rewards are not taken away!

When you read the verses of (1 Corinthians 13), how does it make you feel? Can you see the depth never ending in true love? These words written by Paul and inspired by God are the roots of our foundation. When individuals begin to neglect the true meaning of love and charity, they will have relationships causing struggles and lack of direction! It is imperative to teach and show the true meaning of love to our children and to everyone else in life! There is nothing more encouraging and uplifting than when we are touched by love in our life!

The Lord Jesus taught us love beyond our full comprehension. True love comes only through sacrifice, and often this is overlooked in our relationships today! In every successful relationship you will find dedication, loyalty and even sacrifice. By learning how to place ourselves behind another is how we lift love to unlimited levels! The Lord taught this throughout the entire Old Testament in individual lives, but we struggled to get the message. In the New Testament, we were taught true love and how to achieve through the sacrifice of Jesus Christ! Think about it! What are you willing to do for the love in your life? It is one thing to say something, but totally another to follow through! Often we can witness relationships that take love for granted by someone just expecting the ones in their life to just go along in any direction they choose without considering the other people involved, and this can be unhealthy if we don't explain our decisions in life.

Can you even begin to imagine the motivation and love that was needed on the individual levels from our ancestors to leave what they knew and sail the unknown to form this country? Do you think they involved the family and individuals affected in their decision process? Of course, their decision was truly a major example of pulling up the cross in Christianity compared to our life today. The overall importance of discussing matters in our directions in life, are vital to receive positive results! By sharing our feelings, our dreams, and our desires with those who surround us, in the areas they pertain to, will open the door to others in helping us all achieve our goals. This gives loyalty between all parties involved to work together as one! If we neglect or overlook sharing our goals with others, then we not only hurt ourselves, but also can hurt others beyond our recognition. There are far more benefits to involve all parties directly affected than to not include the family before someone may set sail. When we don't explain ourselves and leave someone wondering "why" without understanding how scars in life can be formed, then this is misguiding other individuals in the darkness of this world!

To attain true love is not something we can do on our own, only through our freewill! The Lord teaches us to build a relationship with Him first, through Jesus Christ, and then learn how to share His love with others. By teaching the Word of God to our children, we show them from where the roots of this creation derive. Not only do we teach them the roots of love, but also there is great wisdom in the Holy Bible that He gave in love for each one of us today! When we build a relationship with the Lord, He teaches us how to accept each individual for who they are and how to maintain a healthy relationship. It is crucial to the life of every individual to understand who they are under God, to accept their position and be filled with the confidence they need to succeed in life!

It can be very easy to allow our children to exist in our lives but it is our responsibility, out of love, to teach the importance of principles and the Word of God in our children's lives. There is a balance needed but it is very vital to stay in tune with the life of our children. Don't forget that the tune of love is played and taught from the heart and achieved through freewill without being directed! In our position of parenting, there will be times of needed discipline that is required in love for the child, and many individuals neglect or even abuse physical discipline in never understanding the importance of teaching. Discipline is a very important factor of love and requires patience and understanding to achieve positive results.

On some occasions individuals face obstacles or discipline in all different types of levels and it can be very discouraging at times. This is where we must recall our love for life to help us overcome our issue and learn to look beyond our circumstance to see the light in the future. In every obstacle there is a lesson to learn, but often when stuck in the darkness, we can't see the answer or even recognize the root of the problem! Often when we get stuck in our own valley of death, the overall picture of eternal life is overlooked! One of the hardest things to ever face is the loss of a loved one, and the Lord teaches us how to continue on facing this sad part of life. If you ever are faced with this unfortunate fact of life, I pray to God that you pick yourself up after the fall. In times like this is where the love for the others in our life is very important. When we struggle to pick ourselves up and show love, our children will learn from us how to overcome major heartache. There is a time and a place for remorse, but for the sake of love in Jesus Christ, allow love to shine through! This is where the importance of love comes in, of not only thinking of ourselves, but the others we touch in life.

Rarely in life will we find individuals who address the factor of death or tragic circumstances, but it is vital to the future that we never lose sight of the end! Out of love, it helps to prepare our families for the unfortunate. When we neglect death, we neglect life! Because if we are not ready to die, then we are not ready to live! Why do you think Moses wandered in the wilderness for forty years? One of the many lessons taught with the life of Moses points out our very weakness within ourselves by losing faith and taking God for granted. It is important to acknowledge this weakness in our human nature, and recognize how easy it is to become lost in this world, or wilderness, to maintain our future. The Lord taught discipline out of love in the training of each individual to achieve their goals in reaching their promised land.

Sometimes in love we must allow discipline to play its course in order to achieve the proper respect required and needed to maintain our focus. This is the sad part, not only to the person receiving discipline, but also to the individual giving the discipline in return. A gentleman once shared this story with me that is a great example on a simple scale, in allowing discipline to achieve respect for the love given. He was warning his son not to stomp on the end of the shovel making the handle fly up. The child continued and the father warned him again that he was going to get hurt if he continued. Rather than taking the shovel away he observed his son continuing against his instructions. It was just a matter of minutes before the handle struck the child in the head and he began to look for comfort from his father.

There is a wise lesson in this when we open our eyes to the Lord and His instructions on how to live and gain respect. Just because the father allowed his son to continue and eventually get hit does not mean there was no love shown. If the father would have just taken the shovel away and protected his son, how do you think this would have prepared the child for his life ahead? If the child never suffered consequences for his actions, then could you see worse possible issues in the future? This relates to the principle taught from the Lord to the people of Israel, as one body, and Moses for not following God's instructions. Moses addressed the people on how to avoid discipline after he received discipline himself for acting upon his emotions.

In love we must believe and have faith to move forward to the eternal rewards and to reach certain goals in life with God bringing them together! If we lack confidence in our belief, then prepare for weak faith in our foundation! If we keep our eye on the goal of sacrifice, then we will move in a forward direction even when we are standing still! Some individuals must wait for love to develop and this is where the true rewards are gained in believing in the love within life that has been given by Jesus Christ.

On many occasions love is abused in lacking the proper understanding of the meaning behind the word. You can overhear individuals saying, "I love this or I love that", and this is where the word love is used inappropriately in life. If we are <u>not</u> willing to sacrifice our desires for the sake of love then we should say, "I like this or I like that." Think about it! What are you willing to do for your children? What are you willing to do to have life? Or what are you willing to do for your freedom?

This is where the true definition of love is gained in life and the Lord not only taught this, He reveals better words for the sake of love in the Holy Bible. There is nothing more uplifting than the spirit of love and it is vital to be disciplined to maintain the understanding. Rather than hardening our hearts from our sins, we should open our hearts and minds to receive the purpose of how we can learn to overcome where we neglected something in life. Sometimes in love we will face mountains and sometimes we may get stuck in the valley. But what matters is the love in our heart and never giving up faith in teaching others how to start! There is no mountain too high or no valley too low when we open our eyes and ears in letting our love flow. The hardest step is facing the facts however once we do this the Lord will show us the path!

Whatever we face in life, if we open our heart and accept the truth, this is how we will rise above the situation to regain growth with direction. If we neglect the truth, then we will possibly lose our appreciation and eventually it will affect our homes or foundation! If you ever feel your love suffering or not understanding, then don't hesitate to communicate with the one in whom you love and respect. A relationship with anyone cannot grow when there are issues to be addressed. Can you recall a time of how you felt after facing the facts or sharing your feelings with someone in whom can relate or they directly affect? When we carry or harbor our feelings, they will affect our life beyond our recognition. This will not only affect the person our feelings are directed to, but will also affect others in our actions. The important part in life is teaching our children how to share their feelings in communication and to prepare them for their life ahead.

It is important to show emotion because if we neglect our own feelings, then our own children may never learn how to address theirs.

The Lord teaches us that when we harbor our issues they will affect our relationship and worship. In the book of (Matthew 18), Jesus teaches each of us how to treat and forgive others that may have caused conflict or disturbance in our life. This is where so many individuals get hung up in their Christian faith. Because once we forgive, that means we are to move on and not hold someone down in their sin. If they continue the same path, then Jesus also gives us instructions on how to address in (Matthew 18), but never are we to not forgive another in life. For if we don't forgive, we are placing ourselves as the judge before God!

In facing issues it is important to control our emotions and show love. Because when you open your door to emotion it can be very dangerous in allowing the others to enter and control your words. Have you ever said something and then regretted it later? We all fall subject to this at times, but what matters is being aware of this to understand the importance to possibly control ourselves to not hurt others. Love is very delicate, and when we use harsh words without understanding then hearts can be wounded beyond recognition! Think about it! What part of our body is the most vital to stay in tune? There is no other part of the body that can exist without the heart, and when your heart suffers the life of the body will suffer too! Our heart is not only in our body but it is expressed in our touch! And when our heart is right, there is nothing that can stop your fight! The object in our life is to strengthen our heart with Jesus Christ and we will improve our life beyond our sight!

One of the best things about love is how we can feel it on our heart! It is easy in this world to only focus on the negatives, but when we look for the positives which have touched or continue to touch our heart, there is a beautiful fragrance that will carry us through every negative circumstance when you acknowledge the love to whom the love is due and learn how to overcome our negatives in life. Can you recall a time of smelling something and it taking you to another place in your life? What is it that you felt or could see from your heart?

With the love of the Lord in our hearts, we learn to appreciate even the simple things in life. Because with the roots of love we can smell it in the air, see it in the sky, feel it in the touch, see it in life, and grow in sacrifice with Jesus Christ!

If our heart is not right in understanding love, then what type of life will we provide and show others? Let's go another step farther; can you see the importance of understanding love when experiencing the miracle of God in giving life at birth? Isn't the purpose of bringing someone into this world to share our love and improve from where we have been? In everything we do, isn't there a purpose and a responsibility within love to grow in positive directions? With the Lord knowing us in our mother's womb and giving us life for a reason, then shouldn't we look for the purpose in our children to help them grow in God's direction? The Lord stresses the importance of children in solid homes with both their biological parents throughout the entire Holy Bible and reveals the consequences of what to expect from children out of wedlock or broken homes. In the very first part of the Old Testament, the Lord gives us great wisdom to learn from and apply to our lives in understanding not only what to expect, but how to be fair in raising our children.

You can see how Abraham, the book of Genesis, acted upon his desires by taking matters into his own hands with his wife's servant Hagar and then the jealousies that came, not only from his wife Sara, but even the rebellion of Ishmael. In addition to what this lesson gives to us, we are even shown the line Abraham had to walk between all parties that were affected for not properly seeing the outcome of acting upon our emotions or desires.

There are many lessons of wisdom from the very beginning in God's Word to each of us today on what to expect and how to handle relationships in a broken home. Take some time to study the life of Abraham, the life of Isaac, the life of Jacob, and the life of Joseph, to recognize the struggles that we go through in children out of wedlock or broken homes. The Lord plainly tells us this right out of the gate due to He knew our human weakness of desires and the deceitfulness that can follow.

These lessons are so vital to teach, not only to our children, but to even apply to us. Due to marriage being taken for granted and us following our fleshly desires over waiting for God to bring things together as we should, often when we take matters into our own hands without first understanding the principle of two being one under God, love can suffer in many ways! This doesn't mean love can't be achieved once again, but it does mean there is a difference in love not being restricted verses love being a line to walk with discipline and understanding for our children's future.

There is a great responsibility in raising a child and understanding what they go through in broken homes and many parents overlook the effect on their children. The parents get so wrapped up in their lives they forget how their actions influence their children's lives, and even break their hearts when their home is broken. Rather than focusing on settlement agreements in divorce, they should first go through a course on how to act in front of their children in order to teach their children maturity in compromise. Have you ever witnessed parents fighting physically or verbally in front of children? How do you think it makes that child feel when they witness this? I pray to God, your children never go through this in life! For it is very easy to bring a child into life but it is very difficult at times to get them through it!!!

One of the most common issues that can occur in re-marriages with existing children is learning how to be fair and give equal discipline between the children. A very important factor to always remember in this situation is, "You not only marry your spouse; you also marry the children!" If you can't equally love the children, then you will have heartache and struggles in your home! We can witness this everywhere in our society today with children being pulled into whatever direction the parents choose without properly considering how to positively teach their children based upon their level of maturity. There is no doubt our children should follow us as parents and this is the law of God in His commandment of, "Honoring thy father and thy mother." But the life of the child is different than just expecting them to just go along with our wrong decisions and treating them like a pet from home to home. It is vital to recall that our children don't or did not ask for our issues in life that we place on them, and it is crucial to teach them from our past to positively influence their future!

It is vital in a broken home to not put a child in the middle of making decisions which are between the adults, or to put pressure on them to decide who they love the most. There is one thing a child never wants to do and that is to choose between the ones he or she loves. Many adults fail to handle things maturely between themselves and use their children as bargaining tools in negotiation without recognizing what they are doing to their child. A child is not a bargaining chip, but and innocent life given in a blessing by God! For any parent who does this is not showing proper love for their child and will answer for this upon that final day! It is imperative to recall love is not directed, but flows freely within structure to give comfort and security in order to have respect!

It can be very tough at times to allow our love to travel freely when or if we feel that there is a fine line to keep everyone happy. When this takes place our love can become restricted! The only way to ever love freely is to have an understanding of how love works, and to never feel we can't express ourselves in life. The Lord gave us this instruction throughout the entire Holy Bible and it will allow our love to flow freely when we see the picture of life through Jesus Christ! Life is not something we create and love is not given without complete freedom of choice. Everything we need was given and created from the love of God, and it is our job to build out of love on our foundation to improve God's creation! When you look at life upon this earth, what do you see? Everywhere in birth we can witness joyous life! Have you ever thought about how the only thing in life which neglects its purpose is the human race? There is a cycle in love for everything in life, and this is where we can find no other depths in all of the living art within all of mankind!

There is a rise and fall to every human race when they fail to acknowledge or neglect the word of God. We can read this in history and even witness it today by opening our eyes and ears to the facts of life! With love taught and reflected from our homes to our workplace, we will find much more appreciation for what has been given and provided in life. Not only will we witness more appreciation, but also we will even see a direction with a purpose in life! Can you even imagine the hurt that God must feel when He observes the lives being lived in His creation? Think about it! You love life so much that you give life and then you witness life being destroyed or neglected! If you were to put your heart and soul into something, how would you feel when you provided everything needed to build upon, with instruction, and only to see it neglected or not even appreciated?

We can take this thought to all types of levels in our society. It is vital to the life of each individual, each home, each business, and even to each nation to understand our position in love to maintain peace in proper order. Love can never be unbroken, but can be forgotten when we don't allow our hearts to be open!

Previously it was mentioned on how love can motivate and how people love as they have been loved. Have you witnessed or can you recall a time of watching love motivate a child? There is great joy that warms our heart when we watch a child reflect love in their actions. A child will reach for high rewards in attempting to please the one that gives them support and encouragement in everything they do. Have you ever witnessed a child's smile and joy when they are just learning to draw and they hand you that picture? What about when they build their first model and show you their work? At this point of life is where our time as parents should stop and encourage them in giving them our undivided attention without outside distractions. This will promote positive growth of a young child and teach them to push for higher levels in their works.

Think about it! When an infant is learning to walk and you are cheering them on. Can't you feel the love within their expression as they reach out to you? Don't they try to reach out to you in every step they make? How do you reward them when they make their first step? There is so much wisdom in this when we really look at it and begin to apply it. The simplest things in life are often the most overlooked or neglected! Teaching a child to walk begins first by them feeling the security of holding our hands. It is pure joy in watching a child and feeling their grip in their first steps. Then as they gain strength and confidence there will be a point to let go. When we place ourselves in front of our child, this gives them a goal to reach. Have you ever felt the joy of the infant upon arriving in your arms and witnessed the confidence they gained? As they grow strength and have faith in knowing that we will catch them in case of a fall, they will begin to step out on their own covering more ground than ever before. This is the most important principle in learning where to have faith and belief in case of a fall. Once they become confident in their walk, they will move on to new goals, reaching a piece of furniture, a wall, but always looking for that solid structure to give them confidence in their steps.

This is where they begin to mature and take in what's being taught and shown at home. These are very crucial years in a child's life due to needing and requiring attention in love to continue their walk. If we don't teach them from the beginning of where to give thanks and how to gain confidence in life, then can you see a possible loss of direction?

The teenage years are often guided by the younger years. Our involvement at home and in their lives will determine the roads ahead. There will be times when we do our part as a parent and our children still mess up from their own inexperience. This is where we need to know in our heart that we did everything we could from the start.

Never is there a time to leave our children behind. We never know how or when their eyes and ears may open for their love to grow! By teaching our roots from God's creation, we will have much more appreciation and even enjoy the freedom within our beautiful nation! It is easy when a child neglects or abuses life to not search the roots of the problem and go our own way. But this is where our love is tested to every length that no matter what, we will say, "I love you and I'll always be here for you!"

When a child can't see their goals, or that solid structure of a loving home, then they will possibly begin to roam. This is like the child being blind when they begin to walk in life. If we don't stay close and help teach them the proper way, then how can anyone expect them not to have bumps or falls in their path. It is our responsibility as a parent to maintain control and give proper guidance to our children. The Lord is waiting above with His arms open and tears of joy on the heart for each child to return to Him. This is the most important structure to ever teach and show in life. There is no connection as solid as the rock in knowing where to stand in life!

Our children see us as their rock in their first steps in life and then they begin to observe our foundation in which we stand. If we sway from side to side then what example are we teaching? Or if their rock cracks or breaks in their foundation, their heart can be broken. If this happens, it is vital to rebuild a solid foundation to give our children the assurance of love to motivate their future. When we show lack of faith or stability, then how will they remain content and ever feel safe? There is no question that even in a broken home that love and respect can be obtained but this is where our love must be unchained! If we restrict or neglect controlling our emotions, then how will our children learn to overcome their circumstances or heartache in pain?

Out of love, we as parents need to teach and stay close to the Word of God. This will give our children the true foundation of where love begins and ends. If they only feel that love only comes from you, then where will they go when they lose the love they once knew? There is a proven cycle of events when you open your eyes and ears to the Word of God in the Holy Bible. For example, when we neglect what we have in life, can you see our children neglecting what they have in life? As parents, how long do we put up with our children abusing something that we have given as a gift? Do you ever see a point of taking something away in order to regain the appreciation needed? For the life of our children and their future, think about your position in life to insure the proper connections being made in your actions to positively guide their future!

Love is not bound in life and only comes from being set free! If we restrict love, then we restrict life and this is never what the Lord intended life to be! When you look upon your children, ask yourself, "What do I want for their future?" And then apply your knowledge and love to help them obtain their goals. The last thing any loving parent wants is for their children to not have their direction tomorrow if they are left in great sorrow!

When we believe and stay close to our children, our children will stay close to us as they mature. This is the message throughout the Holy Bible, for the Lord never left His children in all their defiance, and we are not to leave Him! It is a proven fact that when we begin to leave God out of our lives, then our love and faith becomes very shallow. Think about it! There is nothing worse than walking on thin ice and to not know how or where to step! In our steps without God, our focus is limited to only our steps or those walking with us. At some point man will fall through the ice! Then there will be a point of being humbled and we must look up to grab the Word of God to overcome our fall in hearing God's call!

Our children watch our walks in life to find their direction and purpose in life. So, out of love, talk with them to share your feelings to keep them away from that thin ice and this will teach our children how to communicate their feelings in their future.

Love is not bound in life and only comes from being set free. If you restrict love then you restrict life and this is never what the Lord intended life to be. When you see your children, what do you want for their future? Because what you teach and show will guide their directions in life and this is where you must think of the generations of tomorrow to eliminate great sorrow.

Believe in your children and they will believe in you. This is better taught in the Word of God in the Holy Bible of staying close and involved with our children's walk of life. The Lord never left us and we are not to leave Him. There is so much wisdom when we look at things from the beginning stages in life. Due to our human nature we often complicate or make things more difficult than they really are. In everything there is a beginning that gives us the principles to build upon and when we neglect those founding principles is when our life can become confused! Think about it! Haven't you ever felt the motivation in love to reach goals? Love is not something only in intimacy with another, but it is in everything we set out to achieve! We can take the same process of love and compassion in a relationship and teach it within everything we do. When we care, others will begin to care! But if we neglect, then what do you honestly expect?

The same goals of learning to walk as an infant and feeling the security in our parents can be applied to the workplace. It is as simple as our superior at work being there to help you in achieving common goals. They can't hold our hand the entire time or how will we ever learn to walk on our own? If we abuse our position to reach farther in our walk, then prepare for stumbles or no ground to be covered! The goal in walking and thinking is to reach higher levels beyond previous steps in life!

By having love and caring for others our heart, we will find a desire to achieve more in life. There is no amount of money in compensation that can compare to having a strong unity or team in the workplace. The environment will be more understanding in knowing that as we reach for higher goals there will be obstacles and this is where the team grabs the other by the hand to help one another. If we don't encourage individuals when they fall, the competition can penetrate our business and then we will begin to suffer in our goals in many ways. Have you ever experienced working with individuals that are happy in life and understand how to handle the bad with the good? They take challenges as they come, and don't complain about the job they have or must do. You can witness a difference in working with someone having a humbled heart compared to someone with a hardened heart in the workplace. Think about it! Who would you rather work beside, someone who appreciates their position or someone who steadily complains about their position? We can't forget about those who abuse their position also, because there is anything worse than working or living with someone who abuses their position mentally and/or physically! There is nothing more uplifting than working and living with individuals that you respect and care for in life and this was inspired by Jesus Christ!

When an individual understands the true meaning of love from (Corinthians 13), and applies it to their work environment, you will see a positive outlook within the business team. There is no company that will excel socially and economically without this true understanding. When you remove the love and care from the workplace, then what purpose or goals are you trying to reach? Isn't the purpose of any business to make or provide something better for the employees, customers and even the community?

We can see many companies that exist like stagnant couples. Their relationships are dry and selfish! This happens when they lose their appreciation for what they have and their respect for love in life. It can be very easy to take our work or relationship for granted, and when this happens prepare for the competition! Because we never know who may be sitting on the sideline waiting for that opportunity to arrive! The moment we begin to not take our job or life serious is when we could have the breath knocked out of our position in life, and just like our relationships, "what we put into it, we can expect it in return." The more positives we grow, the more we will catch! Focus on the positives and build upon them! If we only focus on the negatives, then what do we expect in return? There are great rewards in giving something positive in life to others and helping someone achieve their goals.

We can find in the workplace with individuals who truly understand the meaning of caring for others that they will strive to maintain the company moral when times become tough and be willing to sacrifice for others. Because they understand the meaning of when one suffers, we all suffer, and when the company thrives, we all thrive! This parallels the way love works in a relationship in everything we do. By accepting responsibility and putting ourselves behind the other will maintain strength in time of need in order for everyone to succeed!!! Think about it! A captain of a ship in a time of going down or taking on water! Who would gain more respect and admiration between the two, the captain who jumps in the life raft when he sees something before others or the captain who remains with his people and does everything he can to save the ship and maintain their lives? In any circumstance like this, there will be the unfortunate of some being affected but what truly matters is the love and care in the captain's heart to rebuild what was lost. There is no honor in running from others and only caring about oneself.

If, or when, we build something in life, it should be done out of love and focus on the principles of our foundation to maintain the longevity of its future. There is no doubt that when we build on the principle of love it will outlast any other thing in this world. This is like watching our child take those first steps and then maturing to watch them walk on their own. The important factor to remember in love is respecting time and understanding how to balance. Our lives consist of enough chaos in our society without love being shown and if we don't add the positives daily then it will only become worse! What we have is a beautiful thing when we learn to appreciate life for what it is! There is no more beauty than when we open our eyes and ears to what God has created in life!

Have you ever thought about where we would be without the female that God created in life? Each individual has their strong points in a relationship and it is important to recognize them. The male can give strength and protection while the female can give love and affection. There is nothing like a gentle touch on the hand by the one you love. If you were to take away the male's sexual desire and remove the female touch in life, then what type of life would we have? By removing the female compassion in a relationship, men would only be soldiers with no care! Where would we be without caring? It would be nothing but a ruthless life of survival with no joy of birth. Women help us stay in tune with love and affection. The Lord created the female out of love and compassion to not be alone. The Lord knew there was a needed balance to stay in tune and touch with His will and creation.

The love in our heart felt at birth gives us true rewards from God. In everything we do, do it out of love to touch others. Our Father gave us everything we ever needed and even more. Not only did He give us our needs, we receive rewards for the love we show. He could have just left us here on earth like some people do this day and throw their children away. The Lord, our Creator, has more love and mercy than we will ever know in the physical world.

As you build your life look for that touch of God's love, and when you receive this touch you will feel it on your heart! It will grow when you learn to express your love in return from the start! It is when we neglect our gift of love that we lose touch in life for the Lord has given. Love is not a one-way street. It is shown in passing every time they meet! So don't neglect the gift of love in life because this is where we can feel the touch of God from our loving wife.

Marriage is a beautiful thing when two people come together as one. There is nothing more satisfying in a marriage of when each partner understands the meaning of love in serving the other. When one person struggles, the other supports and lifts. This is needed on both sides of a successful marriage. In marriage you learn to love someone for the very little things they do or even don't do. Marriage was never meant for one-sided thinking and this is vital in understanding the meaning of for better or worse. When an individual drops their selfish ways and learns to be compassionate for the other, the marriage will rise to new levels in understanding that true love doesn't come from only one direction.

A very vital part of this understanding is shown and taught to our children at home. When a couple doesn't reflect a healthy relationship in compassion for the other, then how would you expect the child to handle or act in their future relationships? Our children learn from what we show in our actions and how we treat the ones we love. If an individual only thinks of himself in a marriage, then the chances are very high that the child will act the same in their life ahead. It is imperative to teach balance in a relationship and to always give quality time. Our children live off of our love until they begin to understand where true love really begins. When our children understand that there are always two sides to understand, then they will be better prepared to balance their love in the future. In the book of (Matthew19 and Genesis 2), we were taught how a true relationship is two becoming one and the importance of not allowing anyone to split apart what God has joined together!

There is nothing more vital and motivating than sharing love in life. From our children to our workplace and to our adulthood we can see how love plays a major roll in our future. If we are not careful and begin to only think of love in certain sectors of life, then eventually someone could miss out. There is a cycle to love that begins at birth and continues as we grow old. True love even becomes more beautiful in age as we mature in life. It begins in unity and then ends in harmony! When couples share the same spirit of God, we can see the harmony within each movement they make in reflecting their love towards others! (To God All Glory, Amen)

* * *

Riding a Wave

Marriage is like riding a wave. Some individuals become anxious and fail to wait on the right one. While some just drift looking for the perfect wave that never comes or just passes them by. There is no perfect wave but only the one of God. The object to locating your wave that will fit is learning how to accept what you have and learning how to commit.

Before you begin, it is best to start out slow. First on your stomach, then to your knees and when you feel the time is right, you learn to stand, hand in hand.

As you both begin to balance, riding the same wave and traveling the same common direction, you never take your focus off the one you love to maintain your balance in affection. Sometimes the waves may get choppy but you can learn how to ride keeping your love always by your side.

There will be times when you must part, but this does not mean that it is any different from the start. You can always feel their presence no matter the distance in your heart.

In these times that you aren't physically together, you are still traveling the same direction. This is like you are in a love tunnel inside the same wave. While the other may be on top and you are in the tunnel, you both stand strong maintaining your balance.

Sometimes the rolls may reverse from who is on top but where the confidence comes in is knowing that neither will stop!

A relationship takes daily nourishment to stay on the same wave. It is when you neglect this when you can begin to drift apart. If you truly want your love to grow, then feed it with the love of Christ and your love will never part! (Amen)

Respecting and Understanding

*I*n order for us to regain the momentum and the strength we need as a nation and as a man under God there is a needed understanding of differences between all individuals that is required in order to maintain our respect, our liberty, and our purpose in order to move forward in life. By reading the past two chapters, we can easily see how many different cultures came together out of love and sacrifice for a united purpose in their immediate and future goals for our lives today. This should be uplifting to every American when we look at our history and see how our American heritage understood the roots of Christianity and respected one another for their own differences to unite for a common purpose. In addition, we should give honor and respect to those who gave their lives for our children's future generation while we maintain the historical sights of our previous battles to always remember where we have been in order to give our children a sense of American pride within our country.

Based on our human characteristics, it is very easy to lose sight of God's creation and the principle's He has given in this beautiful nation when we continue to remove God from the center of our lives. The unity shown among all individuals in the American Revolution reveals their dedication to our freedom and the importance of having equal rights under God. The Lord teaches each of us in the book of (Matthew 12), **"That any part of a body, which is divided by civil war, is doomed and a family splintered by feuding will fall apart."** There is so much wisdom in what Jesus taught and fulfilled in the Word of God, and when we drift away from following the law of God, our lives will become splintered and fall apart! The evidence is all around us when we are truly honest within ourselves, and quit trying to please man rather than God! Think about it! You are a parent with many children, and they all have different strengths and weaknesses. Does this mean you love any of your children any differently than the other? Absolutely not! As God loves us, we are to love each other for who we are under God and uplift each individual in their strengths to mature within their God given talents. But far too often, we tend to separate ourselves from others in only giving attention to those who either believe as we do, dress as we do, live as we do, talk as we do, think as we do, and the list of separation can go on and on. There comes a point in order to grow, we must learn to look beyond our life to understand the Lord's instruction in how to have the unity we need to move forward and never forget how we all are Americans with a common interest of freedom within this country!

One of the most difficult issues we continue to face in this world since the beginning of time is the pushing of ones will or belief on another, and this is not right under the law of God! It is in our human nature to push our ways on someone else and this is where we often get tripped up in life. Due to true Christianity understanding that our choices are based on our individual freewill without force on another and allowing someone to choose as they please. Recently, an Indian ancestor once shared these words with me that not only brought a laugh, but also even had wisdom that relates to this human characteristic mentioned above. He said, *"If we would have known*

back then what we know now, then we would have sunk that Mayflower before it ever landed." It is sad when we look at how individuals force their way of life on another without allowing them to live as they choose, and we see others taking advantage of situations for personal gain while others may suffer. This understanding of our individual freewill should be respected among all individuals in life to be whomever they set out to be in order to be truly free.

Fortunately over the years our society has grown and improved in understanding and respecting each individual for whom they are, but we still have work to do. We all make mistakes, but what matters is how we learn from them to overcome them. When we dwell on the past rather than learning from it to move forward this produces negative affects on our children in not teaching them how to learn and improve from where we have been. History is a beautiful subject when we learn from it, learn to apply it, and always respect it to maintain a strong foundation for our children's future. But if we continue to overlook the current facts before us and neglect our history along with removing God from our foundation not only will we lose our unity within the body, but we will also see the division, which Jesus warned us of in (Matthew 12).

How can we ever move forward when we are constantly debating where to stand when this has already been established within our foundation? When we only look back at history to point out what went wrong in order to point blame then is this truly knowing how to move forward? This is vital to understand and respect in how to analyze ourselves in learning to apply our past wrong directions to regain our right direction under the Word of God in the Holy Bible. Often individuals want to blame society on what guided their path, but this is honestly just an excuse! For we all make our own decisions within our own freewill, and it is our choice in the direction we choose to take. But it is imperative to know that everything starts from a single decision and when we wait on others to make the first moves then we just become stagnant or can possibly become stuck in our own ways without seeing others.

Think of this animal characteristic in cattle compared to our human nature to see our similarity. Have you ever watched a herd of cattle to see how they adapt to new areas? When they become complacent or comfortable within their surroundings we can open a gate right before them to new fields, and they will either not see it, while some just seem to gaze upon it and others will simply overlook it unless they are enticed to walk through it. While the gate is open in allowing access to new pastures we can find that certain cattle will still cross the line and put their head through a fence in trying to get what is on the other side while searching for that temporary food that soon fades away.

In addition to these traits above, we can also witness some of the herd will still keep their heads so buried up in the hay before them that they lose sight of what is taking place all around them in causing others to lose their direction also due to only seeing what the other has before them. This complacency can occur when they become either set in their ways, lazy, short sighted, or if they may seem to think that they have everything they need before them. Can you see a relation yet to our human nature? It is in our human characteristics to want what we don't have and some are even willing to cross certain lines to obtain it on occasions to only find out they had everything already before them but never understood it. In addition, can you see how the gate of our country is open in the freedom within the United States of America but many people still complain or become stuck without understanding how to move forward in what we already have been given?

Here's another relation to our human nature in how our characteristics parallel the cattle in the pasture. When a gate or opportunity is before us, how long do we look at it before we act upon it? Some individuals just look at it, while some sit back not even caring for it, and some are just waiting on that one to start the process of movement before they move to new areas in life. There is depth in this for personal growth when you really think about it! Our lives can be compared to the herd and America has given us our gate in opportunity and freedom through Jesus Christ! How we teach our children to respect what we have and to move to new territories in proper timing will go a long way in our future generations. The eternal gate is only opened by Jesus Christ and we can see the same characteristics of people in choosing to be where they are verses crossing into the ultimate freedom field within the Holy Spirit of Jesus Christ.

When we become complacent in our life and don't learn from our history, then how can we ever begin to understand what it takes to move forward by not taking for granted what we have already been given? Our children watch us in how we take care of our own pasture and especially in how we move to the unknown areas ahead! When we move forward or decide to cross into new areas, it is crucial to teach our children the importance of planning and especially how to stay focused on their priorities. In this process it is vital to teach them how to respect others for whom they are and how to work together united as one to achieve our goals. We are all of the same species and just because someone may look different or act different doesn't mean to treat them any differently! We were all created equal under God, and we are nothing more than living art with a physical timetable that never stops ticking.

Have you ever thought about the beauty in living art? We are all made by the same heavenly hands and each piece makes its own expression. It is not one particular color that makes the art, but the unity in life working together as one. True art is in the expression and message given in each reflection that paints a beautiful picture that moves graciously within love. For true art has many colors that blend together without contrast in learning how to come together in forming that larger painting in life. In order to be content in life we must learn to understand ourselves in every way possible like a piece of art or mechanical device. But none of this is worth anything unless we understand ourselves spiritually in the word of God to respect our position in this life to the next. For if we don't know ourselves then how can we honestly even begin to understand someone else? Being content in life with who we are under God is the key to finding that true happiness that so many seek, but never find. This is vital for not only us but for our children to learn how to look within themselves rather than something else in this world that never gives them what they will be searching for without Jesus Christ.

There is an understanding to recognize in being content before looking to move to new areas, and the Lord teaches us this in the Holy Bible. But due to our human nature there continues to be a repetitive cycle of events. Our objective in life should be to always be content with who we are and with what we have been given. When this takes place, it is amazing at the happiness we can experience in life! There is nothing wrong with seeking different goals within the will of the Lord, as long as we maintain our perspective within our foundation by keeping God in focus!

Not everyone may choose the same path to take, and this is fine as long as each individual respects another for who they are. It is our job under God to find ourselves and be the person we were set out to be with a common interest of love in our hearts to leave this place a better place than the way we found it. This is a privilege in our country to have this freedom, which derived from our Christian heritage in giving each of us equal opportunities to grow no matter our background when we are willing to work for it. One problem that is easy to recognize daily is the jealousy that derives from our human nature of competition. Due to our human competition, and not listening to the Word of God, we often get tripped up in life by tearing others down rather than picking them up when they are trying to improve their lives or do their jobs to the best of their abilities in their talents given. It is very common when climbing within your ladder of life that someone will always try to knock it out from under you or tell you it can't be done. We should never allow this negative attitude to stop us from moving forward or hold us back in life when individuals don't understand the Word of God in encouragement verses discouragement. We are taught that when we build on the right foundation and serve God's will that everything else will fall into place once we understand our position and know how to move forward in life. If we only focus on the negatives or what if's, then it is only a matter of time before we are passed up in life.

Think of your life like the Super Bowl to make the most of each day! Everyday you are given, have an attitude of a champion to win and overcome your obstacles in your path! Just because your day may seem like a loss doesn't mean you can't win tomorrow! If you lose today, then learn from it and improve your game tomorrow! This attitude is vital to the life of not only our selves but to our children. If we only talk negative or feel like a loser then what do you expect in return from our future players of tomorrow? Don't forget, when it comes time for you to retire from the game, who do you expect to take care of you or continue what you may have began? Our attitude is so vital in teaching our children how to prepare for their future and ours. Don't be fooled into thinking they aren't paying attention to our actions, because they are like a sponge in absorbing everything we say and do! There are many vital lessons to teach our children in the Word of God on how to respect each other for who we are individually and to understand how everyone has different positions in order to serve others.

In the book of (Luke 10), Jesus taught us a valuable lesson on different positions and jealousies. But due to our human nature, we often don't apply this to our lives as we should and teach it to our children in our words or actions. It is easy to get caught up in self-serving events and fail to recall who we all are serving in our positions in life. When we allow ourselves to constantly seek someone else's position in life verses our own, then how can we honestly say we are focused on the proper goals in life? The Lord taught this lesson over and over to the disciples, and they still argued in whom would be the greatest in (Mark 9), by Jesus telling them, **"If anyone desires to be first, he shall be last of all and servant of all."** And in (Mark 10), the Lord teaches us how to grow by serving others to reach our goals in Heaven. Far too often, individuals become jealous in personal achievements, rather than doing the best they can with their talents and to possibly help others in their path. When we allow jealousies or envy to enter our lives then the goals we seek in love, peace, and honor will suffer due to individuals not helping others, as they should under God. This just creates a negative cycle of events in selfish survival by working against one another instead of working together in unity to have productivity. What do you see in our country since our government began removing the lord from our doors? Can you see a negative cycle of events or poor productivity?

When we learn to put ourselves second to others, rather than always trying to be first, we will learn the art within life. It might hurt at first by having to sacrifice our wants or desires on a selfish side, but true rewards are not in material means or in achievements. There are no greater rewards than through the love of Jesus Christ in helping others overcome where they have been and uplifting others to achieve their goals to help someone else in life. We can witness a positive chain reaction in sacrificing our desires for the next when we apply this living art to our lives, but we first must cleanse any sins before we can truly ever begin to understand the freedom within the Holy Spirit of God.

In the book of (Genesis 13) there is a great lesson in the very beginning that teaches us how to place ourselves behind another and then was fulfilled by Jesus Christ in the New Testament. Abraham taught us this lesson of personal sacrifice with his nephew Lott to eliminate future problems. This lesson is taught for us to apply to our lives before our differences can become a problem. Abraham taught us that love within the family is far more important than fighting over something else in ultimately destroying or splintering the family. When we learn to place ourselves behind others then greater rewards shall come whether in this life or the next. There is a great lesson in this to apply to ourselves and to teach to our children. If all we do is fight over what we have, then what do we have? Some things are worth standing up for, but nothing is worth losing the unity in love for what we have been given. There comes a point in life when we all need to learn how to sacrifice something for our children of tomorrow. Can't you see this in the love of God and the sacrifice of Jesus Christ? When we learn to give, then we learn to receive!

The Lord Jesus taught each of us what every successful leader teaches and puts into place in every strong organization. ***"A true leader or teacher does not act like they are any better than the other.***

They put themselves behind others to help and serve the purpose of reaching a common goal. By learning the art of sacrifice, they learn how to attain new levels in uplifting others."

Can you recall a time of someone uplifting you, and a time that another individual put you down? Which one is easier to recall? Why is it we can remember a negative over a positive when the negative is far from being positive? There are two completely opposite emotions in this that are crucial to always recall in order to keep our selves in tune. One causes us to look up verses the other causes us to look down. Uplifting is the art in teaching that will excel our children to new levels in feeling not only encouragement, but also even knowing they are cared for. As they mature in encouraging ways this will play a major roll in their relationships and in their attitude with others. Think about it! Aren't you more responsive to someone who uplifts positively within love verses someone teaching negatively without any sign of compassion? Don't you respect them more as an individual when they have this understanding? Often people overlook their words and actions in how they can affect others not only in the moment but even in the future. There is a great lesson in the book of (1Samuel 1) in how someone can be hurt by others and we should teach this lesson to our children as the Lord has given it to teach us. By sitting down with our children and painting this picture of Herroh as a young child in their imagination will allow our children to see how taunting others is wrong by allowing them to feel the pain of Herroh as a child under God. By teaching our children how other individuals who pick on or gossip about someone else due to their own iniquities will teach our children how to rise above this negative society. The patience and faith Herroh displayed within this lesson is among many other lessons that we should not only apply to ourselves as an adult but even to our children. This will teach them how to have respect for others and most of all who to stay focused on while not falling into the negativity of this world. When we see children constantly chasing society rather than the Word of God then we will continue to see them taking matters into their own hands and even hurting others with little remorse. An individual can carry a negative comment or negative teaching their entire life until they learn how to overcome it by letting it go in the Word of God and understanding how other individuals who tear down are only hurting themselves in the future.

There is nothing more uplifting to a child than someone encouraging them within their talents to reach higher levels if they choose. But often we can witness parents who try and guide their children to follow their own desires instead of looking for their child's own personal talents. This can hold a child back and even cause them to rebel if not addressed properly. By observing our children and learning to listen to their words we can recognize the strengths in which they carry. There is no difference in the successful Leaders traits in business than a parent or leader at home. Both positions learn to help someone develop their strengths with guidance and encouragement to reach their goals. Every child under God may interpret something different than the other and it is how we express ourselves that can set us apart.

I'll never forget sitting in my living room floor and teaching my son how to build a model rocket one afternoon. The rocket came in a kit with full directions to follow and even decals to make it match the picture on the front of the box. When it came time to apply the decals, I stood the box up and told my six-year old son, "Let's match the picture of the rocket on the box." As he would begin to place a decal in the wrong spot, I would stop him and direct him to match the picture once again. After several attempts to place the stickers where he wanted and myself trying to direct him, he looked up to me saying, "Why do we have to do it like they did? Can't we do it our own way?" (Talk about a lesson from a six year old) I then thought about his comment and said, "You are right, we sure can."

This brings joy in my heart to recall this lesson that I will never forget because when you really think about it in more depth we can begin to see the true picture being developed. Think about it! The rocket body was built properly and intact due to following the directions for the foundation of the structure. It was within the decals in how we expressed ourselves differently. Do you think the looks of the rocket had any impact on how high or how well it flew? Absolutely not! What mattered were the principles and the belief behind the foundation that determined how high and safe it would fly. This can be directly related to our lives and how we teach our children in building from the directions in the Word of God. The Lord instructs us to build from His foundation in our own unique way and always monitor our life during flight.

Many other fallen leaders in our country like Martin Luther King Jr. has taught this same message that was taught to me from my six-year-old son several years ago. Martin Luther King thought along the same lines as my son, "Why do we have to follow someone else who restricts us from being the individual we were set out to be?" Martin Luther King then played a major roll in crossing into new territories with others soon to follow the Christian principle of everyone being equal in having the same opportunity to fly as high as the next man!

Our children can see things in life more clearly than adults at times due to the fact that our vision becomes restricted as we mature. As adults, our vision should be multiplied rather than restricted due to our previous experiences and wisdom gained. But due to becoming complacent or set in our ways, we often allow ourselves to not look beyond our own circumstances to see how things may be affecting others and even ourselves. In the book of (Hebrews 5) we are taught to move from our comfort zone to look beyond ourselves in order to grow. This practice of maturity in the spirit should also be applied in every aspect of our lives to not only grow, but to help others who may be living on milk to one day move to the solid food in the bread of life. By teaching our children and supporting them in their strengths as they mature will develop a relationship that will assist them in their future. One of the most difficult things to do is teach someone without forcing our will upon them and then becoming aggravated when they can't see what we may understand. We often forget our trials in different levels of maturity as we grow mentally, physically, and most of all spiritually when we are trying to help other individuals to see the light and improve their life!

The apostle Paul taught us how to adjust our speech based upon the different levels of maturity. In (1 Corinthians 2), Paul spoke of this wisdom in teaching the basics in order to not overwhelm the crowds with intellectual conversations and cause many to fall asleep due to not understanding, or dragging out the message. How many times have you ever read a book or listened to a speaker who put so much emphasis on showing their intellect that they lost the crowd, or reader, in hearing the message? It is in our human nature to want recognition for our knowledge or achievements, but this is very dangerous if we don't understand how to go from one extreme or to the other in relating with all individuals to keep our perspective on the simple things in life. In the end, it is the simple things in life that we cherish the most!

One of the most disappointing, or hurtful things in life is witnessing other individuals discouraging someone else by negative teaching. In (Colossians 3) we are taught the proper way to teach is to uplift and not tear someone down to possibly lose their self-respect or motivation to carry on. But over the years of drifting away from the Word of God, our society has become ruthless in the lack of caring in how their words or actions may hurt another individual. Everyone grows the same way but we often neglect this based upon our own selfish desires and acting within our emotions in our circumstances in life. It is sad when we see individuals who enjoy tearing someone down instead of treating their neighbor as thyself, and uplifting each other. It is in our human nature of sin to feed on the negatives instead of the positives and we can plainly witness this in the media all around us. Throughout life we need to stop ourselves regularly to not only keep in touch with ourselves but to honestly evaluate what or how we may be teaching our children in order to correct something that may not be right under God. When we don't do this, we are only teaching our children how easy it is to quit or tolerate something not right under God rather than standing up and addressing the real issue at hand. Our children need to know that the easy way is now always the right way and to never give up in life.

When we allow our society or environment to cloud the big picture in life then it can become very easy to only focus on ourselves and not see the big picture from our little picture that we are under

God. It is imperative to the life of our children to be open and teach them with flexibility to expand based on their level of maturity. This is not only good for our children, but also even healthy for the adult to exercise our minds in having flexibility from a child to an adult to stay in tune with life. Think about it! How can an athlete ever grow? Don't they have basic principles or rules to follow? If they played the same opponent all the time, could you see their game staying the same or even limited?

It is very easy to see individuals who simply neglect how to mentally balance in life, and only take the path in which they know without being open to expanding in other directions. We often fall to this due to the work it requires to listen and the work it takes to improve. But the most common problem in our society is with individuals who don't know how to spiritually listen and recognize what is right before them. When someone fails to listen then it is only a matter of time before we will see a separation beginning to take place. It is sad how so many individuals are overlooked due to others not listening or to busy judging while some just plainly forget who they are under God. We all are created equal under God, and the Lord Jesus plainly tells us in (Matthew 10) that no man is above another.

It is very important in negative circumstances to not focus on ourselves but on the life of others. Because when individuals feel as if no one cares then they go into a state of survival in creating circum-stances even worse than they really are. This is a very dangerous state to be in and this is exactly where Satan wants each and every one of us to be emotionally in feeling all-alone. Throughout history we can find many tests on our human strengths and can see where the faithful remained strong to overcome what was before them. We can see this throughout the lessons in the Holy Bible to even in the more recent history of the holocaust of World War II with many other historical events of individuals surviving through horrific events. Our country today is facing some very difficult times in our economy and will continue until we purge all the mistakes that have been put into place by those who did not properly think about the outcome in the future which is now the present time.

Due to our human nature, we often tend to neglect our wrong decisions and not face them with sincerity in thinking we can just move on. But this only prolongs the agony for there is a day we all must face what is before us to truly overcome our issues in life. This plays such a major roll in teaching our children how to handle their differences, their heartaches, and even their obstacles before them. For when we do not think about others and try to cover up where we have been then what does this teach our children of tomorrow?

It is normal to hurt when we are trying to overcome or improve ourselves because if we don't push ourselves, then how can we ever grow stronger? *"As a child, we used to have physical growing pains and as we mature we have mental and aching pains."* The problem that often occurs is the lack of understanding in how to overcome our issues in the Word of God and becoming lazy to do what it takes to really improve our lives. By never addressing our issues or keeping our lives in check under the Word of God, we can cause even more pains in the future and even cause our children to suffer beyond our recognition.

It is easy to fall into a repetitive cycle of trying to patch a problem or run from the real issue at hand, but when this takes place it is only a matter of time before the cycle will be broken. Everyday we pass individuals who are running from something or covering up their hurt with only a fake smile or agenda in not understanding how to stand on their own and search within themselves by listening to the Word of God to find the answers they need. As an individual and as a nation our society has fallen to trying to buy our way out of crisis verses facing the truth in the work that it takes to overcome a serious problem. When we throw money at our children to pacify them, what are we teaching? It is very easy to fall into this negative behavior but it is setting us up for worse problems in the future! Our society has, in large numbers, fallen into thinking that money will solve our problems and there's no doubt it helps. But when we really face the facts, all it is doing is causing us not to address the real issues at hand! The Lord teaches us this principle throughout the Word of God, but often we fall subject to neglecting His wisdom in wanting the attention on ourselves rather than God! This is where we have it backwards!!!

Sometimes, no matter the pain, we must address our issues to rise above where we have been no matter what it takes if it is within the will of God! It is crucial that we teach this to our children for them to apply to their future and to understand how change cannot only affect our lives but also theirs in return. It is very important to consider the affects of change on others but even more importantly to our children. Over the years of personal observation and studying the affects of change on children, the Lord has blessed me with wisdom in developing a chart on understanding the cycles of change based on the age and maturity of a child. There can be a plus or minus by a year or two due to the hands around the child. But on average, we can see this process in our children when we open our eyes to their lives and how they react during change. Below is a chart to study and to look at how our lives can affect our children at different ages from birth. Don't forget each child can be different, but what matters is growing with our children and paying attention to their needs at every stage of their life.

Infant	5 – 6	Young Child	12 – 13	Young Teen	17 – 18	Young Adult
1 – 4	Transition Stage	7 – 11	Transition Stage	14 – 16	Adult Teen	19 - 26

It is imperative to try and understand our children at every age of their life to insure we are not hurting them in their life ahead. There is no way that we will ever understand the maturity process fully due to we are not the Creator or do we have all the answers. All we can do is learn from paying attention to history and the cycles of events in order to possibly improve our future. Let's look at the chart in more depth by recalling our own personal feelings as a child and in acknowledging our own children. Whether we have children or not, we are all children of God and we were once a child in facing different affects of our emotions or needs at different stages of our lives. When we put ourselves mentally back as a child during certain ages, we can recall what is most important to understand and help our children mature. This is only a brief breakdown without going into great detail, and there is something else very important to remember in maturity. Maturity is a process that equals three different parts of physical, mental, and spiritual growth. When we neglect one part the others will suffer. Do you remember when you were a child and you wished you were older? Did your parents ever tell you to enjoy your current time, and as you mature other things will come or develop in time?

Now think about spiritual growth. As we age and study the Word of God we can continuously see things as a child learning from their parent with a humbled heart. Like seeking our parents for answers, we are to seek God through Jesus Christ in order to open our eyes and ears to grow. When we allow man to guide our spiritual maturity, we are not allowing God to be the teacher He can be. Our spiritual experiences are often pushed on another in forgetting how we received the clarity in our own timing verses someone else's. We all want someone to see when he or she may be spiritually blind but when we push our will on another then we are forgetting how this can push others away. Spiritual maturity parallels our physical and mental maturity if we really open our eyes to recall how we matured as a child to an adult.

As you read over the next few paragraphs of how change can influence our children at different ages, also imagine this process of maturity in your mind to better understand the Holy Bible. View the Holy Bible as our Father speaking directly with a single child. He gives birth to the child in the book of Genesis and then gives instruction to Moses in the transition stage of 5 – 6 through the 12-13 age brackets. Once the single child under God reached the teenage years he then gave his child judges and kings upon their wishes throughout their teenage life. During this time period the teenager neglects what he was previously taught and made many promises to get what they desired. There were numerous warnings to return from their rebellion but the teenager refused to listen. Finally our Father had enough of the rebellion in the Old Testament and delivered us in the New Testament in setting us free to mature on our own but with the Holy Spirit to help guide us in life. There is a time in every child's life that they must be set free to see how they will live on their own. You can parallel the overall body of maturity in the Holy Bible from Genesis to Revelation from birth to physical death but far too often we are blinded to the time frame of God's mercy and grace due to only paying attention to the story verses of the lesson in life! Can you now see this parallel of life in the Holy Bible to our life as an individual as we mature in one generation to the next?

The infant years from 1 – 4 are the least affected by change within our entire life. These are the years that we as a child only recognize hunger, pain and love given in compassion from our parents or others. At this particular stage the mother and child's bond is beyond what man can even begin to understand, and a child's cries can be soothed with a melody from the heart. During these years, a child grows comfortable with the familiar faces and grows securely in the arms which surround them, and comfort them. Think about it! Where is the child receiving their security from, in love or in their material items which surround them? How can a child at this age miss something they've never had? We are the ones as the adults who try to pacify or give comfort from something of material means. Do you really think the infant judges the thread count of their blanket or the quality of the crib? All that matters to this innocent child is the care given from the ones who surround them. They can do without all luxuries in life, and live on the necessities to survive in the arms of those who comfort them.

As they mature in this infant bracket they begin to understand yes and no and begin to learn the basics of their surroundings. They begin to pair individuals with one another and witness the love between them. These early years of a child are so vital going forward into their teenage years to give them the time and attention they need.

Our children are very dependent upon us at this stage of life, and most parents recognize this while unfortunately some chose to neglect it. In these years it is vital to teach them with patience and not pacify with something else for our own selfish interest. There is a balance in this that both parents need to recognize in helping one another and understanding the importance of stability. There can be a time to give a pacifier and a time to not. What is more important? Comfort and security in love, or something patching an issue? Who is more important? The child or the adult?

The transition stage from the infant to a young child is where a child begins to look beyond what they have to wanting something else. This is a vulnerable point in teaching a child discipline and the principles of God through the love of Jesus Christ due to it will play a major roll in years ahead. A child in this stage of life may act like they care more about what they receive from immediate gratification because they have no sense of long-term fulfillment. Fulfillment is something gained in maturity of faith and the attention given or not given is vital during these years. It is important to recognize the new influence of change on our children at these ages and how to handle their different emotions. This is where we begin to guide and teach them rather than just picking them up in our arms to nurture when they cry out. It is our duty as a loving parent to not put our responsibility off on someone else, because there is no one that a child would rather have close to him or her than the ones who love them. Think about it! If a child is put off on others, then how or who will they follow in the future?

The Lord Jesus taught us this in the lesson of the donkey and the colt when arriving in Jerusalem in the book of (Matthew 21). Have you ever thought about why He requested her colt by her side? Think about it! What better way to teach a child, when going into new areas of life than to have someone they love and trust by their side? At this age the colt was sure not going to leave his mother but only drew closer when faced with the change of an environment. Not only did the colt receive comfort and security by being close to the one he or she loved, but also by observing how his mother acted in the emotion of the crowd taught a valuable lesson in how they were to act. There is much wisdom in this when we open our eyes to the Lord in raising our children and staying beside them to give them strength in their times of need.

This lesson should be applied and taught throughout our life with our children to give them support in their changes. Because our children are a product of what we teach and show in life that molds them into the individual they are. The difference between a parent and the child is that we can rationalize our thoughts from our own education and experiences while our children are unable to maturely rationalize theirs due to their immaturity in education and lack of experiences.

It is vital to remember that how we live our life and carry ourselves each day will guide our children in their walk of life and even shape them in their character from the transition stage moving through the young child ages of 7 – 11. In these years our children begin to be shaped like a piece of art. Not only being a reflection of the hands around them, but even their environment in which they live. Think about it! Once you begin to build and develop anything in life how we apply pressure and attention will develop its future.

These years of 7 – 11 are beyond crucial in teaching their foundation in life to shape their future. It is one thing to say something, but how we apply it is vital in the message we teach in our actions. Why do you think Moses stressed in (Deuteronomy 6) the importance to teach our children wholeheartedly where to commit in our homes and whom to acknowledge on our doorposts? We can see Israel as a young child at this time under Moses and the Lord was giving them instructions to follow. Can you relate to this, as a parent, to your child in telling them how to stay focused and return home when they become lost in this world? At this age as a young child we can't fully understand, or see the purpose, but we can understand instruction and guidance.

In the maturity of a child, we can notice a sense of separation as they grow. They begin to get caught up in other things, besides being under our feet all the time. There are different levels of this separation based on the maturity of the child. The main thing our children want to know is that we are there for them and we can see them as they watch us in the distance. We can notice them when they play once their excitement begins to diminish in how they begin to look for their comfort and security in love all over again. Have you ever witnessed a child's reaction when they could not locate their security in love? That split second of being alone and scared frightens them, and there is nothing that can fill that void they seek in sincere love which they experience only as a child in the familiar arms around them.

At this stage of childhood it was taught in the book of Exodus through the book of Deuteronomy when you view our Father instructing the entire body as one. The Lord traveled with His children instructing and even remaining close in sight. Like our children when they loose sight, they loose their direction. This weakness in our human nature was revealed in the book of (Exodus 32) after Moses left them at the foot of the mountain while he received further instructions from God. If we don't teach our children the Word of God and the understanding of growing within our weaknesses, then how can someone expect them to have security and strength in their foundation when we are gone? At this stage of our children's life it is vital to teach them where true security comes from. If they rely on man they will only be let down in their future. In this stage of childhood we should begin to release pressure from our hands that surround our child, and observe their actions of when to apply pressure if needed to keep them in tune in the spin of this world. Every loving parent, like our Father in Heaven, wants that piece of perfect living art but due to our human nature of sin the Lord had to send His only begotten Son to show us the way to cover our iniquities.

The transition years between the young child and a teenager are where we begin to see even a further separation between our children and their parents. This is where our foundation and teaching from the previous years will come into play in how we have shaped our children. Let's think about our children in another direction to see the overall joy of growing with our children. Raising a child is like building an airplane and preparing them for flight as they mature into their early teenager years. In the beginning we build and shape them then we become the pilot to guide their direction and then to step a side to be the co-pilot to help when needed. There will come a time as a parent or co-pilot that we must not even board the plane. Only to watch them fly on their own and praying they always remember the foundation from where they began.

During these transition years and teenage years it is very important to step back or loosen the reigns but always remaining in the shadows in their time of need. Don't fall short sighted in thinking we still don't have an influence in their lives because the security in love we give and show will give them the strength more than we ever know!

The years moving forward from the transition stage into the young teen ages of 14 to 16 are totally different from the earlier stages of childhood. At this point, we move from teaching the foundation to maintaining our foundation. This is where we begin to take the co-pilot's seat in observing the new pilot in training, and correcting them and encouraging them when needed to stay on coarse while always providing them a solid foundation in which to land. During this stage we learn to be their friend in addition to being their parent. This is another fine line to balance to insure proper respect of all positions. For instance, if our children or we don't understand our position of seniority, then what happens when our child veers off of course? Can you see how God, our Father, has given us our heading in the Holy Bible? Can you feel this guidance from within when you drift off course? Or, can you feel the power when on course in the Spirit of God?

During these years of a young teen our environment and their immediate surroundings easily influence our children's minds. By not teaching the Word of God in the earlier years will leave a void in their foundation of never knowing how to come home and this is dangerous for our children's sake. Our children, while in flight, will face storms in their path and this is where we are in the control tower at a distance only observing their flight with no actual control. Our radio connection is in prayer and our prayer should be that our guidance of teaching our children where to look will be recalled to guide them through whatever they face in their path. Upon their return, we provide the needed nourishment and maintenance for their future flights to take off all over again.

In the next stage of a child from 17 to the young adult years the roll of a parent changes due to our children seeking further independence. This maturity stage has now moved from the co pilot seat to allowing them to be the pilot they were set out to be. Their roots have been established and this is where every parent prays for their child to find the love they have shared with them as they matured in life. When a child never receives love how will they know how to give love in return?

These are the years that will begin to show their family values as they begin to mature into adulthood in their reflection of the love they show to others. As parents we must begin to teach independence and responsibility in every way we can for our children to handle their future without having to rely on others. This doesn't mean to fully let go, but always be there in case of a fall, because we never know when our child may need to call. Can you see in the Holy Bible and even in today how God is the One in control while we received the instructions to fly in the Word of God and the Holy Spirit being our radio connection to stay on coarse? How about through the love of Jesus Christ personally teaching each of us the way to return home? Here is another thought to never forget, "Don't ever forget the logbook on judgment day in keeping record of our flight, now that we as our children have been set free!"

At this stage from 17 to young adult, their direction has been programmed from their earlier years and this will guide them in their own independence or freedom in flight. It is very important to discuss the facts of life with our children as they mature for them to know the truth and to understand our feelings as we understand theirs. By doing this they will respect our relationship with our honesty and will learn how to be open in their future with others to build stronger relationships when times may become turbulent. It is our duty as a loving parent to constantly try and understand what our children are going through at every stage of their life. By doing this it creates a relation-ship that is inseparable which is a bond of God who gives the love we all share through Jesus Christ.

When we look at the young teen years to the years from 17 to young adult years think about the life of Christ. Jesus came here due to our minds being easily influenced by our environment and our weakness to human nature. Not only did He teach us as we walked with Him, Jesus Christ prepared us for our freedom in our flight. There comes a point in all children that they must learn to fly on their own. If we continue to stand over our children and do everything for them, then how will they ever grow up? Can you see the purpose of Christ in teaching us in whom to believe and how to mentally mature? When you think about planning or taking steps in life what would you honestly expect if you never knew how to achieve your goals or even worse not even know your direction to follow?

The Lord Jesus came here to teach the maturity within freedom in understanding how to not only act, how to think, but even have everlasting life! When we look at the Holy Bible as a single body with a distinct direction, then we can see the overall maturity of a child throughout the Word of God. First learning to crawl with Abraham, and then walk with Moses, then working with the child through their teenage years in giving judges, kings and even prophets to instruct His children when off path. Never did the Lord our Father ever leave or abandon His child throughout the ages. But He observed His children in their freedom over many generations to see how they would return once they learned they could no more stand on their own in thinking they had all the answers in needing no help from God above. All children must be set free to properly mature over time. For when this does not take place they never learn who they are individually under God due to always relying on something or someone else. It is very easy to look at the violence in the Holy Bible in such cruel or drastic measures, but when we really open our mind and think about the entire body of believers being one body under God then how large do we see the body and how minor do we see the discipline to re-align the overall child of God? We can see the discipline on a drastic scale to us individually, but on a small scale to God being the Creator of mankind.

After all the physical discipline in the Old Testament, there came a point in maturity where our Father had to let go physically and begin to teach in love through spirituality to properly mature. This process takes place in the transition years from seventeen through the young adult years of a child and parallels the time period between the Old Testament to the New Testament when we look at the big picture from the little picture we are.

These years during this stage of a child are considered the window of their independence in their individual freedom. But many adults struggle in this stage also, by not wanting to let go of their child. And when this takes place, it only creates a negative dependency in their future by causing our children to not properly understand how to survive on their own and take the easy way out unless they are motivated by something else in their life.

During these years, a child needs to always know their parents are right there for them in advice and comfort to help them grow in their flight of freedom. This is exactly what God our Father did for each of us in giving direction, purpose, comfort, joy, love, and the way home through the blood of Jesus Christ His only begotten Son. But there comes a point in every child's life they must mature, and face their own consequences in their decisions in life. This is where everyone should praise God our Father for loving each of us so much that He never turned His back on the rebellious child, and gave us the bread of life to nourish our souls in (John 6) to fill our needs.

One thing the Lord demonstrates beyond our comprehension is patience, and it is our duty as loving parents to do the same with our children in order to teach obedience as they mature. If we neglect this responsibility, then our children will possibly take shortcuts or never understand the purpose of life and even worse they could possibly miss the eternal life. It is very easy to guide our children to fit our desires but this is where we need to understand their talents and most of all their needs. Often in life we can witness parents who try to mold their children into their desires rather than the child's, and this can cause rebellion or even restrict a child from developing to their full potential. The Lord teaches us that love is not directed, but only by free will, and children are often never taught this. Parents always want their children to have it better than they did as a child, and this can cause a vital lesson to be missed if they don't teach their children how to earn their rewards. Earlier in the book we mentioned the purpose of discipline in only eating enough manna for the day and this is vital to teach at a young age to prepare them for their days ahead.

Rather than having our children try to conform to our desires, we should learn to help our children in conforming to their natural talents. By always holding firm on our values and standards in our foundation we can help our children develop their talents within the ground rules. Observe your children as they mature and recognize their strengths to help encourage them in positive ways to develop their talents. When a child sees you get excited over their works, then they will find motivation in love to do better.

Frequently we can observe many parents who give their children the freedom or material items that they may have missed as a child. But when this takes place the respect for what is given is very difficult to maintain in overlooking what it truly took to achieve their goals in life. Look at the lesson of the two sons of Eli in (1 Samuel) in how they never understood what it truly took to follow the Word of God in achieving their rewards verses understanding the self discipline required and the faith to succeed in life. By giving without properly teaching we are only setting ourselves and our children up for struggles in the future which we are now experiencing in the United States of America. This is unhealthy for the parent, for the child, and even our nation when we lose our perspective in the Word of God, which maintains our balance in life. When we give without work then we lose the appreciation and respect for what we have in life. It is not about what we may give our children in material items but what we give them in the sincere love within our time of life. On most occasions children who receive genuine love but once lose it will search for it until they find it while there are some who never do. A child who knows the feeling of love never wants to let down the ones around them but most of all, the One above them. All they want is their love and attention in growing up! When this is neglected by a parent, then expect to see a child to possibly have a void in love that they may not understand until they receive their own answers in life. This is where the foundation is vital in teaching where love truly comes from in the Word of God. If they know where love comes from, they won't wander in the wilderness of life with no direction.

As we mature in life we are to always grow mentally, physically and most of all spiritually. Within this growth of our freedom, and standing on our foundation the Lord teaches us to follow Him as we grow in life. The apostle Paul instructs each of us to be more like Christ as we mature in our actions and thoughts. There is no doubt we will all stumble or even fall short but this doesn't mean to ever not pick ourselves up and especially to not improve our lives under God! In every aspect of life there is always someone who may excel over others and when we understand the art of this, then we will learn to help others when they show a willingness to learn and receive. We all can learn from each other when we seek the same purpose through the blood of Christ. When we seek to please God in everything we do then the approval of others won't seem so important in our goals. By doing right for God we will be doing better for man!!!

Throughout a child's life even into adulthood, they all seek the same thing in which we all need in love and compassion. When a child only receives discipline how will they know to ever show their feelings? And when they only receive compassion or tolerance how will they know to have discipline? There is a major lesson in this taught throughout the Word of God in two becoming one and each part plays a roll in order to maintain balance.

When a single parent plays the roll of the mother and the father it is imperative that they learn the importance of both rolls. A mother must have firm discipline and still give compassion. Like the father must have compassion while he gives proper discipline. If there is a void neglected in either of these rolls then our children could possibly miss something vital in life. This is a very difficult situation for any parent but the main thing is that we recognize each other's roll to do our best to teach our children proper balance.

Let's change gears to open our eyes further before we come to a close in this chapter of the book. When is the last time you have really opened your eyes to nature? Have you ever paid attention and noticed specific behaviors between the different species of life? You will find that each one has its own beauty and even shares the same purpose of sustaining life. Rarely will you witness animals encroaching on others and when they do the predator side will show. Animals within the same species rarely fight over life and when this happens it is often a test for leadership and/or territories. Can you see a relation from this to our human nature?

In all common species there is peace among the herds excluding the ones who want to rule or have power. Each individual animal is territorial of their space but they learn to respect the others by not invading or pushing their individual zones. When one animal begins to get too close, there is always some sort of scuffle. You rarely see the same species fighting with one another when they have plenty to eat and room to grow. Why is it with our thinking capabilities we can't learn to put aside our personal differences and focus on the common interest of having peace in life?

You would think that with the capabilities, which we all have, this issue of understanding should not be a problem to achieve. We have the means to communicate and reason in our thinking process beyond any other animal species on earth. The Lord has given us all natural instincts, the Holy Spirit, and even His wisdom in the Word of God. But where we get into trouble is in our desires. There is nothing wrong with desires as long as we maintain our focus on the Will of God. When our desires take over our long range plans in understanding life, then someone always gets hurt or left behind. These desires are often enticed by Satan in wanting us to take our eyes off of what we know and whom we love.

Our common traits among men can be observed in male animals and the same can be witnessed between the females. Think about it! How many men do you see searching for something with power or pushing themselves on someone else? What about men who cannot control their sexual desires? How about witnessing the common trait of a mother nursing and caring for an infant at birth? There are different levels of male or female characteristics within each individual and this development of a child's character can be witnessed from a young age when we look at it. There should be a level of respect and understanding on all differences. Neither should force their way on the other but we all should recognize the natural pattern in life. When we try to force our desires of the flesh into the natural cycle of life, then there will be constant struggles with restricted directions going forward.

On a large part, majorities of people don't take the time to study the similarities between animals and humans. But when we look at it up close we can see many common characteristics between the species of life. Take for instance a head of horses in the wild. There is always one stallion that will stand out and if he had it his way he would be the only one among all the mares. The mares on the other hand mostly get along but then there are some who try to attract the stallion by certain walks or even revealing more than they should show. Solomon wrote on this in (Proverbs 7) to warn our children and ourselves of how to avoid this behavior, and control our emotions.

There are many characteristics of animals, which we can find in humans but our major difference is our mind in deciphering right and wrong. It has been proven in how animals can retain learned behavior by repetition and discipline. But we not only have this capability, we have the wisdom from God on forward thinking and the capability to rationalize our thoughts. Often where we fall short is not looking at our future affects of our decisions on others and only caring about our immediate desires. This is crucial for our children to understand and witness for their proper growth in how our decisions create a ripple affect on others.

In the Old Testament the scriptures are full of men with many wives and/or concubines. The Lord plainly teaches us in the beginning the sanctity in two being one in marriage with the consequences of what to expect when someone is unfaithful. Look at Abraham for instance on his troubles between Sara his wife and Hagar in the book of Genesis to relate to a divided home. Throughout the Word of God we can see the hurt that can be caused by sexual misbehavior. This not only takes place in the males but also in the females. One of the male's weakest links since the beginning of time is their desire to be that stallion amongst the herd. Rather than understanding their position as they mature they still seek to observe either from a distance by their walk or even their talk. It is one thing to recognize the beauty of a woman but another to not respect her or what you already have. The Lord Jesus taught a great lesson in taking our actions to our thinking and this is crucial to teach to our children.

Throughout the Word of God from Abraham to David to King Herod we are taught the consequences of sexual desires and this is vital to keep in mind. Like King Herod many men have underestimated the power of sexual enticement and been willing at the moment to give away everything they have only for pain in return at a later date. Don't fall short into thinking you can resist any temptation of evil, because if we are not careful without Christ our head could be the one on the platter when we allow our weakness to be tempted too closely!

Our children need to recognize through proper teaching and see the strength of their parents in staying true to their partners in life. This will not only affect them in their lives but in their future in how they respect their position in a relationship. No loving parent wants his or her children to suffer heartaches. By teaching them in our actions the sanctity of love with honor and loyalty to one another they will see the importance of being true to everyone around them!

There is a very important factor to always remember and understand in life. ***"Just because someone may have failed previously, does not mean to quit but learn how to overcome in understanding what went wrong."*** This is done by learning to rebuild ourselves and always put emphasis on teaching our lessons, in order to respect life! Our children watch and learn from what we teach and show. The Lord teaches us more on this understanding in the Holy Bible beyond our comprehension. We are all his children and when we take the time to read the Word of God imagine yourself as the child you are to allow the Lord's hands to shape your life or improve it with direction and purpose to move forward!

It is vital to teach our children how to recognize the differences in human desires and recognizing the Will of God in our relationships. By allowing God to shape our lives with patience and understanding in how to respect others, our children will find strength in true love. Just look at how things built of man-made desires deteriorate over time verses what is built out of love and discipline are still standing till this day. When we build on the love of Christ and on God's foundation we can attain love beyond our imagination.

Our differences in talents and even cultures can be related to the many sunsets in which we see. Each sunset has its own beauty based on the position and perspective from which we observe it. In each one we will find specific patterns and even colors that reach beyond mankind. Do not neglect your sunset in life and begin to think yours is the only one. Because before you know it your life or vision could be little to none. The Lord penetrates with rays of light that never change unlike a sunset in every second of life. Each one has its own purpose to reveal God's Glory to his name!

In the book of (Exodus 28), we are taught that the Lord blesses and fills individuals with certain talents different than others. We all have the capability to learn a talent but there is a major difference in someone who learns to build on their own natural talents of God. You will be able to feel the depth of the Lord in bringing to life whatever their talents may be! The love of the Lord is something we feel and not something that stops with only us. Do not get caught up in all the other different ways certain individuals are portraying success. True success comes from the heart and only through Jesus Christ! There are many different messages being taught and shown in this world, but if we cannot understand our position in life then we will struggle to maintain our balance. The Lord Jesus Christ taught us this understanding in everyone being equal beyond our full comprehension.

In all differences it is imperative to remember what unites each and every one of us. Unity does not just happen without understanding. We must work at it each and every day to form harmony within the spirit of life. Harmony is not something achieved in a single note. It takes two or more to learn the harmony of being one. When we find that one person carrying the entire load, be careful because the life of the note could eventually fade. Each individual can find harmony within the spirit of God when they learn how to unite through Jesus Christ. The Lord is there waiting on the sideline to hear our call, and when we surrender our will, we will discover harmony by dropping our wall.

When two work together as one, their harmony in love will build to last. In your life touch others out of kindness to create your note in passing to the next. It is all in how your notes meet in your touch that will determine the life of the future. So, as you teach your children and touch others, show respect to help others appreciate the differences in each generation to come. This will help other people in their balance and their walk to stay united for the peace in love which is needed to reach harmony in their individual music of life.

In some circumstances we will find that when two or more cannot come together in learning how to work together for the common purpose of life, then their music can be one sided in not understanding how to truly unite. Respect each individual for who they are and allow the Holy Spirit to teach us the music to be played. This will allow our children to open their eyes and ears beyond our sight. The purpose in love is to not just stop with us but to affect others through each step of life. The object of each parent's life, like our Fathers in Heaven above, is for each generation to learn and improve from where we began. So always remember this in your actions and where you stand!

(To God All Glory, Amen)

The Keys of a Piano

Our character traits are like keys on a piano when you really think about it! If we only learn one way then how can we expect to learn the art of living? There is a balance to stay in tune along with certain lines not to cross. But the important factor to remember is if we miss a certain note, then that trait may struggle or possibly never develop. No one can play the perfect tune due to each individual has a difference. What matters is the common ground in which we all stand and learn to love what God has given in the land. Learn the character traits to promote growth and watch the music of your child come to life. There is nothing more gratifying than the love of a child looking up to its parents. This is what the Lord enjoys when we focus on Him and learn how to live each and every day. The Lord rejoices when He hears and sees the music on our hearts. So as you develop your character, don't overlook certain keys because you never know when we could get knocked to our knees.

It is crucial to know our children and realize that our lives guide their future. There is only one Perfect Father and one Perfect Son who taught us the meaning of two being one. Life does not stop with us and we have already been given everything we need. So search the Word of God and follow Jesus' lead. (To God All Glory, Amen)

CHAPTER 7

Time Out

*T*he life and sanity of every individual in this world is vital in knowing when to call time out to maintain our focus, balance, and future. This can seem very difficult at times to do when we become wrapped up in the pressures of our society, and forget how to breathe in life. Our lives can seem very complicated in learning how to balance when we separate ourselves from God, but often we neglect how simple it is when we become lost in the world. The Lord has given us numerous instructions on how to maintain every aspect within life in the Holy Bible, but we tend to always neglect what we already have looking for something new. This whole process of taking time out daily is vital mentally, physically, and spiritually not only to us, but also to every other individual in this world.

It is very wise to always know where, when, and how to stand mentally, physically, and spiritually before we ever begin to venture into new areas. Not only do we need to know our position under God through Jesus Christ, it pays to look at the overall picture that our world is painting all around us. Because when we step forward, we better_know_ how to stay in control, face our obstacles and especially whom to watch out for! If we are not prepared in our decisions in life, then would you say we are not thinking or believing, as we should be?

Can you recall a time when feeling overwhelmed and even struggling to catch your breath? How about making a decision based on pressure, and later regretting your choice? This is a common characteristic among all individuals, and this is where we should learn to listen to God in our hearts to keep our focus in giving us peace in every circumstance in life. For when we don't have God in our lives then there is no peace, no direction, nor even purpose but only existence in a temporary life!

In all positions that we seek to attain, there is no excuse to drop our standards or values which the Lord has given to achieve our objectives, and this is where Satan wants us to feel the pressure in causing us to think we have no other choice when we really do! For if we don't properly think our decisions through we are not only hurting ourselves but our children of tomorrow.

We all have made wrong decisions, and some even more frequent or larger than others at times. But what matters is what we learn from them and apply to our lives to possibly share with others to prevent the same cycle from reoccurring all over again. The objective in every circumstance in life is to be mature enough to take time out to maintain our perspective before we lose our balance and possibly fall. During this time out, it helps to focus or refocus in where we are going or where we went wrong in our goals to maintain our unity with God to receive our understanding in order to move forward again. Have you ever witnessed an athlete or a team who came from behind after halftime? What do you think they did during this time out period? Do you think they took the time to review the plays, study the rulebook and refocus in where they lost control? How about learning to listen to the coach and refocusing on the art of the game? Where you see a team or individual place their heart in belief is where they find strength to overcome where they are or where they have been. The object during time out is to breathe, focus, and understand our position in order to grow. All things are possible with the Lord on our side and in our hearts, no matter how far behind we may have fallen. The Lord plainly tells us in (Luke 16) **"No one can serve two masters"**, this is where we understand the art of focusing on our goals while keeping our perspective on God first and everything else second.

There is strength in numbers when united for a common goal, and a true team can recognize an athlete who has fallen and picks them self back up again with a true repentant heart with an understanding going forward. For if a team or a coach doesn't help or support a player when down, then who do you feel is guiding their actions and spiritual behavior?

In every sector of life whether in our homes, in our work, in our church, and even in our nation, there is no better feeling than individuals whom uplift and support one another in giving them strength like they can't explain in proper words. The reason we can't explain is because it is of God and not man! Why do you think we see more and more of those whom tear others down verses lifting them up? Can you see this growth since our government began removing God from our foundation in our schools, in our work, and now it is happening in our homes even with the currency, which God provides or can take away? The goal of every individual should be to learn how to move together and encourage one another in unity for our children's future. But if we can't learn to breathe together, walk together, and serve together than how can we honestly expect to live together? Our actions daily affect our children beyond our recognition, and especially when they witness our trials in life. It is up to every mature adult to be the example they should be under God through the love of Jesus Christ to teach them how to live and go forward while encouraging others along the way. Not only in the moment around others, but even when we are all alone with the eyes of God watching our actions in revealing our true faith.

It is very easy to neglect what we have when we get too wrapped up in our own box of life, and don't pay attention to our surroundings. By getting caught up in the emotion of our circumstance we often overlook our standards, which guide our children's future. But what truly matters is how we recognize and apply ourselves to overcome our stumbles, to possibly prevent others from making the same mistake twice.

Over the years we have witnessed individuals losing control, when they get so wrapped up in pressure, and don't know how to handle it. If we don't learn how to take time out and breathe, we will never overcome the same cycle of events from our history. This whole struggle has been going on since the beginning of time and many individuals still don't recognize how to stop and truly listen. Some just neglect what they know while others just don't understand or let's say "See the light" in recognizing the importance of slowing down to keep their focus in life. You can witness this in history throughout the Word of God to our present time in our children to adults losing control and even taking someone else's life.

Let's look at this scenario of a game being played like football and the other team is behind so they begin to run their mouth or trash talk. What do you think the team who is talking trash is trying to do? Do you think maybe they are trying to affect their opponent psychologically in causing them to lose their focus in the game? What do you think the purpose or motive of the losing team is in calling time out just before you kick the possible field goal, seconds before the clock runs out?

This is exactly the same type of scenario Satan works in the spiritual world. The Lord teaches us to stay focused and Satan is steadily trying to use someone to persuade or remove our focus during our lifetime. There's always someone trying to misguide us in the wrong directions in order to tear us down, and you will meet many individuals who don't even recognize whom is guiding their actions spiritually until it is too late. Have you ever stopped and really thought about the wisdom the Lord teaches us in stopping ourselves to prepare and the importance of taking one day to observe the Lord in proper order? The Lord Jesus plainly teaches us about the Sabbath day in (Matthew 12), and He directly shared with us how the Sabbath day was given for each of us due to our needs of the flesh. Don't you think God our Creator knows more about our human nature than we do? Everyone needs time out to not only stay focused daily, but ultimately to remove ourselves weekly to re-nourish our souls and keep our perspective where it should be on God rather than on man!

If you listen to a majority of the specialist in this world, they all seem to be repeating the same message already given from God who gives the answers in the Holy Bible. But we tend to search physically, rather than believing spiritually due to our weakness in this world and lack of proper faith. By giving us the commandment of the Sabbath day in order to rest, the Lord knew that if we continuously worked then we would begin to neglect not only what we have in our health, our relationships, but even in His creation in which He is sharing with each of us.

When we don't stop, we lose touch with not only ourselves, but with our environment around us causing us to ultimately neglect our Creator and Supreme Judge in heaven above. Our society likes to call this Eco Friendly or Going Green, and that is where Satan has caused us to remove our focus from God the Creator. Everything in this world has a natural coarse, a purpose, and a reason under God. But more often than not, we tend to neglect or not appreciate what God has given to each of us due to getting lost in our own box of life.

Prior to Noah in the Holy Bible, we can see how the world fell to sin in losing their perspective, their morals, and even falling to unnatural events causing complete disrespect for what the Lord has given. At this point in time the world had free reign to see how we would act with very long life spans, but the earth became corrupted with evil due to our lack of control in the flesh of man. This is why our life spans were shortened; due to the amount of evil we could produce over several generations. Think about it! When we feel like sin or pressure is everywhere, where does time go? For whether we are living in sin or surrounded by sin, our focus is removed from where it should be and we lose track of what is really taking place all around us. When we allow the pressures of this world to control our emotions and actions without understanding time through the Word of God, then our physical lives can pass by with a blink of an eye. At this stage prior to Noah, the human race had no control and had to be corrected in order to start again. Ask yourself before it is too late, How often do you truly stop and spend quality time with the ones you love daily? What about helping or encouraging others in need? Life is too short when we lose our perspective within the time we are given. We are weak in the flesh and need reassurance daily in order to maintain our perspective, relationships, and spiritual life. Why do you think the Lord in (John 12) said **"I have both glorified it and will glorify it again?"** Why is it that once we are told something it is not enough to understand and believe? Why must we be reminded over and over as an adult like an immature child being told to do something in responsibility and not to question? There is only one answer to all of this in the deception of Satan in causing us to waver from what and whom we know is right under the law of God!

The Lord, Jesus Christ, gave us explicit directions on how to serve in the book of (Matthew 25) and we all fall short in taking time to abide to His message. Our human nature is easy to allow ourselves to become self-centered when we get so wound up mentally in thinking we don't have time, and causing us to neglect our purpose of serving the Lord, which in turn guides us to serve others in need. Ask yourself when you feel pressured or pulled in many directions, Am I doing this according to my freewill or am I doing it to please man? We all have responsibilities in serving, but not to please man in the flesh but only God in heaven. If we are not careful we can easily become overwhelmed in our society and taking on too much at one time. This can be related personally, financially, and even spiritually. Often we fall subject to thinking we can handle something without properly respecting the purpose of shaping and molding in proper timing. How many times have you ever heard a child say, "I'm mature enough, I can handle it?" This character trait doesn't just happen with our children you can see it in adults all around us. It is in our human nature to want something before we may be really ready for it and this can be compared in the process of making pottery. For there is great wisdom in the process of forming clay pots when you compare it to our lives when we really open our eyes and ear's to hear Gods' message in which He gives.

In this process of shaping, molding, and curing the pottery that all clay pots must go through before they are complete there is one crucial factor to understand, having time to cure before they can receive. If we neglect or overlook the purpose in this entire process then there can be cracks that eventually cause them to break. Our lives parallel the clay pots on the turntable of earth, and if we don't learn to respect the maturing process in the principles behind time, then how do we honestly expect our children to ever maintain Gods' foundation in life? It is so easy to become distracted when we follow the world in feeling that we don't have enough time in the day. Honestly, the days and nights over a twenty-four hour period couldn't be any better than what we have, and our biological clock, that only God can fully explain, gives us the signs of our needs when we pay attention to our health.

There is a cycle of productivity in every sector of life throughout the day when you really think about it. The morning sunrise brings life and the evening sunset brings rest. It is how we learn to prioritize our goals based on our timing throughout the day with the Lord in our focus and He will show us the way to bring things together that won't fall apart! Think about it! Everyone starts out sluggish in the morning and then begins to rise. There is a peak period during the day where we all maximize our strengths and then begin to tire due to our limitations of the flesh. It is imperative to our health to take time-out periodically to maintain our productivity and stay in touch with life.

Over the years of personal observation the Lord has blessed me with the wisdom to recognize these characteristics of productivity during the day, to the week, and even recognizing certain traits during different seasons of the year. When we do nothing but rush through life, what message do you feel this teaches our children? How can we learn to relax and truly focus if we are always worried about the time? It is vital to our child's maturity that we teach our children what the Lord gives in true balance with Christ in letting other things go and focusing on the moment in which we are given. Based on past observations, and now with a clearer understanding from the Word of God in the Holy Bible, the Lord teaches us how to balance time while it is our responsibility to recognize our own emotional patterns. We can see a direct pattern each week in our emotional productive state when we really pay attention to ourselves and we can even recognize the need of stopping ourselves on the seventh day in our week to stay in touch with life through Jesus Christ.

On average, Mondays are common for struggles in restarting where we left off the week before. Tuesdays seem to always pick up in productivity and our energy levels tend to increase. On Wednesdays we can see strength and creativity moving forward in the week. Thursdays seem to be, on average, the most productive day of the week mentally and physically. The reason for this is because we have gained momentum from earlier in the week, and because we know what tomorrow brings. Fridays are always good no matter where we are in life, but often people tend to not maximize the day due to their mind begins to wander off on tomorrow. Saturdays are still productive and our mind can run just as strong if we choose to not stop and begin to slow down. When we don't stop on the Sabbath day our minds continue to run and not relax to properly receive what the Lord gives causing us to lose touch spiritually and even begin to neglect life all around us.

Not everyone has the same work week and some even may not relate to this pattern, but the importance of this is to recognize how we learn our own individual needs to maximize our time in productive ways. Our work week is a race and if we can't learn to control it, then it will begin to control us! By not prioritizing our time daily based on our personal and spiritual needs, we are limiting what we are given in life. This will not only affect us, but everyone else in our environment. There is great satisfaction gained in learning to balance time in different levels of life and making the most of everyday in every positive way no matter where we are in life or what we are going through! When we have God in our lives, there is a joy that no man can take away, and you will find this joy causing envy to those who don't truly understand the Word of God in the Holy Bible. This is why the true Christians have been martyred throughout history, but it is our job to love and pray for every lost soul in this world to see the light in Jesus Christ.

Many individuals tend to just drift through the week, while others push the week to improve something in their life and even others. The object in personal growth is to recognize our strength's and acknowledge our weaknesses to build upon them with God in our focus to maintain our mental, physical, and spiritual strength in every aspect of our life. In order to grow and maintain strength we must know our roots and goals to properly address them daily. If we don't know our roots or our goals, then where is our meaning in life?

With every new day we are given, we should strive to nourish every part of our lives to reach our maximum potential in every way we can. In addition to ourselves, we should seek the same growth in our relationships, in our work, and most importantly with God through Jesus Christ. There is a balance in this daily, and it is important to not neglect any sector of our life in order to maintain our perspectives. This balance is vital to the life of our children in not only how we give them quality time, but also how we teach them to maintain their lives as they mature. Remember the pottery, on the turntable of earth? There is a vital part required from both male and female parents in their hands in how they shape their children into the adults they become. What happens when we apply too much pressure or not enough touch to the clay being shaped on a turntable of earth? Or even worse, when we allow our children or the clay to mature completely on there own without any hands around them? Think about it! Picture yourself as a gardener and you are working in a large greenhouse. Your greenhouse is earth and it is your responsibility to take care of the plants or people in your life. Within the environment of the greenhouse there are rows and rows of other plants of all species from young to old. Within these rows they represent your spouse, your children, your parents, your grandparents, your friends, people you don't even know, your job, your church, your relationship with God, and the list goes on and on when you open your eyes and ears to the message given. Within these rows from young to old plants in life, each has a point of birth from the seed, and a point of physical death before passing another seed to the soil to replenish hope before they move on. The young to the old can represent the beginning and end of not only our lives, but also our goals in life. Just like life, our goals are planted and carried out from the ones we leave behind when we properly teach and share them with others. This message parallels the message in (John 12) when Jesus said, "Unless a grain of wheat falls into the ground and dies, it remains alone, but if it dies, it produces much grain."

Now ask yourself what happens when the gardener neglects the environment of the greenhouse? What about when the gardener overlooks or neglects certain infections in plants that may be spreading to others? How about when the gardener neglects one of the rows of children, they're spouse, work, or even our Creator? Could you possibly see one of the neglected rows either fading away or growing out of control? Can you see possible consequences to follow? How you maintain and observe is crucial to the longevity and growth of every row in life. Think about the best way to water your plants in life. Do you hit them directly with a direct line of approach or can you see the importance of taking your time with a gentle mist? There is a time to be direct but if you neglect the need for a gentle mist, then how would anyone believe you ever cared? How about the gardener who only acknowledges the pretty flowers, and neglects the others that may look different or may need help? Would the gardener be doing his or her job properly in only giving attention to those certain individuals in life?

Now think about yourself as the owner of the greenhouse and you returned from a trip only to see how the plants were neglected. Would you fire the gardener or possibly try to teach him the importance of not neglecting life? Your approach and actions will reveal your heart in your love for life. So now I ask you, can you feel the mist or did it bounce right off?

There is another important factor to remember in gardening and that is to watch out for all the different fertilizers in this world. Because everyone is searching for that miracle grow and they never learn the art of certain amounts in proper timing to gain the true fruits in life. If they are not careful when using false nutrients, they could either stunt the growth or even worse, burn the plants up! The most important part of gardening is giving proper nourishment in due time, never neglecting the roots and always maintaining the soil in the foundation.

Each individual who reads this analogy should take time out to analyze their own greenhouse and every row within their life. The first step in ever improving our relationships and reaching our goals is crucial in how we learn to nourish properly in the right soil of God with the gentle mist within time. This will lead to a much happier life and fulfillment in knowing when our superior and supreme judge returns that our jobs are being done properly or to be the best of our capabilities. There is no way in the flesh to be perfect or to not miss something, but the important part is striving to maintain every row and plant in our life to grow stronger. When we feel that we only have so much time, then how can we give proper attention? In addition to all of this above, when we feel something is not right under God then nip it in the bud before it grows or possibly spreads beyond our control.

This can seem very difficult at times to do when we are wrapped up in the pressures of our surroundings. In the book of (Exodus 18), Moses teaches us how to overcome the feeling of being overwhelmed and to maintain our productivity. This whole process exists within two elements of prioritizing our time and learning how to let it go, and how to delegate to others. If we struggle with this process, then we will find our productivity either being restricted or even falling behind, before our lives move to chaos. Every successful leader has learned the art of prioritizing and letting go of certain task in proper delegation. Moses' father-in-law taught us this in how to delegate to others who are qualified to handle the job. Many successful teachers like Napoleon Hill, Earl Nightingale, have repeated this quality and the list continues to travel. But we must remember who originally gave us this instruction, for it was not man, but God! Over the years of removing Gods' Word in our society there has been a downward spiral of no loyalty and proper teaching that creates weak relationships in every sector of life. When we fall to pressure without the proper under-standing of following God, and lack understanding of discernment in individuals we tend to give task to certain individuals who don't properly understand nor have God in their lives allowing them to receive what they need in instruction to move forward in their task. When you give someone a task understand their level of experience and their willingness to be loyal in achieving your objectives. Many individuals can talk a good game, but never comprehend how to play.

Even when we are in a position to delegate doesn't mean to abuse your title, and begin to think someone is less than you. It is very easy to separate ourselves if we are not careful and this is where we need to recall that a common goal of unity in moving forward does not happen with separation. All parties must feel important as the next and this will improve the productivity of the overall objectives. As Moses taught in the book of Exodus, if certain individuals can't resolve an issue, then no one is neglected the right to go higher up with proper order and discipline. Nor did Moses exclude himself from the crowd, but walked with them every step of the way. When we begin to separate ourselves, people will begin to lose focus and not properly care for the steps ahead. The closer you stay with the ones around you, you will find that they will learn to respect you and even help you. Don't ever fail to think that someone else is not being influenced by your actions!

One of the most difficult times to manage is how to maintain control during change. Everywhere we look, something is changing and this is normal due to the cycle of life. But as the world continues to turn, it is imperative to find your level of contentment before you ever begin to move forward. Can't you see the importance of preparation prior to change? The Word of God throughout the entire Holy Bible teaches us not only what to expect, but how to handle and prepare. It is so easy for each of us to put off issues that we must face in time and this only makes matters worse not only for ourselves but also for our children ahead. Very few people want to ever face change due to becoming complacent in their life or for the work that it will require. When have you ever witnessed a game that was won where the players stood around with their hands in their pockets neglecting the effort to improve the overall game? Think about it, if you know what is coming at you in change, wouldn't it be wise to prepare your skills before the change takes place?

This is where it is important to take time out and evaluate what you must do to not only be prepared but also be on top of the game. The last thing anyone wants is to be blind sided when you possibly had time to prepare. There is nothing wrong in change, and it is healthy for the mind, as long as you are content with who you are. But when you have no foundation, the affects of change can be horrendous to your health and even knowing how to breathe. The pendulum of life can be balanced when prepared and properly anchored! It is very easy for our picture to become foggy when we get caught up in our society and we don't take time out daily to keep our priorities in focus.

Life today can be very easy to get sidetracked with how fast everyone has been pushed in this new technology age and with all the negativity being shown or discussed everywhere we turn. It is vital, like our ancestors, to anchor our homes and lives with God in our focus. By keeping our attention on the Lord first, our goals will remain clear as an individual, as a Christian, and as a nation. The lives of our children are at stake if we don't learn to stay focused on our priorities and teach them how to carry out certain standards in life. Our children not only watch us in how we spend our time, but they also are influenced by our culture. Can't you see the love our Father had for each of us in leaving us explicit instructions to build upon within the Word of God? No loving parent wants their child to just be thrown into the swimming pool without learning how to swim first through proper direction. How we teach our children relates to how the Lord teaches us. Don't neglect the time to build your home and family on God's foundation to improve our children's future.

Change or growth needs to be treated like opening a door with a chain latch behind it for security and control. You open it one link at a time and sometimes two, based on the strength in maturity. When the door is just left open without understanding of proper discipline, then what do you think will happen? This can be a disaster due to our human nature without understanding the importance of restrictions and guidelines to follow. Our founding fathers armed our door with the strength of God, our Creator, and supreme judge. In addition, we need to run our home the same way.

In the book of (Romans 12), the apostle Paul warns us not to fall into the customs of this world and be content with the Lord. He was not telling us to be stagnant, but never lose sight of our Creator. Throughout the entire Word of God, it continuously points out how we can become lost and neglect what we already have been given. It is in our nature to become lost in numbers or in false desires causing us to neglect the truth behind the Word of God. It is very important to recognize the difference in passing something positive through the love and teachings of Christ verses trying to gain temporary satisfaction in pleasures of this world. Pleasures are very tempting because they can be so easily achieved. True love is often neglected due to it requiring discipline and sometimes even sacrifice. This causes many individuals and couples to stumble and even fall. The sad part of pleasures, or false desires, is how they reflect false hope. This can be related directly to what our society has been displaying throughout our history. When you study the Word of God, this is plainly pointed out throughout the Old Testament to the New Testament.

Why is it that some individuals and nations haven't figured this out? Why is there a continuous repetitive cycle of struggles throughout our history and in the Holy Bible? Is it because of greed? Is it because of not being content? Is it not for respecting someone else? Is it not for respecting the Word of God? Or is it all of the above? Many of the issues that we see or encounter begin on an individual basis and then grow to our homes, places of work, and ultimately to our nation. Over the last sixty years, America has faced some drastic changes in our society. For our own personal stability and health, let's look at our culture of today verses the culture of our past. To give us a better understanding of what we face in today's society, and what our children will encounter in the years to come. Keeping our perspective in life and focus on God has become a tougher task due to many distractions being put right in front of our face daily. Let alone the fact of individuals removing or moving away from the true teachings of the

Word of God in their homes, in our schools, and now even to our government neglecting the truth. There is a balance that we must strive towards. For this to happen it is going to take individual sacrifice and unity in the purpose of love for our children.

The luxuries of today are in no comparison of where we were in the last thirty years much less the last sixty years. The items that we now recognize as a necessity are nothing more than an amenity. My children panic now when I ground them from a cell phone. How would they handle it if they were grounded from A/C? Or how would the modern home react without a microwave? Our luxuries of today are very nice to have over what it used to be and they continue to get better. The vital part of our luxuries is remembering the essentials to live, learning how to be content with whom and what we have. Always keeping focus and appreciation to God for giving us what He has. In the book of (Matthew 6), Jesus teaches us not to serve two masters. When you fall into this materialistic trap, you find a continuous cycle that never ends and eventually someone can get hurt. Do you think the marketing side of our culture wants you to believe or understand this? Absolutely not! They want us to make spur of the moment purchases and not care about the affect. You can see the same in our lending institutions, since they lobbied Congress to drop regulations in lending, creating a very competitive banking market. These changes, creating softer regulations, opened up new doors and territories that were previously controlled and restricted. I guess our government was thinking or counting on proper leadership in discipline and social responsibilities within the lending industry to maintain proper control. Well, we can see the results from this course of action. These softer regulations eventually caught up with, not only our economy, our personal debt, but now even affecting our neighboring nations. What example are we showing, not only to our children, but also to our neighbors? It is bad enough to have debt at home, much less owe our foreign countries.

David Walker, the US comptroller general, stated on July 23, 2007 that, *"Foreign interests have more control over the US economy than Americans, leaving the country in a state that is financially imprudent. More and more of our debt are held by foreign countries, some of which are our allies and some are not."* This statement of fact isn't very encouraging, but to improve, we must face the truth, even though it may hurt.

Our nation's founders were against debt like many of our ancestors. Over the last forty years, and especially the past ten to twenty years, debt has become just a common thing in our society. Borrowing capability is good as long as there is a plan to pay it back. Sometimes the plans just become a little more risky, but if we didn't take risk, where would we be? Due to the moral downfall and the ease of previous bankruptcy laws, many individuals have lost out. Any and every individual should search every alternative or excusable means before bankruptcy is taken. Not only does this affect the debtor, the consumer, and the taxpayer, it also places a burden on the person who cares. Thomas Jefferson once wrote, "I place economy among the first and most important of republican virtues, and public debt as the greatest dangers to be feared."

In the book of (Matthew 18), Jesus taught an excellent lesson in the parable of the unforgiving debtor, not only in monies, but also in their unforgiving hearts. Each and every lost individual is bankrupt without the acceptance of Jesus Christ whether you have money or not, you will be broke without the blood of "Christ.

Our economy has taken such a ride over the past thirty years with all the economic changes. It would have been nice if we would have been told to at least prepare ourselves for the fall of the seesaw when the other party jumped off. Someone in leadership surely looked beyond just the immediate transaction and saw the possible consequences that would follow the deregulation in lending, global trade, and the Internet highway which took place in the late 80's and early 90's. If the technology boom would not have hit, we would have been in a big mess with the loss of our American jobs. Based on this, we need to thank God for taking care of us, not man. Regarding the softer lending restrictions, this just took a longer cycle to show up or let's say, "Hit the fan." You can only trade paper so long before someone calls the debt, like the king in the parable Jesus spoke of in

(Matthew 18). One very important lesson to remember is that when the access to money becomes easy, there will be consequences to follow.

Our children of today and of tomorrow face some of the most difficult moral and financial issues that this country has ever had to face. The most important thing to remember during these times ahead is our relationship with God and following His directions. No matter where we are in life, with God, we can overcome and face any situation. In the book of 1 John, we are taught that, "Greater is He that is within us, then he that is in the world." Recently there was a book published titled, "How Would Jesus Vote?" It should have been, "Are You Ready for Jesus to Convict?" If Jesus was present physically, He would do more than kick the tables clearing the temple, He would clean house! Jesus is passing His vote on our hearts but very few are listening. Everyone is fighting to be the artist in a painting that has already been determined, and forgetting or neglecting the Word of God, our Creator, and our Supreme Judge.

When you look at how fast our technology market has sped, not only us up, but everything else also. The only thing that keeps them alive is how fast they can develop and sell the next item. It was great at first, but now the technology market has hit a plateau with spikes every now and then keeping them going. The main technology focus has turned to speed and how much we can get out of a compact device. They need to take this technology to different levels rather than to our children trying to drive, text, and now watch videos on the phone. This technology is really neat, but what purpose does it serve? Are our children growing from it or are they being distracted by it? Don't take me out of context of being against this technology or change. These things are great as long as we respect them and use them to productive manners. There is a time for there use and a time not. Based on what the videos and media continue showing, the use is more of not.

Many individuals in our society have fallen into this speed of trying to keep up and forgetting where they even began. They continue watching for the next latest and greatest. The sad part is that when individuals lose their focus they find themselves running in circles.

When this happens, you will witness them losing touch with life, their families, their friends, their savings, their purpose, and their very appreciation for freedom. The Lord taught this lesson throughout the entire Holy Bible, but again many have failed to listen. You could say, "These individuals who have lost their focus on Christ are lost in the wilderness."

When you compare the economy of today to the economy of yesterday, you can recognize the mental impact on the individual and the family. It would have been nice if our leaders would have said, "Okay America, upon us loosening our lending restrictions, opening the global market, and introducing the Internet, we need to prepare for change and discipline. It is imperative that you control your children in their spending and restrict their access to certain websites. Oh yeah, don't forget to train, for our new economy because the one you know is leaving, and while you are at it, we are going to begin to remove God from where we stand." "Be prepared for the temptations of money and sex due to the door that is being kicked wide open." If our government or leaders haven't learned something by now, then they need to quit where they are and figure out whom they are working for. Are they working for themselves, or properly serving others?

Have you ever considered the differences in our previous industrial or manufacturing economy and how they affected us mentally verses how our economy of today affects us? In our previous economy there was a sense of balance by having time to get away and stay focused. Individuals didn't have as much trouble balancing work, their relationships, their worship, and their own needed time to get away. In other words, they could pay attention to when something was getting out of control or when they needed to fertilize a certain section for proper growth. Now days, it is very difficult to get away. There is always a connection and someone getting upset if you don't answer their call or email in adequate timing. Individuals should not be offended when someone says, "This is a bad time, and I'll contact you later" or if they don't answer your call. There is no excuse not to contact someone back within a respectful time period, but the other individual needs to respect the others life also. Many business owners feel as if they don't work 24/7 that they will lose their marketing edge or value. There was a reason for rest in our work week and I believe our Creator knows more than man. A vast majority of people have become lost in the numbers and they have put them in front of God. It is easy to let someone else fertilize your own yard in life, but before you know it they could be fertilizing more than you want causing you to lose your proper nourishment, and eventually fade away. As we are instructed by the Holy Spirit in (Hebrews 3), be careful not to neglect or harden your heart away from God. When this happens there will be no eternal rest. In the book of (Mark 6), Jesus instructs us to go off by ourselves to a quiet place and rest. When we do this and keep focused on God, our Father, we can maintain life in balance by letting this world go.

When you look at these two economy models, you can see how time management is not just crucial to this temporary physical life, but life threatening to our eternal spiritual life. Before you know it, when you get caught up in this whirlwind of life, your life will be over. Then just before you take your last breath, you see only your surroundings but no depth of love in your picture. This could be a very sad moment for some. To prevent this, it is imperative to understand the meaning of being content, how to look at desires, and the principles of setting goals.

Let's begin to understand on an individual basis of how to stay strong and always keep life in balance. This is a daily task, but when individuals stay focused on the very principles in life, they won't seem to lose their direction or their purpose. Many individuals get wrapped up or caught up in this world in their own problems or in their false desires that sidetrack them from what they truly need. Then before they know it they don't know how to get out or stop. So let's look at some basic fundamentals to help prevent or overcome this from either occurring or re-occurring. There is nothing wrong with change as long as we respect it, understand it, and we are content with whom and where we are in life in case of a fall. We are not placed here to sit still! We are here to grow and climb in life through the love of Christ. We should always strive for peace and wisdom in everything we do.

In this process we need to understand and respect the fact of our individual differences in life. This does not mean to not expect differences of opinions, but it does mean that true loving Christians will work together despite our differences. As long as we keep our perspective in change, we should be supportive, rather than against.

This is often where we fail in change, because when we fail to honestly evaluate the affects, we are being self-centered. This is where we face dangers, because before we do anything we need to truly understand how we may be affecting someone else. We should always try to learn and grow daily being motivated by love, and not for or pride. Check yourself on contentment. Are you constantly complaining and searching or are you thankful for what you have. Think about your life as a ladder and the most important part is the foundation from where you place it before you begin to climb. First, you need to know that it will stand on it's own without you having to continuously hold it. Then you need to examine it for stability for the winds of this world. Can you see the importance of knowing where you stand? How about the importance of keeping check on the footing to insure not slipping sway? There will come a time that you must step aside and allow someone else to climb. Can you see the importance of teaching your children or the ones below you how to climb and always maintain their foundation?

If you don't take time out to teach the basics in climbing, then how high can we expect them to reach without a fall? There is only one true foundation which gives us the contentment in case a slip and this solid ground is rock solid being Jesus Christ. Everything we ever needed to build upon has been already given and now it ever dwells within us. This love, through Christ, will strengthen and motivate more than we can ever explain. With Christ, our personal ladder of life will be filled every step of the way when we maintain our focus day by day. It is important to understand that the answer to being content is in our perspective, our priorities and most of all our source of power, Jesus Christ. No matter where we are or what we may or may not have, if we stay focused on Christ, we will be content within our heart. When we are not content, there is a void like a bottomless pit.

This void can be dangerous if we are not careful. With the armor of God we can stand strong! "For if a man has hope, he can find his purpose."

In examining our goals and desires it is important to make a list and separate them per the different categories of life. For example: before I came into this place I set a goal to grow mentally, physically, and most of all spiritually. To leave here a better man than the one that walked in. When we set goals in life, it is one thing to talk about them but another to accomplish them. Ask yourself, "When you say that you are going to do something, do you do it?" This is a priority step in accomplishing goals. No matter what our circumstances may be in life, we need to always list our desires and goals to keep ourselves on tract! "What you put into it, you can plan to get out of it. If you don't plan, you will be planned for." This is where so many fail to understand the principles behind listing our goals and replaying them over and over in our head. Just because you hit a wall or even bottom out doesn't mean you give up! You pick yourself up, and go again! But this time smarter and wiser than before. I firmly believe we can do anything when we set our mind to it! The difference is that everyone is blessed with their own God given talents and we need to accept that certain people will excel when they match their talents with their goals in life. The reality of life is that we often get lost in this world attempting to fit everything else into our mold verses into the mold already predetermined and assigned by our Creator. This causes us to loose our perspective of our goals, our responsibilities and our appreciation for what we have already been given.

Don't make this task of listing your goals and desires harder than it really is. It is as simple as grabbing a Napkin and listing them. When you list your goals, always remember your priorities, point out what you wish to achieve in life, but remember to analyze your goals to insure they are of no negative consequences to yourself or possibly to others. Solomon wrote, in the book of (Proverbs 3:6) **"Seek his will in all you do, and He will show you which path to take."**

These are three main states of reaching our goals in life. One, listing our desires we wish to achieve. Two, defining how to achieve our desires with proper planning, and three putting our plans into action with hard work and dedication. This is where we get weak, because everyone wants an easy way out. I am a firm believer that if our goals and intentions are based on (Proverbs 3:6), that no matter our circumstance, our goals can be achieved with hard work and dedication. But, this is not possible without faith! "If you can't seem to find or take the time to improve or grow, then how do you expect something better?"

It is very important to examine every row in our greenhouse of life and our walk along each path. When we fail or neglect to do this daily, we could possibly be setting our ladder up for a fall. Just think how everyone would be if we all took the time to do this in our life daily, examining our paths and teaching our children how to reach their goals. Don't allow our society to overwhelm you and feel you can't get away. Everyone can find that moment of peace daily where you learn to control your mind and maintain your focus on your priorities. Everywhere we turn, someone is connected electronically, but the question is "Are they connected spiritually?" Do you recall the cell phone provider commercial saying, "Can you hear me now...Can you hear me now?" Here what we need to be paying attention to, being the Holy Spirit and the Lord saying, "Can you feel me now?" There is no better long distance provider than Jesus Christ, and when you accept and receive the true operator in life, your connection will become clearer than ever before.

Try to have your electronic connections off one day and see how you feel. If you feel disconnected, then maybe you really are! Technology is great but when we can't control it, then it can be hazardous to our health. Think about it, does your life or technology control you or do you have control of them? There is a balance that each individual must strive for everyday to maintain their life. When we don't put our goals on paper and guard the doors of our lives with the armor of God, then we can easily be affected by the world around us. The Lord has repeatedly warned us of this in the Holy Bible and we all fall short! The goal is to understand the importance of taking time out and preparing for the days ahead. When you feel you can't get control of your life, don't do like me and almost wait until it is too late. No matter your pressure, never sacrifice what is right for something wrong! It does matter how we play the game of life. And learning to breathe during the game is vital to the life around us.

Teach your children through your actions how to give time and attention to those in need. When we neglect our children the quality time they need as a child, they will struggle with this in their future. It is very easy in our culture today to overlook this and where it could possibly hurt is when we grow old all alone. The Lord teaches us and instructs us to honor our father and mother. When we don't take the time for our parents, how can we honestly expect our children to treat us in the future?

There is a very important cycle to follow in life and not only to the sectors that are convenient for us. The Lord repeatedly teaches us the importance of preparation in order to clear our minds and focus on what is before us. When all we do is worry about the time, then how can you honestly learn how to have a clear mind? When we take time out to focus, it is important to have your mind directed towards what you want to receive or give in life. It is easy in our human nature to become arrogant in achievements and it is important to remember that just because you may reach a particular level or goal doesn't mean you will overcome the next without proper consultation and preparation. It is vital to allow the Lord time in our hearts before we ever start. In every move you make stay focused on the Lord and don't allow your emotions to cause disobedience. The Lord is of time and order without shortcuts! So every time you feel rushed, take a breath to maintain your focus and strength.

There is nothing better than preparation in time and just look at how good things are when you allow time to take its coarse. Think about it, look at our meals in how fat and easy they are with a microwave, but taste the difference in a dish made from scratch that is properly cooked in time. This can be related to everything we build from relationships to structures. Look at the differences in the ones that are still standing today verses those that are quickly fabricated of man made products or desires. We all see the sin before us, but look at how the generations of love still carry us. When we follow the Lord's instruction and take time to prepare and grow, the love of the Lord will always show! Don't look for shortcuts that can jeopardize your relationship, not only with others, but also with the Lord! Taking short cuts will only move our minds to wrong thoughts or actions. By taking time out to study the path and our objectives will give us more appreciation for what we attain in life. When things come easy, it is easier to let it go, but when you earn something in proper maturity, then prepare for strength beyond what you ever know. Teach your children how to spend quality time with others and this begins in our homes in allowing your sincere love to flow.

Treat your children as that perfect dish. Prepare them in time with that gentle mist. As they mature your strokes may become tougher but always keep your eyes on that perfect dish. Teach them how to reach their goals and stay in focus in life. There will be times when the oven can overheat, but guide them on how to balance their emotions in taking time out. Remember, they look to you for help and learn from your actions. So keep your eye on the goal to stay in balance and maintain controls. (To God All Glory, Amen)

Balance

The hardest part of life
Is learning how to balance.
If we are not careful,
We can lose sight.
Then life becomes nothing,
But a worthless fight.
Eventually becoming lost,
And facing all types of cost.
When we stay focused,
On the life of Christ,
We will find
The true desires
To all of Mankind
(To God All Glory, Amen)

CHAPTER 8

Thinking and Believing

*I*n every step of our lives, from young to old, it is imperative to think forward in our direction and most importantly to have belief in where we are going. Within this whole process of growth we must accept and understand how to reach our goals in proper timing along with the maturity required maintaining them. Due to our human nature it is easy to become sidetracked or even discouraged away from our belief when our goals don't seem to be within reach or they may seem to be in another lifetime. By allowing this discouragement to consume our thoughts, it can cloud our vision, and cause us to become weak in ourselves or in faith when we overlook the lessons in our trials that give us the strength we need to grow stronger for our future.

Throughout the entire Holy Bible there are numerous lessons from men, women, and even children who teach us how to maintain our faith during difficult times along with those who teach us how to make the most out of every circumstance in life. In addition, there are numerous teachings from individuals who never understood how to live and not only destroyed themselves but also destroyed others. The most important lesson throughout the Word of God is that we are to maintain our faith no matter the circumstance and understand our human characteristics with a one on one relationship with God through the Holy Spirit of Jesus Christ. Think about it! If we fail to have faith in something, then how can we honestly believe in what we set out to achieve? The Lord teaches us how to focus and to think about our goals with proper planning throughout the Word of God in understanding in who brings them together.

We all face trials in life and how we handle them will reveal our heart for the person we are under God. There is never a point to quit when we properly believe, but there is a point we must learn the art of surrender in order to maintain and properly understand the principles in life. Once we learn the art of surrendering each and every day, we will find that the Lord will show us the way! At this point of surrendering our will of the flesh, in realizing that we are not the ones in control, our life will begin to be shaped or molded into the person we were set out to be and this is where we learn the art of being free!

Freedom is not only being allowed to do as we please, and it is sad how it is taken so for granted in life. Many individuals never understand the true meaning of freedom in only thinking physically verses spiritually in this world. For there is only one complete freedom, and that is being spiritually free through the Holy Spirit with the understanding of obedience in controlling ourselves mentally and physically as we move forward in life. True freedom is gained by keeping ourselves humble as that child under God and by helping those in need once we fall to your knees. At this point of spiritual maturity we can learn the art of complete freedom in forgiveness through the blood of Jesus Christ who gives us the eternal key. By surrendering our freewill we can be set free!

Everyday we are given in this physical life we should strive to maintain our foundation of freedom and improve our children's future. If we neglect or fail to think forward in proper planning, then how would our actions be toward teaching our children for their life ahead? Our children need to reach for the stars, and understand the meaning of true faith in believing in themselves with Jesus Christ in their hearts to give them the strength they need to succeed. If we allow our society to take God away from our foundation then it is only a matter of time before the fall of our country in causing weak faith and falling to anyone with a false since of direction. With God in our heart and soul we can feel the difference in true belief that never quits even in our physical death by knowing there is eternal life!

Think about it! Can you imagine a team going to the super bowl of life and the emotional high they would have inside? Let's take this a few steps further, in now you are the athlete on the team in the locker room just before the game begins. Can you see the importance of first knowing the turf of the field and knowing your surroundings before you even begin to play? It is vital to not only know and understand our position, but even the location of where we chose to move in life! Now back to the locker room just before the game, can you see the importance of a positive attitude? How would you feel if others who claim to be on your team have a negative attitude and weak faith? How would you handle this positively or negatively? If we fail to uplift our teammates when down, then we are neglecting our position on the team!

Now the clock is ticking and we are about to enter the stadium for the game to begin, but the coach hasn't arrived to brief us and encourage us. While this wait is taking place some of the stronger players begin to lose their direction and faith, while others don't take the game seriously in understanding what it truly takes daily to maintain our belief and strength. Can you see the importance of proper faith and a positive attitude no matter the wait? What about daily training to stay focused and in shape mentally, physically, and spiritually?

Finally before the game begins and our team is losing their unity, our coach sends us a message stating, "This is what you have been trained for your whole life and I have given you everything you ever needed and more. So why are you becoming weak when you know what is right in your hearts? You have the Word of instruction and you know my love in your hearts for each of you. So what excuse do you have for becoming tolerant or losing your direction? There is no excuse for weakness in faith and what you know in your hearts! I have never told you how long your wait would be for the specific reason of testing your faith, which is the whole lesson behind time. I am hurt that those of you whom are leaders have fallen weak and now even you have to be lifted up! Now, get up before you fall down and reconcile yourselves to rejoin the unity within the body and regain your direction for our children's future! Stay strong in faith with no waver of what is right under God, and enjoy every day as if it were your last! You will never know the time, or the hour in which the game begins!"

Can you see the purpose in the encouragement speech prior to moving from the locker room onto the field? How about preparing us for the opponent prior to the game or during time out? Can you see the importance of proper planning and reviewing how to achieve our goals? How about the importance of a strong coach who doesn't take your challenges lightly? Won't you feel more secure with a coach who genuinely cares and keeps order on the field in understanding the art of the game? What does it really matter in who is right or wrong when we know what is right under the law of God in moving forward?

The time now has come once again to re-enter the field with a solid foundation of being united as one under God with direction and purpose within the freedom of the game. Then as the game carries on over periods of time large majorities of people begin to play once again within their own misguided or selfish direction while neglecting the unity of the team in respecting their position under the coach. Finally, halftime arrives and it is time to re-enter the locker room to refocus on the principles of the game to regain control. What do you think will happen to the team who doesn't properly focus on the game upon their return?

Now let us switch gears and we are no longer the player on the field. We are the parent or coach in the locker room with our child. Can you see the importance of our children humbling themselves to regain their direction and begin to listen? Can you see the importance of being there for them even when they fall behind? Would you not leave them instructions on how to continue or regain control when they went back into the game on their own? Can you see the purpose in the Holy Bible, and the beauty of the wisdom taught directly by Jesus Christ?

Now take it a step further in being able to attend if you choose, and stand on the sideline while you watch your child move forward. As they run on the field they stop and look for you in the stands or on the sideline to only know that you are there. When your eyes meet there is something neither can explain in the love, and confidence felt within. This confidence comes from properly teaching them where to find the answers within themselves in the Word of God to receive their answers in their questions or trials in life. Can you see a time in maturity that children must learn how to believe and do it on their own? Did you teach your child how to reach their goals and to expect obstacles in their path? How can a Child ever mature if we always give them what they want and don't teach them how to use their own mind in order to seek the true answers in life? Don't take the game lightly and become carefree in not thinking about our children's future! For if we continue to remove God from our foundation the game will come to an end in only a matter of time.

Our attitude is vital to keep in check daily and understanding how it can influence others! Our children absorb our moods like a sponge to be squeezed and played at a later date. This not only applies to our children but to everyone else who surrounds us in life. So the next time you begin to reflect a negative attitude, think about how you would feel if someone acted this way in front of your child. Our attitude plays the same roll on our children as it does on adults, and it is sad how short sighted we can be at times.

There are two parts in belief that are crucial to understand individually and vital to teach to our children. One is how to believe in ourselves and two is how to believe in our goals. In (Matthew 23) the Lord Jesus tells us to first wash the inside, and then the outside will become clean too. But far too often we only want to clean the outside or the high spots, which we see due to the amount of work that is truly needed on the inside. Many individuals never understand how to truly cleanse themselves and this is where we not only learn ourselves in the Word of God, but we are set free. The most important lesson in attaining our goals is how to receive and achieve them in our works for our eternal future! If we don't do this, then think back to the locker room and be the player. Would the coach be doing his or her job if they didn't prepare the team and only took it half hearted? Out of love we should prepare and teach our children how to live for the day that we can no longer play! We never know when we may not have another day.

In the book of (Matthew 24), Jesus teaches us this lesson better than anyone can explain. We are told that the day and hour is known by no man, not of the angels, but only by our Father in Heaven above. Think about it! How do you act prior to knowing something that you must face? Don't you treat the urgency level differently based on the time left on the play clock? Is there a difference when you take your eyes off the goal and lose sight of the time left in a game? Let's go further in thought, "If you were testing your child to behave on their own while you go out to dinner, would you feel it would be wise to tell them the time of your return for a proper test? Another step further, you own a business and return to your office. How do you expect your employees to perform on their own? Now in another thought, you are the employee. How do you want to be respected when your superior returns? All of this is said for the message of Christ, "You better be prepared on your heart because you never know when the clouds may part!"

Don't allow other individuals clouded vision without God in their lives to cloud your view and discourage you from performing the best you can each day mentally, physically and most of all spiritually. It is easy to get trapped in our own box of life and forget the overall picture that has already been painted. Think about your team who is in that locker room. Each individual can represent an individual family, a city, a state, and a nation. The entire body of believers from the entire earth makes the team and your job daily is to work together for a common goal to improve life under God. Always keeping your focus and perspectives because no one knows the time or day that our Father will say, "Come home!" It is our duty to do our best daily with what we are given in life without complaints and serve God in everything we do in turn then we even serve you.

There is no doubt that when we think about our lives coming to an end we all want to overlook this stage in the cycle in life. On a selfish side, no one wants to leave the one's in whom they love and even those that they care for outside of their family circle but where it hurts the most are the ones who are close to us. Everyone will face this at some point in their physical life and unfortunately even before many will be prepared. It won't be for the lack of not knowing but for their neglect in life. Everyday we all can see someone who never makes it home after stepping out in this world and thinking they will return at a later date. Don't allow this to happen to you and prepare your children for their walk in life to understand the joys in the next. There is emotional hurt in our physical death of missing the ones we love, but most importantly we need to recognize the glory received to those who know God through Jesus Christ and prepare the ones who surround them. This only comes through understanding, respecting, and the single most important part, believing! Everyday we should treat everything we do and the ones we love as if it was our last. Doing the best we can in every possible way to not allow someone to hurt no longer than they may need once we have passed. And this is how the Lords true love will last.

Many individuals in our society neglect the lesson and the wisdom given of the ten bridesmaids in (Matthew 25). When we loose site of why we are here due to our sinful nature of being cast out from the Garden of Eden the depth of our personal picture can become very faint or even lost. In other words, when we believe and keep our lives in focus we can see beyond our box of life to the next. Imagine this scenario to get a better picture. You have a child that is dear to your heart. Wouldn't you want them to live making the most of every day they receive and to be prepared for tomorrow? If someone didn't want this for their child, then would they be doing their job as a parent? We all fall short at times of neglecting our purpose and our full responsibilities in life under God. Especially when we don't have an understanding or when the other team may be guiding our direction. But what matters is discovering our purpose before it is too late and teaching what and whom we know in order to help someone else in life. Where we need to strive daily is how to recognize our own emotional state in order to stop when needed and give attention not only to ourselves, but most of all to whom it is due.

One of the worst enemies of the mind is the infection of worry. This is where so many individuals overlook the art of properly surrendering and knowing who is in control. Our minds can destroy us if we don't learn how to overcome our negative thoughts. How many times can you recall your negative thinking causing you not to take a step in life and later wishing you did? How about the thought process of fearing something for a period of time, to only kick yourself in the rear after you discovered that it never was an issue? Have you ever worried about how people look at you or maybe perceive you? All of this comes from a lack of confidence in your belief and in yourself. We all have these moments in life and when we keep our focus on Christ we can gain strength to overcome any issue. Can you imagine His steps and especially knowing what He faced? This did not stop Jesus though, due to his love and belief in what and whom He knew. When we worry, study the real reason why and begin to understand how to remove it in helping you overcome the obstacles in your path. If we do nothing about it then our worries or troubles only grow, but when we learn to face them with an attitude of a champion under God our worries will fade away. The first step in removing our worries is sincere prayer from our knees in seeking guidance and strength to overcome what we you have before us. Often when we only focus on the negatives, we will only see the negative side. But when we look for the positives in every negative then they will overtake our negative thoughts, which cause our worry and can even lead to depression.

In our decisions in life it helps to place them on a mental scale to insure the positives far out weigh the negatives before we ever move forward. In those decisions though, they should not have negative effects on others. It is one thing to have a negative that we can overcome in a normal process, but never when it can eternally cause someone else to fall. It is imperative to think about the outcome of all our decisions before we act. When we teach this to our children they will have more confidence in their steps in life, and receive the proper nourishment needed to maintain their healthy relationships going forward. There is a complete cycle to this from generation to generation in the Holy Bible to our present day, and when we fail to understand this then it is only a matter of time before someone gets hurt.

So many individuals allow their worry to almost destroy them to the point they lose sight of what is really taking place all around them. This occurs easily when we neglect the purpose of communication, and we only hear what we want to hear. How can we ever improve something if we aren't willing to openly discuss it? The first thing we must realize is how to recognize it and then dissect it in order to improve. When we just overstep the problem or only hit the high spots on the outside then what do you honestly expect to happen? This is what our problem is within our homes, our churches, and even in our nation. When we remove the Word of God from our lives then we only neglect the truth from what it takes to repair within the inside. As a parent or even as a loving individual, we must learn how to communicate spiritually with others to eliminate the possibility of walls being raised and restricting what we may need to say or even hear. Often when someone recognizes a problem they aren't the only one who sees it, but they are only waiting to properly understand it in order to overcome it. It doesn't matter who gives the answers for all the answers have already been given in the Holy Bible, but far too often we want the recognition rather than giving the praise to who it is really due. As long as the answers follow the Word of God then that is the correct way to follow.

By teaching our children how to communicate and express themselves in proper order they will build positive relationships and make more positive decisions in life. If we neglect this lesson then we are not only setting ourselves up, but also our children up for possible heartaches in the future. Because when that cycle of life comes back around, don't fail to think we won't want our children to be there for us. All we can do is pray that when our children are set free that they remember their priorities, and most of all their belief. When we think about the cycle of life coming back around in our repercussions for our actions, we can see the relation to what the Lord taught in the Old Testament in how our future generations were affected by our sins? There was a message in this indirectly taught but later taught directly from Jesus Christ. Throughout the Old Testament we see a continuous cycle of rise and fall in every sector life due to individuals not learning how their actions affected their future generations. The Lord Jesus Christ taught us directly that our children are affected by the fruit we bare. There is a specific parallel in the Holy Bible indirectly in the Old Testament to directly in the New Testament to see if we could follow and put the pieces together from the overall body in life. Our children are affected by our actions and what we show them will influence more of there future than actually what is taught verbally. In other words, we can say our children will suffer for our neglect of proper teaching in our actions until the chain is broken. The only way for this chain to be broken is by returning to the Lord in our focus and applying His instruction to our lives in order to maintain or even grow.

The Lord teaches us in the Holy Bible that it should be our priority to watch our actions in how they influence our children's future, and how we are to grow with our children ultimately pointing them in the right directions. Have you considered the responsibilities of a parent today verses yesterday. Nothing has changed from our priorities but what we feel and see in our society is what makes a difference from all the false pressures around us. When we look at how fast everyone seems to be going in this new technology age, we can see constant struggles and personal anxieties on the increase. Many individuals have trouble keeping up with them, much less when we get caught up in the technology trap without being able to control it. Our economy today is a wild river with little remorse and when we fall into this raging river without a foundation of God or understanding then prepare for it to cause us to lose touch even further from where we may be.

In the past it was much simpler to micromanage our children and keep up with what they may have been going through. We could just pick up the phone in another room to hear whom they were talking with, but now unless we regulate it we never know when they are even using it much less who they are communicating with. Even if they aren't talking, they are using modern day Morris code in text messaging in not thinking they can leave their phones alone. When you really think about this whole cycle of technology in the Internet, not only do we not know whom they are conversing with, but also they sometimes don't even know themselves. All of this technology is good but can be very bad also when we don't stay in touch with our children. On a lighter note, little do my children know my private eye skills. This is no longer a task for Andy Griffith or Magnum PI. We have even gone past Dick Tracey to the James Bond parent of the future. In addition, I was influenced by Barnie Fife to Hawaii Five-O and even tempted by Charlie's Angels. Then I was left on an island all alone looking for Mary Ann and beginning to think it was Mission Impossible. Before receiving the ultimate training in life taught and given by Jesus Christ. I no longer surrender to Mary Ann, but now I understand and surrender to Christ! Once I learned the art of surrender, little did I ever know that I would meet and marry "Wonder Woman"? Now making me feel like the Bionic Man playing football with my son while "Remembering the Titans", and even writing in The Notebook of love. I just wish my wife sometimes didn't have that bionic ear and I had the power to remove all her fears. With all this being said in being trained from the rest, now my family better prepare for I have been retrained by the best!

Technology is great, but it can be very dangerous to young immature minds with full access. There is a balance in this that each parent should always seek to stay involved with personally in our children's lives to insure their understanding of what is priority within the family time we all need together. It is good to promote growth but only in proper timing while our children learn how to manage their time, which they are given. Our children's lives are being taken from us everyday and this is so sad when we see this tragedy. We must prepare our children and teach them to believe in our Creator for comfort and strength in their days ahead. Like mentioned previously, there will be a day we may not return or we may be called home, and what a joy that will be if our children properly believe!

One of the most difficult parts in our thinking process is learning how to rationalize between our thoughts and hear God's whisper within our hearts guiding our direction. It is in our human nature to act on our emotions and like mentioned previously there is a great lesson on this in the book of Joshua that teaches everything we need in this sector of life. The Lord gives us our direction to follow but often we tend to rely on man rather than on God. We only want to believe what we see, rather than believing what we don't even comprehend in the Word of God. This separation is the difference between our human side and spiritual side. We become impatient and feel that we have the answers by neglecting who is in control or the true artist of the picture.

In the book of (1 Corinthians 1) the Lord teaches us about the wisdom of God and it is sad how we often neglect or fail to listen to the Word of God in the Holy Bible. Many individuals seek a pedestal of knowledge and this can show dedication. But the Lord gives each of us particular strengths and anyone can achieve rewards when they put their focus on the task. The Lord, Jesus Christ, teaches us firsthand how to concentrate on what is before us to achieve our goals. Not only are we taught how to focus but we are instructed to control our thoughts. When you really think about it, our mind is not much different than a computer. At birth someone else enters the data by their influence and teaching. As our computer ages, it begins to mature and take life on its own. During this process, it begins to download whatever it may choose. Our mind or hard drive can only hold so much before it must be purged. If we are not careful, it can even crash. The data entry is vital to the life of the computer and being able to detect certain viruses before they infect. Without firewalls the life of the computer can become restricted and even be contagious. In addition to all of this our idle time is crucial to protect and help guide our future.

Our life without understanding from the Word of God is like a computer with no power, and without Jesus in our hearts we are vulnerable to all the viruses in this world with no firewall protection. Without the spirit of God in our breath, all we ever have is limited life like the battery back up that eventually will be cut off. In the book of (Ezekiel 37) we are taught in better words of the true power source in the word of God spoken in the valley of death. There was no life until the Lord gave His breath and the Lord teaches us in (Matthew 21) that He knows our intentions in our heart as in (Jeremiah 17) we are taught how desperately wicked our heart can be. So we should always stop and think about our decisions before we act, and this will allow us to hear God's whisper on our heart before we begin to even start. In addition, this will teach others how to follow God rather than man and we will see things in the right way by following the will of the Lord.

Our children are on line with us everyday of their lives and they can feel our presence when we are all spiritually connected as one. So whatever we do, we should download their minds with positives in teaching them how to overcome the negatives in life. Teach them how to purge themselves in repentance and prayer to maintain their relationship not only with God but also even with others. The last thing any loving parent should want is to become disconnected from their child in this world, and lose the most precious gift we are given in life with our children. Remember our facial expression is the screensaver that continues throughout the day and night, which plays a roll even when not in use because it can uplift others when they see our smile or joy, which comes from within.

In the previous chapter of taking time out, we addressed the importance of recognizing our personal characteristics per day and the need to plan according to our daily emotions affecting our overall productivity. Have you ever considered the affects of seasonal change? What about the affects of a full moon? Don't overlook how these two cycles in our environment can affect our moods and our productivity. We all are affected by the rain, storms, and even sunshine in this world. The personal art that we should seek within ourselves is learning how our days can affect us along with the natural environment, which surrounds us. Throughout the Word of God we are taught the importance of precise order and respecting discipline within boundaries. The guidelines that were set in the Old Testament were precise with no waver without major ramifications to follow. Now, open your mind to see how everything in life has a specific pattern and the ramifications when that pattern is broken? What would happen if the earth's orbit sped up or slowed down? What if the earth tilted more on its axis? Or what would happen if the moon's cycle with earth becomes more distant? There is a distinct and necessary pattern in life and when it gets interrupted, we will always see a negative reaction.

This fact does not only apply to outer space, but even in our environment in which we live. Based on our current level of limited knowledge and capabilities, we are restricted from the upper atmospheres and this is fortunately prolonging our negative impact in space. But this negative impact that derives from our sinful nature of overlooking the future affects is critical to understand, recognize, and to help our children's future. This lack of previous attention and moral obligations is leading to the deterioration of our environment and upper atmosphere right in our own backyards. Can this be corrected? No, but we can learn from our past mistakes to improve the future. By neglecting the overall impact of our pollution this only increases the normal process of maturity and deterioration. There is a necessary cycle to our environment that we must understand and respect to maintain our homes for our children's future. There is no way to not produce some negative impact due to we will never be perfect in this physical world. But we can be responsible and learn to limit our waste in thinking about the future. Maybe one day we can develop a car like in "Back to the Future" that will run on what we recycle that will be affordable verses the manufacturer trying to capitalize on something needed to help their future generations. It is sad how individuals try to capitalize on our environment verses really caring about our environment and costing us millions of dollars that will not turn back the hand of time. There are really only two natural parts in our environment that we must learn to maintain when you simplify the issue. One being human and two being everything in nature, without these two parts in balance there is a negative cycle in our environment. By teaching our children to respect what God has given to each of us in this world they will be better prepared to carry it even further in the future. It can be as simple as when we see scattered trash in picking it up to show our children we care.

When you study the earth and moons' orbit we can learn something from what God has created. Think of your daily attitude and how it can be affected with negative impacts of another. Here is the lesson on the cycle of earth, "The pattern does not alter, but slightly before correcting itself to hold its purpose." Can you relate this to what the Lord teaches in the Holy Bible in believing and always holding firm? This orbit has a distinct pattern which the Lord put in place and to maintain life. Now, how does your attitude reflect a pattern in your mood? Are you the same daily or do people have to enter your presence in caution? How do your children see your attitude negatively or positively? When someone may strike or interrupt your normal daily pattern of joy how do react? Do you return to your axis or do you get warped in space in losing yourself? Can you see how Jesus taught us how to maintain our patterns of joy to keep our lives in tune with God?

Everyone has ups and downs daily, but in God's Word we are taught to correct ourselves before we may alter someone else. In other words, like the earth on its axis, be consistent in your actions and if you become altered, return back to the cross to maintain life. There is a major lesson in the earth's pattern and in the Word of God when you open your eyes and begin to see what the Lord has given to you and me. There is a beautiful piece of living art in life and within our environment. Our impact needs to flow first on our spiritual level, and then it will maintain our human level. By staying in tune with the Lord in our daily walk, we will find in our works that He will provide everything we need to ever succeed. Our rewards from our works come from the heart and not from material means. True success comes when you believe and learn to serve others in need.

When we look at the cycle of life here on earth, we can see how many individuals are looking for that miracle or even those fifteen minutes of fame in some idiotic action. This is caused from lack of understanding in the Word of God in being content within ourselves and searching our positive talents to excel in life while helping others. Can you see the importance of showing people or your children the time they need instead of telling them to search other directions to find what they need within themselves? When individuals can feel their need in life, then they will discover their purpose in life. But when we neglect to show we care, then how short lived will this be? Think about it! There is a natural pattern in growth and maturity not only in people, but also in everything else within our environment. What happens to the human body when we don't pay attention to what we consume or the type of medications we take? Can you see any possible side affects on our physical conditions? Or, how about the negative impact of pesticides and growth enhancement chemicals in our agriculture being consumed by our livestock, and then given to human consumption? There is a balance in all of this to seek to understand the possible side affects over long-term reactions and the affects they can have over natural growth patterns. It may look good at first, only because the money that can be made in speeding things up but what happens when things return to normal or the natural state? Can you see the side affects or even the consequences of what happens when we lose our focus?

Every individual in life has his or her own level of appetite, but it pays to understand the negative impact over time. When we don't do this we are only selling ourselves short. Our children consume what we provide and when we don't teach them to respect their health, then how will this affect their children of the future? The King of this world Jesus Christ teaches us in the book of (Matthew 15) that it is not what we put in our body, but the affects of what we consume in how it leaves our body. If what we consume takes root then be prepared for whatever level of impact we will receive. All of this is only said to teach us how to be aware of what we take in and how it can affect our cycle of life in our future. We all have a choice to consume what we desire in our own freewill, but it is wise and vital to understand the risk in what can take place if it takes root within our bodies ultimately affecting the heart.

There is a distinct pattern in our emotions during the cycle of the moons' orbit and especially when it is full. The moons orbit has a purpose that is easy to overlook due to just taking it for granted. It plays a roll in the cycle of life not only in the oceans, in the plants during growth, but also even in our personal cycle throughout its orbit when we study our emotions. We can observe a pattern within certain weeks of being more productive than the others just like the patterns of our emotions on particular days during the week when we really pay attention to ourselves. There is a distinct parallel between the weeks and months that we can even see in the seasons of the year when we dissect the patterns from the large to the small.

One of the easiest ways to prove this fact above on our human emotion during the cycle of a full moon is by speaking with anyone who works in the emergency room of any hospital. Or, ask a farmer who plants according to the cycle of the seed opening just in the precise timing of the full moon to see the affects. Our emotions can appear to be much more prominent during this time frame and there is a distinct connection between all of this that one day we will understand in the kingdom of God. We know that if the cycle of the moon can affect the tides of the ocean then surely it has some type of reaction even on us. By observing our personal characteristics we can plan accordingly, and this can help us stay in tune with God to further understand ourselves.

We can see natural affects from our environment beyond our understanding when we open our eyes and begin to observe life on this earth. There is a pattern and reason for every move in life, from our solar system to even the insects in their roll to survive. When we neglect to recognize these patterns and their purpose, then we are beginning to lose our focus in life. Every living organism has a cycle in this life with a natural distinct pattern, which the Lord has given to feed another purpose. There is nothing we can do to create or prolong life without having consequences to follow. We can research all day long trying to figure it out or debate how everything came together, but what does this really matter? We all have a birth and a death in this physical life, and every moment we spend trying to prove one another wrong is only taking something away from someone else that we could be giving in positive time verses negative debates that can't be fully proven. In (Psalm 49) we can read the facts of life from birth to our physical death that were better stated in the Holy Bible for us to understand what it is like to be in the hand of God.

We all have natural instincts to survive, but often we neglect God's desires for our own. Like mentioned previously, humans are the only ones who interrupt the natural cycle of life and this is why the Lord has given us our directions to follow in the Holy Bible. All of this is only said to look outside our box of life and learn to appreciate God's creation. When we do that ourselves and begin to teach our children to look at the big picture, then they will begin to think about their impact from the little picture. Think about it! What roll does the honeybee play in the overall picture in life? Would you say this is the little picture within the overall big picture? What economic impact does the bee have in our environment? Have you ever noticed their natural patterns?

Can you see the importance in teaching the value from something small to something large? If you remove the honeybee, there will be a chain of events just as if we removed the moon within our orbit. The only difference is the level and time frame of the impact then creating a chain reaction of events. If we don't teach our children the value of life and how to respect each position from small to large, then we will continue to see an increased negative impact in the orbit or cycle of life. When we look upon the honeybee compared to the solar system, would you relate this to a gentle whisper compared to a loud thunderous voice? Like mentioned previously and stated by Jesus Christ in the Holy Bible, no one knows when the time will arrive but only the Father in Heaven. But I would like to share something with you that have been shared with me to now pass on to you. When you seek the Lord where do you hear or see Him in life? Can you hear Him spiritually or see Him throughout His creation? How about feeling the love of Jesus within your heart and soul?

We can hear the Lord in a gentle whisper when in the spirit of God and in (Psalm 46) we are instructed to **"Be still and know that I am God."** The Lord speaks to us when we learn to be still and listen to what is before us. You can hear and see His works from big to small when we surrender in understanding our position to serve. By returning to the Lord in proper repentance, then we will be saved before the ultimate fight? It could be tomorrow or many generations ahead, but what matters most is that it could be tonight? There are no worries when prepared within our heart and doing our best daily to do things right within the Lords sight. As we lay down at night, we are to give honor to who it's due and thanks for each day for the Lord providing the way. Thanking our Father in Heaven above for sending His Son, Jesus Christ and asking for mercy in His grace to save us from this place. The Lord will then bless us as we rest and lay down to say goodnight while all the others who don't believe do nothing but continue to fight. May God bless you and give you peace in your rest to always do your very best. (To God All Glory, Amen)

If we do not teach our children the Word of God and how to value not only themselves, but also even others in life, then their life will continue to have struggles in their relationships with little purpose to grow. Everything in this world has a value and purpose in sustaining life when we really look at every aspect from the deep waters of the ocean to the sun above. It is easy to do reverse engineering mechanically and genetically, but the part we will never know until the Lord reveals is how this whole process works and how He creates something from nothing. When we learn to appreciate what we have and who we are then we can learn how to reach higher levels of understanding by keeping God in our primary focus and understanding who is the true Creator in life. Think about how we are to teach our children to build something in their path. Do we tell them to use what they have or do we tell them they cannot do it on their own? The key is teaching them how to follow the directions in the Word of God and to respect what they have to make the most out of everyday in life. When they learn to rely on God and surrender in prayer, then the Lord will provide them along the way everything they ever need to truly succeed.

Prior to my current understanding without proper spiritual maturity, I treated my life and daily time given like a dragster on a racetrack. This is where I eventually got hurt and almost physically lost my life once and for all. Our minds are important to try and understand to not only respect the purpose of time out, but to learn how to start them up and shut them down. The Lord teaches us this lesson in obedience and discipline in order to maintain our perspective in life throughout the Word of God. In order to maintain our balance in our daily routine, it helps to understand how to make the most of our time but most of all to respect the purpose of time. Like the dragster on the track, everyday we are given to start another day there is a warm up period needed in order to move forward. Once we are awake and our eyes are open then we begin our race by keeping our eyes on the days end. Along this path we are to plan and work wisely while keeping our focus on our goals throughout our day. When we begin to understand our personal peaks, then we can learn how to maximize our days in every productive way.

Not only is there an importance to understand the warm up period once we wake, it is also vital to know how to slow down to show we care. Our children watch this in us in how we move and think even when we don't feel that they are even online. In addition to understanding the respect in slowing down, we must learn to even have time for ourselves to even maintain our mental and physical health. It helps tremendously to find some type of hobby completely separate from our work or daily pattern. The Lord teaches us this in His Word for us to stay in touch with life. In the book of (Genesis 43) we are taught this lesson between the Hebrews and the Egyptians. When we become surrounded by our society or works, often it is hard to ever get away. The Lord teaches us this in how to prepare our minds in this chapter. It is imperative daily to keep our focus on God and daily learn how to maximize each day. Here is where the wisdom comes in from my new understanding from studying the Holy Bible; **"There is a reason for each season and a purpose to not take short** *cuts in respecting that only proper things come in understanding the maturity of time within the will of God."*

Once we learn the art of daily surrender and begin to recognize who is really in control, then there is a sweet, sweet aroma in life beyond our understanding. There is wisdom as we mature in learning to respect the time we are given and the talents, which God has given to every individual in this entire world. So, whether our lives are the blown fueled dragsters on the drag strip or the turtle on the track, we must appreciate our position and always keep our eyes on the goal. In addition, it is vital to always understand our risk before we act. Because I can personally tell you the crash hurts badly when laid out on our back and especially when we watch the turtle pass us by while we are stuck on the track. When we begin to understand our personal characteristics throughout the day and even begin to look at them in a cycle of time, we can learn how to plan properly to fit our daily emotions and productivity. For example, if we know Mondays are always tough, and then plan your day according to the way it best fits you and this is how we will learn how to maximize our time. You may observe two Mondays out of the month differently then the others and this is where you must begin to understand yourself without having a feeling of negative productivity. Personally, I have found that my projects productivity is more positive when they open and close during the middle of the week verses the beginning and end of a week. Of course, there are projects that don't carry over or some that take a lot of time over a prolonged period. But what matters is how we plan and follow up accordingly to reach our goals. Everyday we must remain focused and plan our time wisely without losing sight. In today's world, it can cause us to become scattered when our feet are not planted at the cross. Everyone has their own level of performance and even balance in life. But when we don't think about our individual characteristics, how can we maintain our own personal needs? The Lord teaches us all of this in the very beginning of time in the book of Genesis and I thank Him from the bottom of my heart and soul for what He has now done for me in understanding the wisdom of God. Not only are we taught how to plan, but also we are given instruction on how idle time is vital to remain watchful. In (Mark 14) Jesus taught the same lesson in which Moses taught in (Exodus 32) in how we are weak to the flesh in our idle time, and how we can lose sight of what the Lord has given before us.

All of this above was also taught in (Galatians 6) in relation to harvesting what we plant. When we watch our actions and our words throughout the day we can see how they leave impressions on others. The apostle Paul followed as Jesus taught to prepare for the seeds of our actions that we sew because we all want to be included in the great harvest of God returning to the Lords kingdom that will come. In everything we ever do it is important to be cautious in sewing the proper seeds of God, due to one bad seed can destroy a crop if it continues to grow out of control. This does not mean we cannot overcome any circumstance, but prepare for what it takes in daily effort mentally, physically and most of all spiritually in order to grow and be properly delivered!

Our children and our country are suffering some major negative impacts from the lack of our personal time within trying to keep up in today's society. This whole chain of events is not even in our homes but even between several key nations. When we only chase each other then we can only copy so much before we must learn to follow God and learn to create our own individual strength's once again. The growth enhancement of the technology market is now affecting our homes and even our children. This is like the side affects of what we consume in one day interrupting our cycle of life for not reading the fine print in the Word of God to see the results of our actions. Over the last several years the economic high has been on a steady down fall and is now wearing thin in being so distracted by the negative media and even the technology games our children play. With our adult focus being so distracted by the media and our society our children are being taken from us right out from underneath our nose. We are paying more attention to our financial portfolio verses our children's education and future.

This technology market has had a major impact on their concentration level in the lack of understanding the art of patience and respecting time within hard work to achieve their goals. It is very easy to plug our children up to technology when our time seems so limited and this is important to keep in balance but more important to keep in touch within their lives. Another very important factor is the understanding of how the technology games are infecting our children's mental hard drive and their future. This can be related to the teaching in (Matthew 15) taught by Jesus Christ when you open your eyes and ears to the wisdom of God. If you study this lesson and analyze our children in the affects of certain materials influencing their lives at certain ages we can easily see how this can guide their actions and cause them to want everything now verses learning the art of patience. When a child repeatedly witnesses something in front of them that may not be proper and we as parents don't address it, then how will they know what is accepted or not? Are we truly doing our jobs if we don't address something that is not right under God?

It is easy to become tolerant or give our children something to pacify their time but what they need is our time one on one to learn the joys of life. There is no greater joy than watching our children imitate us in a positive way verses a negative way. When our children witness how we use our time wisely, then they will learn from us in how to stop and start within their days to show they care in return. In addition, when they receive our undivided attention, they will learn how to stop and focus on what is before them. A child often hurts internally when they don't receive the attention or encouragement from their parents or the ones around them as they mature. A young child feels secure when living in a structured environment with love shown and often we can witness children who rebel from the lack of attention or even receiving discipline. The longer this is avoided, then the worse it can become. This can be related to any problem or issue in life from our relationships to even our nation as a whole. Why is it so simple but so hard to face the truth?

Our children are like a pressure pot on the stove. If we don't teach them the directions and objectives of respecting pressure, then at some point they can overheat or even blow! There is a wise lesson in understanding pressure and when left unattended, in the possible repercussions. The attention required in the use of a pressure pot on the stove is in direct relation to the attention we give to the ones we love as they grow. Many parents or individuals have some form of regret in their life and it is easy to remember the good over the bad. When we don't address the bad, then how can we find the good? Often, we neglect to think about how our children or others may have been affected by our negatives and this is important to understand. The Lord teaches us throughout the Holy Bible to forgive and address our sins with the ones that are directly affected to overcome any hindrance in worship or prayer. By doing this, it also teaches our children how to overcome and face their pressures in life. When we don't face them then we only run from them, and they eventually will catch up!

As a child, we must listen to our elders when we are out of line, but as adults, very few want to face the truth. When we as adults begin to neglect that we will answer to our Creator for our actions, then there are definite consequences to follow. No one likes to hear where they are out of line, but if we don't take heed to the Word of God in understanding how to stay in line, then how will we ever grow? Neglecting the truth will only build pressure beyond our control. Remember that a problem or an issue is much less costlier when addressed in the early stage. When overlooked, it will only grow as it matures in life affecting others within the environment. By learning to face our issues straightforward with no hesitation in the love of Jesus Christ, we can save ourselves a lot of unnecessary pain. It can hurt or even take years to recover but what matters is our children's future.

In the book of (Luke 7) we are taught a great lesson on forgiveness in our Christian life and it is taught again in (Acts 8) in how to face our sins and regrets in life. When we face our wrongs head on with proper understanding and even remorse, then we will find relief the moment we properly address our sins. Our children carry our pain and suffer when we neglect the truth. By teaching our children how to address their problems or even how to recognize their weakness in the privacy of our homes, then this will be carried over into their workplace as they mature. It is crucial that we find the positives in all negatives and learn how to recognize the negatives that can occur by losing focus on the positives in life.

Over the past twenty years or so, there has been an increased amount of attention deficit disorders among individuals and especially in our children. Can you see any possible side affects of our technology culture on the affects of learning how to focus on time? When something is constantly changing or moving without ever using one item to the full extreme and jumping to the next without ever giving proper time to fully understand, then does this relate or possibly parallel the symptoms of attention deficit disorder? There are a lot of children that could be corrected without medications if we truly gave them the time needed and applied the Word of God properly to our lives. If you have a child who may suffer from an attention disorder, here is something to try as you read further that was originally taught in the book of Genesis on staying in tune with the country and not the culture of the Egyptians. When your child is between the ages of five to ten, they are more receptive to spending time with you and showing interest in what you show to them. These years are vital to a child's innocent mind and what they download during this period is carried for their lifetime. The time we spend with them during these years will play a major roll in how close they will remain to us in the years ahead. There is a balance in this that can differ from each child, but overall a large percentage of children can relate to the time they need at different stages of their life. Everyone has probably witnessed the struggle of children with parents who will not allow them to live, as they should with their own freedom to make choices in life or just not wanting to let go. There is a balance in this that is very difficult to strive for and can vary on the needs of an individual child. One thing to remember about balancing is that sometimes we may get heavy on one side but the point is to recognize and adjust properly to stay in tune to not cause a possible slip or fall.

In addition to witnessing those who are being smothered, we can see many who do not ever restrict in giving too much freedom. When this happens, it often leads our children to have a void of feeling cared for. Think about it! If the person you love just allows you to walk by in passing and does not care if you come or go, then how would you feel? Would you feel wanted or loved? In order to feel the love of an individual, there must be respect and even structure in understanding the purpose of love. Like the pressure pot on the stove, if you just open the valve wide open it will dry up and if you close it too tight, then it can blow! The object is to adjust accordingly and nourish in love, to not allow the pot of love to become dry and despair!

The Lord taught us this right out of the gate in the book of Genesis. If you look at the life of the Holy Bible as the birth of a child to their life as an adult in being free with the birth of Jesus Christ. In this recognition, it helps to try to balance our attention with the ones we love in order to allow our children to learn the art of being free. By teaching our children to stay in focus and in understanding the purpose of keeping our attitudes in check, as Jesus taught, we will be preparing our children how to build on the right foundation and to be there for the ones they love once they are set free in this world.

The young years of a child are vulnerable to constant psychological change and this is the time to help them in teaching how to concentrate on a project outside of their school curriculum with some form of a hobby that you both can enjoy. It is vital to teach the art of patience and how to pay attention in respecting the purpose of time. For instance, can you see the lesson in attention and time in planting a seed in a pot to watch a plant grow in the window seal? How about as they mature the respect for attention in following the moon through a telescope? Not only do you teach them patience in growing a plant, you can teach them the lesson the Lord teaches us in the type of seeds to grow based on the soil conditions. Jesus taught a beautiful lesson of this to us as adults in the book of (Mark 4) that is often overlooked in our path. This is a vital lesson to teach to our children and to follow in our future.

Regarding the lesson in a telescope, can you see this possibly expanding their minds to reach to new levels? How about learning patience in following the moon in its orbit? By teaching our children at the early age the art of focusing on a project or object, will guide them in their direction in life. If we neglect the lesson in focusing, then our children will struggle in space. Think about it! This world is full of objects and with no understanding they can wonder or wander in circles searching for something they do not know. This is no different than traveling in space where you must know your direction, your capabilities and your goal. If we lose sight of one of these important factors, then our trip back home could be a catastrophe!

Another good practice is teaching our children how to build with their hands and understanding the purpose of following the directions. By giving our children the opportunity to construct models or build objects, it can teach them to focus on a project and obtain an eye for detail. Can you see an importance of our children watching a fine point brush while following a narrow line before moving to the next stage of the build? The object to teach is, **"It is not how high we may climb, but the foundation's stability from which we stand."** When they understand the process of time, then they will have more respect for where they stand and even what God is sharing with us in this land. Don't allow your children to lose sight of where they walk, because this is the first lesson they must learn before they ever begin to talk. The best part of all of this is the love shown in time and patience in allowing someone to feel important or even cared for. When children witness the time taken and required in a project to reach a goal, then you will not only teach the art of patience but most of all it will teach them to respect what they have been given. As adults we can learn the art of time management but our children are not mentally developed in their early years to understand the purpose of time. Based on what our culture of today continues to show this is even more important to pay attention too.

It is important to grow with our children and stay close as they mature before setting them free. The Lord taught us this throughout the Old Testament, but our time is not His time and this is where we often fail. In the book of (2 Peter 3) we are told, **"One day with the Lord is as a thousand years and a thousand years as one day."** This is where we must believe and have faith in God's time and not worry about ours. Throughout the Holy Bible, we are shown our weakness in not understanding time and we still to this very day struggle with this in our lives more often than not. Why is it when our spouse tells us they love us one time that it is never enough? How about a friend who never calls to say hello and you are the only one who follows through? Just because someone does not acknowledge or call does not mean anything has ever changed. We all get caught up in our responsibilities throughout a day and we can tell the sincerity in relationships when we cross paths of others in how they act. A true relationship doesn't allow time to affect the sincerity of ever losing sight of what you have missed but picks right up from where you left off. Everyone goes through ups and downs throughout a day and especially over a period of time. A true relationship is based on who you are and not on what someone may have or even accomplished. In the book of Genesis we are taught the true way to handle our relationships under the will of God through the life of Joseph who held no grudges to those who previously hurt him in his earlier years. It is the will of God to have mercy and to forgive each of us, as we are to forgive others to rebuild our families that may have fallen to sin.

When a person has the love of Christ in their heart and soul, you will know on your heart that they will always be there for you no matter what or even how far you may be apart. Can you see this character trait in our belief and faith in the love shown by Jesus Christ? How about in what the Lord teaches us in the Holy Bible in relation to the earth on its axis in always remaining true? All of our relationships face tests but the critical factor is to remember our position as a Christian in how the Lord is always there for you as He is for me. The Lord tells us He is never changing and to always be faithful when we begin to have doubts what we may have before us and I can assure you I have tried all alone when I did not properly understand as I do now. But never again will I fall to this feeling for I now know the truth in the Word of God in knowing He is right there waiting for our call to give us the strength we need to overcome anything in life. Never lose hope in your belief because even when your life is out of balance, you can find the small positives things where the Lord continues to provide when our circumstances seem so bleak.

This message was taught in (1 Kings 17) and then directly taught by the Lord, Jesus Christ, in His life and sacrifice. There is a lesson in our faith taught by Elijah and the widow in how we often overlook the small blessings of daily provisions and focus on the big things in life. The Lord plainly points out to us our need for strong faith when we face something drastic and to never doubt His power. Throughout life, we receive small blessings everyday that often get overlooked or even neglected. All small things add to big things and without the small things, there are no big things! Think about it! Without a human cell, there is no body. Without breath, there is no life. Without daily nourishment, there is no strength. Without the people, there is no nation. And without employees, there is no need for employers.

Don't overlook the small things and only focus on the big things. Because over time, the big things will fade and if we don't remember the small things, then what will we have? There is an important lesson in this story of Elijah with the widow when you open your eyes and search your heart. We are plainly shown our weakness once again in how we neglect who is in control and who provides life. Build your relationships and faith on the small things in life and when the big things come and go, you will remain true to whom you know. In our early years of childhood and even as we mature when set free, we all feel weak over a period of time. This was shown from Abraham to Moses and to many others throughout history. One thing to notice is the time period of their trials and promises from the Lord in what they were told would happen directly and by what they had in faith on their hearts. When we look at the period of time in the many years of sincere faith, we can learn the importance of never giving up or losing focus within this place. The Lord, Jesus Christ, did what no man has ever done before or will do again by remaining completely true and pure to whom He knew!

We all tend to become weak over a period of time and especially when we are facing troubles ahead. We can witness this weakness in

our children in their early years when they don't comprehend
or understand the purpose of time and we will begin to see them
question their future. It is crucial that our children know without
a doubt, that we will always be there for them. This will give them
strength as they grow and prepare them for their life ahead. Can you
see this direct relation of love from God above? In not only caring
for us so much and leaving us His promise book, He sent His only
begotten Son to show us the way in keeping our faith. We all can
become weak when we don't stay or feel close to the ones we love and
especially when we begin to lose sight. The Lord revealed this
weakness over and over throughout the Word of God but when we
overlook His Word, it is easy to lose sight.

Here is a personal experience that still breaks my heart and
even causes me to cry. But I share it with you only to reveal how fast
something can happen and how our children must know our love on
their hearts when they face troubles in life. Over a split second our
mind can cause us to doubt or question and this is where we must
teach and show the love of God to whom we know. When we are faced
with a wait, never give up or lose your faith. One afternoon on a beach
in Florida, my wife and I stood at the edge of the water with our pants
rolled up in the break of the waves. The weather was cloudy and the
beach was vacant as we watched our son playing in the ocean. It was
peaceful and quiet with no one around and only the crash of the waves
making the sound. My son wanted to wade out further and as he
walked backwards into the waves, it warmed our heart to watch him
play. All of this took place over a five to ten minute span, before we
began to wave him back in interrupting his plan. In just a brief
moment, as we motioned for him to come back in, we noticed his
smile turned to fright before our very sight. My heart dropped as
I began to run out to him and I could see the tide had grabbed him in
his fight. The swim seemed like a period of time but was only seconds
in our lifetime. When I reached him his face had tears and relief when
I put my arms around him and said, "Don't worry I am here with
you now and you will be okay!" The part that still breaks my heart is
his moment of fear and wondering how quick I would draw near.

We reached the beach safely and we all had tears facing the ultimate fear. But one thing I assured my son of is to never have a doubt or fear and that I will always be there for him when he needs my help in feeling all alone. How do you feel with your children and can you relate? Because this is how our Father in heaven feels with each of us as we drift away.

There is a distinct parallel of love from God through His Son, Jesus Christ that we carry with the ones in whom we truly love. Can you even begin to imagine the pain of watching your child having to suffer and even be sacrificed? It is so easy to lose faith even when the love is right within our sight. The difference is feeling the power of the spirit within every struggle in life and knowing without a doubt that we are loved for who we are in being saved in the tide of sin. Those few seconds of the swim to reach my son can be related to the generations of time in keeping our belief and faith. We can't comprehend time in this physical world and especially in God's creation. Everyone falls weak or faces some disbelief in some form of wait and this is where we must teach our children the purpose of time and never lose our faith. This lesson is taught continuously in the recorded events of the Holy Bible and when we learn to evaluate our history, we can help others in their future.

Like mentioned throughout this chapter, our children's minds are weak in believing or having faith in their early years and they need our help in developing an understanding of who is truly in control. Our children need to know to not ever feel that God has forgotten or abandoned them and He will always take care of them. In the book of (Isaiah 41) the Lord tells us, **"He is always holding you with His right hand."** When we open our eyes to our surroundings and begin to pay attention to the patterns in life, we can see the purpose of structure and discipline to maintain the cycle of life. Everything has a purpose and value in our sight. If we don't open our eyes to what is taking place in our environment and pay attention to the clouds above, the Lord could appear with no one knowing the time is near! Everything in life has a purpose, all the way to you and to your children of the future. We all become stuck at times and lose our focus of the true artist of the picture in who gives life. It is easy to paint our own picture but our purpose is to help others who may be lost in flight or who can't see the true picture within their sight.

Don't fail to examine your picture before you point something out in others. Because this is a sign within your own picture of life that you may be lost in flight with who gives us light. Everyone wants to be the ultimate artist in life and this is where we must learn to respect our position in what we are given. In looking upon a piece of art, you will find that each segment relates to the next. Never with a contrast that doesn't flow and this is where you find the love of Christ in teaching the art of love in whom you know. A true artist is the one who learns the art of using what he has already been given. Like using only the primary colors learning how to mix each color to create its own beauty. This is in direct relation to God, our Father the true Creator and artist of our picture. The Lord uses each of us as we come to understanding to add another beautiful color that will give more depth to His picture that the Lord already knows.

As we read the Word of God, it may speak differently to each of us due to the different colors of our personality and one of the most beautiful parts of God's art is that it comes to life. As He mixes us in the scripture as an artist mixing one primary color with another, we create our own expression to add further depth to God's picture of living art. Everyone wants that ultimate picture, but we better never overlook the true artist in life and teach our children how to paint in love by the hand of God to carry the depth of love beyond our sight. This was taught first hand by Jesus Christ! All Glory to God our Father in Heaven above, Amen.

Dandelion to a Rose

Have you ever noticed the life of a dandelion flower to a rose? It is bright in yellow with a consistent pattern throughout the day. Unlike the rose, its life consists of a steady glow, opening and closing based on the environment and feeding the roots below.

During the night, the dandelion closes up for rest and during the day it opens to a new life. If it rains or becomes cold, you will see the dandelion close up for protection or share the water to continue its smile of perfection. The beauty of a rose serves no purpose other than its short-lived reflection and is often shown in affection.

The rose lives for the moment before fading away. Unlike the dandelion that learns how to share with the other parts in need. Teaching us the art of how to succeed and how to share what God gives in the nourishment of life rather than being selfish and restricting the growth only in its sight.

Not only does the rose only shine for a while, due to never learning the art of opening and when to close, before deteriorating petal by petal to nothing more than scattered pile. It is important to recall that every rose has a thorn before it is even born and if you only rely on the external beauty rather than the smile that comes from within, you better prepare for your heart to be torn.

Like the life of a dandelion, it is all in the art of learning when to open or when to close. This timing of life is taught by the true artist of the big picture and never forgets the point of return nobody knows! (To God All Glory, Amen)

CHAPTER 9

The Dangers of Pride

Over the years of history and even to today there is one thing that seems to be prevalent throughout history in remaining the same. Our selfish pride is one of the evil team's strongest advocates in our human nature of sin that plays a major roll in our lives today. Why is it so hard to drop our pride when it is so simple to let it go?

There are two sides to pride and one is good while the other is very bad. It is one thing in pride to be proud of our works in giving respect for what we have been given, and totally opposite to take pride in thinking we did it all on our own leading to arrogance in our work. These two sides of pride are critical to understand to maintain our proper balance in life and not to forget our position of who is in control. Always remember life can be compared to a two edged sword with a fine edge that is invisible to our human eye. The object is to find that point and learn how to maintain the edge to keep our life in tune. The instructions to follow and even to find that edge are right in our grasp in the Holy Bible. The only way to see and feel the point in life is with Jesus Christ providing the way and even the light!

When we study the Word of God there are repetitive messages from the very beginning to the end revealing the same warnings of how pride can affect us and even destroy us. It is vital as a sword in the heart to understand it and learn how to control it! In the book of (John 7) we are taught how pride can affect our reasoning and in (Ephesians 2) the apostle Paul tells us how pride even blinds us to our own personal faults. In addition to these two lessons in the Holy Bible there is another very important fact in the book of (Psalm 10) to always remember and place within our heart. The fact to never forget is, ***"Don't allow our pride to cause us to depend on our self and forget that God is watching us."***

Previously it was mentioned how as a child we are accountable to our parents but as we mature in life we lose our accountability when set free in this physical world. This is where so many individuals become blind, even when they can't physically see. By not feeling or thinking they will be held accountable in life causes many individuals to become stuck in their own valley of death and often leads them to not think of how their actions can hurt others. Can you see the message throughout the entire Holy Bible of keeping our hearts humble as a child and never to feel that we are not going to be held accountable even if we feel we are all alone? Because the Lord is always watching from His throne!

The Lord teaches us that selfish pride leads to a hardened heart when we neglect the truth. That is why so many people turn away from the Word of God and search for everything else. Because their own pride has lead them away in not wanting to feel accountable for the person they are and feel they are the ones in control. Everywhere we turn someone is trying to buy time and this is where we all must face the inevitable of the truth. If we overlook or neglect teaching our children the truth in the word of God, then how will our children feel when they are all alone?

One of the hardest parts in life is to face the facts and admit that we may have been wrong in our previous decisions or actions.

Everyone falls subject at times for searching certain individuals or professionals for answers but first they should be honest with themselves and search the Word of God to give an understanding in order to prepare them for the truth. The Lord teaches us to reach out to certain individuals who have been blessed with certain talents to help us through whatever we may face. But it is important to first understand ourselves to be specific about the area we may need to address before ever moving forward. How many times have you ever had an issue and you struggled with an answer? Can you recall a time of discussing it with an individual and before they even spoke you already had the solution? A lot of times we already may have the answer but it takes us having to face the truth on the outside before receiving it on the inside. This can compare to writing our goals on paper verses trying to sort them in our mind. Our thoughts or issues in life can become jumbled as our goals, unless we learn to put them out in front of us to see. There is clarity on the outside but distortion when we become stuck in the middle or if we feel that we have all the answers on the inside. Think about it! If you are trying to solve a mathematical equation, is it easier to put it on paper to figure or to figure in your mind? Every problem has solution but sometimes we may not understand the answer. If we become lost in the solution, then we need to search the Word of God who holds all the answers.

In the book of (Proverbs 20) Solomon tells us, **"A man's steps are of the Lord; how then can a man understand his own way?"** Once we learn the art of surrender and begin to keep our focus on the true artist in life, then He will help us through our day even when we may not have the answer to whatever we must face. By learning to trust in our Fathers' hand in staying close to Him will give us the protection and comfort to see us through.

This is how our life should be in raising our children for the day they are set free. As a parent we protect our children and give them security in love. Teaching them the Word of God as their foundation in our words and actions, showing respect for what we have and how to work for their rewards, never neglecting God in whom we owe all glory towards. As Solomon teaches us in the wisdom of God, we don't always know all the answers nor can we predict the future. But if we teach our children to obey the Word of God in never losing hope and how to be open in being humble to receive help when in doubt, then our children will be better prepared for their future when faced or given more clout!

If we teach our children how to pray in opening our hearts and minds to the Lord, to hear the gentle whisper from the start, they will learn how to search for answers from God before we part. Often when you and your children are whispering in prayer, the Lord will place the answer on your heart in the air. When this happens, teach your children that the answer they received as they spoke did not just come out of nowhere, but from the Lord who hears your heart before you ever even begin to pray from the start. By teaching our children in our actions and words that we don't have all the answers will equip them how to grow in their future through whom we know. This will teach our children to seek God first and look within themselves before taking the easy way out. In addition, it will teach our children that not all answers come directly but they may come through others indirectly.

Can you see this message in the overall picture of the Holy Bible in teaching His children how to grow and what to look out for? The entire Old Testament is full of indirect teachings through certain individual's actions and even the Lord traveling with Moses from the cloud above. The Lord repeatedly over the generations in the Old Testament taught in messages indirectly through other individuals to teach His one body of believers how to live and worship. But over time, the same cycle of events continued to happen over and over even to today. Why is it we must constantly be told something once we have already been told? Have you ever thought about this? The New Testament recording the life of the Lord, Jesus Christ, fulfilled everything the Old Testament ever taught in how to live directly in His walk and talk before His sacrifice in being set free. The Lord taught us directly the way back to God's grace by sending His only Son from the heavenly place. Just taking our children to church and placing a Holy Bible in front of them, is not enough! The Lord teaches us how to live in the light and if we are not careful to teach our children in our walk and talk, then we all could miss Him in flight!

Don't allow your pride to harden your heart and not be open to others in whom you love. Life is full of ups and downs and if we don't teach our children how to be humble, then how will they ever learn to live when they may stumble? As the Lord taught us in lessons of Moses, our children will follow us as we lead when humbled as a young child on their knees. This will prepare them as they mature for the day they are set free. Teach your children patience in prayer to hear the Lord and allow Him to guide you through. Even if you must face pains, this will teach them how to be true!

Why is it we can see continuous struggles in our homes, in our schools, in our workplace, in our economy, in our government, in our lack of leadership and sadly, even in our churches of today? Do you think it could possibly be pride in our human nature of not wanting to face the facts or better yet, the truth? It is so easy to conform to the crowd and not learn to stand on our own in life. We all try to hide or patch our problems, but there is a proven fact that we all must face, *"We can only run from the issue for so long before the truth must be faced!"* There is only one line to follow and it is very straight and narrow in our path. But due to our personal pride or thinking we are the artists of the picture we often tend to neglect the truth. The truth hurts when finally faced, but if you don't face the truth, the truth will face you! Think about it! You are a patient and the doctor calls you in. You haven't been feeling well for some time and your family history has a cycle of certain life threatening conditions that you have always hidden from the ones you love. Your family could see the signs and even knew the history. But no one wanted to address or face the facts. As you enter the physician's office you take your seat with the doctor behind the desk. The whole time you knew what you finally had to address. The time had come to face the truth and there are no words for the pain. All you could do is keep the tears from falling like rain. There was immediate relief from a load that you bared and this is where you begin the process of repair.

The sad part is by neglecting the truth over time the repair process can be much worse, and even cause some to be carried away in a hearse.

Can you see an importance to paying close attention to the ones that are close to you and see how sin can be even infecting you? If we are not honest with our self first when suffering then how can you be truly honest with our physician? If we withhold the truth from our doctor then how will he or she know how to properly treat the issue? Or better yet, if you know the truth but won't speak it then what do you truly expect in the cure? There is a tracking system in every positive or negative circumstance in life, but where many individuals continue to struggle with the same symptoms is where they don't take the time required to trace the issue to where the roots may have begun. The same process is also followed in true success in life. By following the roots of success, many individuals understand the importance of knowing where you stand and especially understanding their position within our Father's land. When the truth is neglected or just patched without understanding the history, then how can we improve the future? Like the doctor and the patient, what if the patient had been honest up front? Could you possibly see the recovering process less intense rather than waiting for the disease to overtake the body? Can you see the importance of understanding the illness and how to recognize the symptoms to possibly prevent the infection from returning once cured?

The awareness is right before us in the Word of God and we can see the same symptoms of destruction or struggles in the Holy Bible compared to today. If you can see a continuous cycle of symptoms, don't you see that it may be time to face the truth and find the cure? Like a physician or a mechanic, they can help you dissect a problem and possibly find a solution to repair, but if you don't take the time to properly understand the problem, then how will you ever know how to possibly prevent the relapse in the future? Our human pride causes many individuals to stumble and even fall. We all face different levels of pride throughout life in overlooking or even neglecting the truth. Everyone falls subject to their pride trying to buy time in some form or fashion and there comes a point that we all must face reality that our time is not our time but only in God's time.

Everyone falls subject to patching a problem or issue in life from their health, in our work, in our relationships, in our economy, and even in our children. The list can go on and on if you really think about it. Our society, by large numbers, has lost the perspective of time and has turned to the easy way out in trying to avoid or patch serious issues in life. You can see this in every level of life from our government to our economy and all the way to a single individual, even my self, falling guilty. Rather than searching the Word of God and standing on the truth, many fall subject to our society in trading debt for debt, trying to throw money to cover up a problem and even patch an illness with medication without properly taking the time to diagnose an issue. What does this teach our children? Better yet, what will this leave for our children? All of this evolves around one thing, in facing the facts to avoid future problems. This whole issue of a quick fix begins with an infant in giving that pacifier, then to toys, and then to money. Can you see where each one of these three items is only a temporary solution to a possible issue in life? There is no difference in this process taught at home as a child than in our life as an adult. As a child, the material things are not understood when given and as an adult, it is easy to fall guilty of not taking the time in hard work with discipline to do what is needed to correct the possible problem. If we don't teach our children how to positively dissect a problem to the smallest detail and how to recognize sin before having time to take root, then how will our children learn how to properly grow in their future? Every issue has a beginning and an end. When we learn with understanding from the Word of God how to recognize and overcome our burdens in life, we will find true joy in moving forward by acknowledging the truth. Think about it! Psychologically as we mature our issues or sins build pressure and hurt us more than when a child. Do you know why? Could it possibly be as adults we feel that we can handle our issues in life on our own? Many adults carry issues from their childhood because they were never taught how to properly address and overcome them. In this recognition, often these adults don't realize how they are still affecting their children when they are blinded by their own pride.

As a young child at home, our wrongs are dealt with on most occasions and then as a child we are to learn from our correction and move forward. Have you ever witnessed a child who knew they were wrong and faced some form of punishment? Did you notice an emotional affect on the child? How about the child who did not receive proper discipline and they continued the same wrong action? As they matured and continued to do as they chose, can you see where the issues still remain, but only may have changed with maturity? The difference between a child and an adult is our understanding of how to deal with our issues in life. The child is accountable to the adult or guardian and after they receive discipline, you will see that child acting happy once they get over their initial pain or correction. On many occasions, you can witness adults who are unhappy or burdened inside because they don't feel they are accountable to anyone except themselves. Their pride keeps them from happiness and having peace in their mental state by not opening their mind to the Word of God in facing the truth that they are still accountable for their actions.

Can you see why the Lord teaches us as adults to repent of our sins as we matured in the Holy Bible? If our pride keeps us from understanding that we are always being held accountable in our life once we mature from childhood, then our pride will begin to harden our hearts away from what is right in God's sight. There is no difference in this process of repair from a young child to an adult except from our understanding in whom we are accountable to and how our pride can cause us to hold things in that only build pressure eventually affecting our emotions and actions. We all, as adults tend to think we are strong enough to handle our issues in life and some occasions we can. But when our pride sets in after we overcome obstacles in our career, in our relationships, and in our everyday life, then we are just setting ourselves up for a hard fall whether in this life or the next.

Everyone male and female on some occasions wants to prove or show how strong mentally or physically they are under certain pressures. This is in our human nature but what we often tend to neglect is where this strength comes from. Like mentioned in the first part of the book, our children look at their parent as Superman or Wonder Woman, but if we don't teach our children that true strength comes from God, through Christ, and power comes from the inside rather than the outside, then how will our children ever know how to appreciate themselves and others for who they are? Because everywhere you look on the outside there is a new Superman or a new Wonder Woman taking the place of the other who fades away.

The Lord teaches us we are to be one body in a common direction in serving His will. If we allow pride to infect our thinking and begin to think we can hold everything together on our own without properly recognizing our weakness or faults, then prepare for pressures like you have never known. There is such a relief when we let go of our pride and submit to God in facing the truth. Think of yourself as a part of the body, like your legs for instance. Can you see the importance and purpose of the legs working together to reach a common direction? What happens in their confusion of which way to go? Would you feel like you were possibly stuck in place or even maybe being pulled apart? Could you see this even tearing your heart in two if the other leg takes its own direction in not understanding you?

Let's add a little more pressure as we mature and begin to think we are so strong on our own. Imagine a rope being attached to each ankle with the rope representing people who look up to you or who may even rely on you. Each rope is pulling in different directions and you are caught in the middle being pulled apart by different individuals causing you to feel stress in your heart. You think of yourself so strong that you can hold it together to bring your legs back in unity for your love in life and this is where you realize it is beyond your might. There must be a time in order to let it go to figure out what it is that you may not properly understand.

Everyone at times falls into thinking they can do it on their own and this is where we neglect or don't understand our position in whom is truly in control from the throne. We all face pressures or obstacles in life and this is where it is crucial to teach our children in our actions that we don't hold all the answers for the day they are left alone. When you think of the analogy of two legs and one body, can you see this relation not only to an individual, to a home, to a church, to business, to a country, but to the overall body of having peace in this world? You can apply this to anything with a common goal as the body and the legs are the direction of moving forward in life.

Have you ever noticed a sports team or a business that struggled in their game internally due to certain individuals serving their own interest and neglecting their position to properly work as a team with a common goal? Let's even go a little further; how about our government in constantly being divided due to their own pride and not learning how to work together for a common goal of unity for the people or by the people. Everyone wants to be right or have the attention on them but they have forgotten or are struggling with the purpose behind sacrifice in love for others. Personally, I had rather lose and my Team wins than win and my Team loses! Can you see how in this analogy that the legs must learn to work together to not become stagnant and work ultimately affecting the body? In your decision process in life you think about what is it going to take to move forward to sustain life? Don't ever feel down over attempting something and it only working for a while because no one has the perfect solution, except for God, and I believe we all fall short and agree on this.

The object is to not sit still and let something fall apart while arguing how to repair it. Repair wisely and then seek while the engine is running what you need to do to carry it further. Rather than just turning it off or shutting it down costing more money to eventually start back up, keep the engine alive by staying in tune with proper service with the people in order to keep the support and moral together when times may become tough. There is nothing worse than when a team begins to fight within their organization resulting in improper behavior by adults. There is a way to handle opposition in life, but if you can't drop your pride to reach a compromise, then how would you see this as being wise?

Everything in life that God has given has a beginning and an end and there is nothing we can do to stop the inevitable. Our job is to stay focused and treat others as we want to be treated, teaching our children how to live their lives ahead. When you open your eyes to what the Lord has provided, you can see that everything has a consistent pattern in constant motion to maintain life. Life mentioned previously, we as humans are the only ones who break that chain of life and if we don't learn how to work together with a common goal or direction, than how will we truly survive? When you study history in the Holy Bible, you can see this constant cycle of events and for some reason we continue to be blind to the facts. Do you think maybe pride could be standing in the way? Study the book of Obadiah sometime and relate to our current time in what you see. In addition, look at the fall of the Roman Empire in how they struggled within the government and the rich to poor. There is wisdom in history when you look at it for positive results to improve your future. Don't just read history to see what happened, but learn why it happened to prevent the same issues in the future!

I remember a story of a father and his son back years ago that still touches my heart to this day. The father was enjoying his peace while reading the morning paper and enjoying a sports game on TV. His son sat beside him on the floor and continued to interrupt the father's moment of peace. As the father continued to overlook his son hoping he would move on, the son never quit interrupting and the father could not overlook him any longer. So in order pacify his son, the father tore a picture of the world out of the paper and then proceeded to tear it into multiple pieces. The father's pride set in thinking he was the smart one and gave the pieces of the worlds picture to his son attempting to pacify his time by telling him, "see if you can put the world back together." The father then returned back to his temporary peace, while his son was occupied with the world in attempting to put it back together. To the father's surprise, the son within seconds said, "I got it!" The father was amazed and then asked his son, "How did you assemble the world back together so quickly?" The young son then looked up to his dad and replied, "It was easy. There was a picture of a man on the opposite side, and when I assembled the man back together, the world came together." Isn't it amazing how children see things but we, as adults, tend to make everything so complicated in life?

No matter your circumstance in life, whether you are struggling in a relationship, raising children, facing health issues, facing issues with leadership or authority, you can find the roadmap to happiness in the Word of God when you drop your pride and learn to surrender your will to Christ. The Holy Bible paints a beautiful living picture from Genesis to Revelation and fortunately for many, they are able to see it without ever reading it completely through with the blessings of God. Often though, you can hear or see the message being distorted when some individuals take a section and read it without understanding the whole message. Especially when they are going through certain emotions, causing the Word to mold to their thoughts and not being open to listen and learn to be shaped in God's hands. The living picture will have better clarity when focused upon daily and meditated upon in your day.

Many individuals, and even people of influence, tend to neglect the full picture in the Holy Bible and use it for personal gains. This is done by not pointing out our weaknesses and only focusing on what someone wants to hear, causing the truth to become cloudy in the picture of life. There is no doubt we all had rather hear the good over the bad, but in order to keep the picture clear, we must be direct in facing the truth. Just think how our world would be if everyone focused on the positive and learned from the negative to be stronger in life!

Why do you leave a will for your children? Is it out of love and possibly direction for guiding their future to serve your will? How about how to handle or take care of what you give? Now, open your eyes to feel the love in your heart and understand that this is what God has done in the Holy Bible from the very start! Our Father loves us so much that we can't even begin to imagine His mercy and grace in what He gives us in this place! Don't allow your pride to blind you from the facts and allow the Lord to guide you in the truth in order to give you strength like you have never known. This is possible through the blood of Christ for your life to keep in balance and return to God's throne!

It is never too late in life to drop our pride while we still have breath! Don't ever feel helpless in pride no matter the age! For I guarantee there is someone who loves you and is just waiting for that special day that you return to God and begin to pray! Can you see where our Father in heaven loved each of us so much that He sent His only begotten Son to show us how to live and return to Him? Can you even begin to imagine the love of God in Jesus Christ that He gave His life for His belief and love all the way to you and me? What are you willing to do for your child or the one you truly love? This is where you need to understand that what you do is not for someone else, but for the love of God in discovering yourself. Then you will begin to learn how to have true unity in your direction and find letting go of your personal strengths will guide you to even stronger levels in the body of the believer, through Jesus Christ.

There is a great lesson on where our strength comes from in the life of Samson and Delilah in the book of Judges in the Holy Bible. In addition to his strength, there is a major lesson of not giving into nagging, and to thinking we can do everything on our own. There are two different views to observe and learn from the life of Samson. One view is as an adult and another as a child of God maturing in the Holy Bible.

When you look upon Samson as an adult, can you see where he became arrogant in his own strength in not understanding where it truly came from? Can you see his own pride taking over in not under-standing his position to be obedient to the Lord's instruction? What did Samson do when tied between the columns of the building that he had not done since a child? When Samson returned to the Lord in prayer, God revealed from where the strength came. Not only did Samson return to prayer, he pressed on through his troubles in his belief of God answering his prayer. There is another lesson about the nagging wife, but due to possible consequences, let's view this as a nagging child in the growth of the single body in the Holy Bible. Have you ever witnessed a child who kept on and on and on....? What happened when the true issue wasn't addressed and they were just given a pacifier to send them on their way? Once the pacifier wore off, did they continue to come back over and over again? If we don't get to the root and understand the objective or issue, then can you see a continuous cycle of events? There is so much wisdom in the Word of God when we drop our pride and begin to see what the Lord has given us!

When you really think about it, why is it so hard to submit to the Word of God in the Holy Bible? Why do so many individuals search so many other teachings or chase nothing but theories? Our pride causes us, at times, to think things are much more complicated than they really are and no one honestly likes to feel accountable to someone above them, not only for their actions, but even their thoughts. Have you ever thought about why so many individuals backslide from the Lord? Do you think it could possibly be not wanting to face the truth and taking the easy way out in conforming to the world of personal desires rather than following God's will? Can you see children who rebel after being overlooked in life? How about children or even employees who return to their same attitude or actions once they have been corrected over time? How many times have you ever addressed an issue with your spouse, but their own pride got in the way of not wanting to listen? How about the husband who only sends the temporary rose?

Think about it! You and your spouse are missing something in your relationship that is very minor. One person tries to address while the other just thinks it is no problem or issue, and continues on their normal way. Then as one attempts to address it at a later date, the other still continues to overlook what their partner is trying to say. As time moves on, the issue, which was little to nothing in the beginning, has now elevated into something, due to not addressing it at the start. The issue in the beginning was only lack of time and proper attention. But now it turns into more, because the other party won't listen!

The problem grows internally until one day the husband realizes he better drop his pride and address the problem. So instead of taking the time to listen and understand what is needed to fill what is missing, he attempts to patch the issue with a gift or even that temporary rose. By not dropping his pride to properly listen this is how the minor problem only continues to grow! When a couple or anyone in a position to serve doesn't drop their pride to fully listen and only tries to cover-up with a patch, then how can you honestly expect something to remain strong with purpose?

The toughest part of life is facing the truth in our reflection of who we truly are and the life we live. This is why so many individuals won't submit to the Lord in trying to understand the Word of God. Because when they hear the message, they face a mirror that only focuses on them, not allowing them to point the finger at someone else. The Lord plainly tells us in (Matthew 7), **"And why do you look at the speck in your brother's eye, but do not consider the plank in your own eye?"** Throughout the Word of God from the Old Testament to the New, we are continuously shown where we are guilty and when an individual doesn't listen to what the message is revealing their pride begins to harden their heart in even affecting others without recognition. If someone is in darkness and blind, then how can that individual lead someone to the light? This can only happen with the love of Christ in giving them sight to feel God's might!

So many people tend to look at the doom and gloom of the Holy Bible and this is where they don't understand the message within learning from our history. Personally, I am thankful to have the opportunity to not only look at history of downfalls or weaknesses, but even proud to know that God has given me another chance through the blood of Christ to not only live, but to learn from my sins to improve my future! This wisdom and history in the Holy Bible and in my personal life of facing the truth is not only for me but for the love of God in being a better person with a proper understanding for everyone else in my life!

When an individual humbles themselves as a child and learns to face a weakness in the truth, they will not only grow stronger but they will receive joy in God's mercy for understanding their position by learning and knowing that they are not alone! Can you see the parallel to your love with your family in never wanting them to feel alone? This is all only said to strengthen your relationship with God and hopefully to reach an individual in the dark.

In the book of (Leviticus 23) the Lord gave instruction to Moses to live outside in shelters for seven days to remind each new creation of their history from their ancestors. The Hebrew call this Sukkoth in relation to the festival of shelters, the Lord revealed our weakness in pride of how easily we can forget where we came from and the importance of keeping our pride in check to maintain appreciation for what we have. There is great wisdom in this to keep our life in tune, especially when our society continues to move at such a fast pace.

A good example of this could be compared to camping and learning how to break away from society spending time with the ones you love with only the nature of God surrounding you. You might not have to spend but a couple of nights and believe me you will appreciate your bed and shower back at home! The Lord taught us in the purpose of staying in tune with life will not only give us respect for our past generations, but will also keep us in touch with the simple things in life.

On a lighter note, speaking of this lesson in (Leviticus 23), and recalling how pride can affect our way of life there is a story from a friend that I must share to give you a laugh as it still humors me to this day. Whether the story was exaggerated or not it really hits home when you think about it. My friend was single and out one night the week prior to the fourth of July. That evening he met someone and they hit it off really well. As the evening progressed, he invited her to meet him at Pickwick Lake to go out in a boat and enjoy the upcoming holiday. She accepted the invitation and they set the time to meet at the boat ramp for him to pick her up. Here's where the laugh begins. My friend did not own a boat at the time and nor did she ask any details to my knowledge. He undoubtedly did not properly plan and thought he could just rent a boat right before the holiday. Can you see the importance of proper planning or even checking the details?

When it came time to locate a boat, just before their date, he was out of luck for all the other boats were taken. In his choices now being slim to none and his date would arrive soon, he had no choice but to drop his pride and rent a flat bottom aluminum fishing boat with an outboard two-stroke motor on the back. After dropping his pride, he loaded the boat and took off to the boat ramp in time for the date. He said the funniest thing was seeing her there waiting, all prim and proper, dressed for the occasion and then he pulled up with the two stroke motor smoking saying, "Jump in!" He said there was definite hesitation, but she also dropped her pride and came back down to reality for them to enjoy the day.

That expression on her face had to be priceless and another funny thing about it was, for some reason, she never answered his future calls. I guess you can say, his flat bottom boat wasn't good enough for who she thought she was in forgetting how to appreciate the small things in life!

It is sad how individuals allow their pride to overlook someone for who they may be on the inside rather than what they have on the outside. Can you see this relation towards the teachings in the Holy Bible of staying in tough with life through the message of Jesus Christ?

There is nothing wrong with the luxury of life, as long as we never forget where we come from and in whom truly provides! If your pride begins to stem your ego and you begin to raise yourself above others, then you better recall your position in realizing that sometimes it is best to do without! This entire message is taught repeatedly throughout the Word of God in order to be proud of our works, to always honor Him and to be careful not to lose our perspective or direction in life.

When you look at the history of our society, you can see how we are continuously pulling away from not only the Word of God, but even struggling with our unity in our American heritage of the United States. An easy way to see this is in our television shows of today verses yesterday. Today they teach our children how to create or cover-up a crime, compared to our history of having morals and lessons to teach our children reinforced lessons in life. Just look at how Zsa Zsa

Gabore in Green Acres had to drop her pride to not be above others in a different culture of life. You can see how her city life struggled with her husband's country life and how her definition of fine living did not quite go together with Arnold the pig. Maybe it would have been good for her to have spent some time with John Candy and Dan Ackeroid in The Great Outdoors and they could have taught her how to water ski!

Since we are on lessons from previous shows, maybe some of these CEO's or executives in office should spend some time with cousin Eddie and Clark Griswold in Christmas Vacation to remember who actually helps them fill their financial portfolio in life. Everyone needs a cousin Eddie in their family to keep their life in check and also teach us how to overlook certain issues to remember the principles in life! It is pathetic in how pride can lead to greed and suppress the ones below in order to make others gain! There is nothing wrong with proper gains when not hurting others, but when individuals begin to achieve financial gain by suppressing others, then would you call these proper gains?

In the book of (Luke 16: 19-31) the Lord Jesus Christ taught a vital lesson to the rich and the poor. There is not only a message in how to treat others in need, but even a look of the torment from Hades being the pits of eternal death. Can you even begin to imagine how much it would hurt to be in eternal death and watch others traveling your same road or path? The Lord reveals in this message how the fallen can always look up while tormenting their soul and we are taught in (Revelation 21: 3-4) how the believer will have their tears wiped away. This means the ones who are lost without true repentance will always suffer for remembering the hurt they not only caused themselves but even others in which they care for. In addition we learn how the believer and follower of Christ will no longer look back on their hurt or pains, but look forward in the eternal life they have gained! Think about it! When does losing hurt? **"Losing hurts the worst when you know you could have done better and you neglected the truth!"** If you have done your best and you still temporally lose, then you still can have or receive peace in your rest. By learning to accept your position and striving to improve, this is how you never lose. Can you even begin to imagine the torment in Hades in always looking back and the beauty in Heaven of only seeing forward? Now, can you see our purpose of being in the middle in order to properly achieve the ultimate eternity.

Due to our society and constant moral downfall being displayed in the media and technology world, we as parents and the overall body need to not only stay involved with our children, but be creative in developing productive ideas to help in our children's future. When individuals continue to dissect in unproductive manners with little reason or solutions while continuing to be tolerant of right and wrong, then there is no doubt what the future will hold for our children ahead. In the book of (2 Kings 10) we are taught not to tolerate sin in our lives and the consequences that follow. This same message is repeated over and over due to our ancestor's lack of under-standing the truth. When you read the story of Israel, don't look at it as a defiant nation, but as an individual, single body, tolerating sin in his or her life. We, as humans, see separation in the differences of people, but the Lord looks down upon each believer as one body without separation, but performing different functions to serve His direction. There was a distinct purpose and reason why the Lord denied Moses access to the Promised Land and a very wise lesson in proper maturity to achieve certain rewards. If you study this story in Exodus, and the Law of God in Leviticus you will see great wisdom in keeping proper order to maintain our perspective in life. This is where I thank and praise God for the ultimate sacrifice of His only begotten Son by fulfilling the law of God, and providing the way for each of us today while breaking all traditions of yesterday.

Based on the above in developing productive ideas to help our children's future and with the wisdom of God of understanding the purpose of guidelines, let us look at a couple ideas on different critical issues to possibly trigger some type of movement back in a positive way for our children and even the life of our country to sustain our positive movement in the overall body. Think of each nation like this, every nation wants to be the head of the body, but this is where each nation is only head of its single body, being a part of the overall large body from God's view. Think about it! We are to use our heads to work together to do what is best, to keep peace, but for everyone to sustain life. Each part of the body has a specific use that relates to the overall body and each part should learn how to work together for a forward direction. Now stop briefly and re-read to think of the depth of thought process to receive a deeper understanding. Sometimes it helps to slow down and re-think of where we have been.

Idea #1 – Technology and Media

Issue: No censorship, nor secure way to properly insure certain access and information being viewed by innocent children, or by age of proper maturity, to not infect their young minds in thinking something is acceptable or not.

How to Solve: Apply the technology already in place, but being used for semi-productive manners. With the technology of infra-red seen on our phones and other web access could be censored automatically with a data base storing, either eye scan or fingerprint scan to securely allow our children access to certain web sites being censored by age.

Who Would Enter: Parents, based on their own access point, and their determination of when their child is ready. In addition, we could create a file being a single file list of where our children are surfing the net if we choose to view as a parent.

Rather than boring you with more details and how it could work, let's think about it like this, "Why are there laws preventing children to buy tobacco, pornography, weapons, or any other controlled substance as a minor?" There is a reason why an eight year old or thirteen year old cannot view certain materials in the physical world due to their vulnerable minds. But in the technology world, there are ways around every access point and even acts of violence being taught over the web. Let alone, how to plot something or build something that can hurt innocent lives. On another level of regaining control of lax restrictions on the web, can you tell me the difference why a cigarette company can still be liable in a lawsuit when they have posted numerous "warnings" on every pack and there are even laws restricting the age of purchase compared to a website provider posting acts of criminal violence, pornography, and other ways to build weapons that can hurt innocent people. For instance, a young child with no parental discipline views a site revealing something adults are doing so they begin to form an opinion that it is acceptable in society.

When you really think about the Internet and consider the benefits in our business or education process, can you see a negative impact on our children with little to no guidance at home? Personally, I have trouble and concerns with my own children even with a strong teaching of right and wrong in their lives while being involved in a Christian home. Because I know that one break-up or that one bully could trigger a chain of events that we may not see and could even affect our children in possibly being free. It is easy to witness how our society without God in focus has affected our divorce rate, our teen birth rate, our economy, our government, our churches, and the list continues to grow even to someone you may know. Due to our tolerance and lack of proper controls we can see how our media world has gone wild in the lack of respect for individual's personal lives. In addition, look at what has happened to our jobs and surplus since the free trade agreements. Now by certain individual's greed and their own pride not wanting to face the truth, we have fallen from a trade surplus country to a trade deficit country. Countries that once looked upon us in how to grow are now looking at us in how we overcome our previous mistakes to regain our position within the overall body. They now see the importance of regulations and what happens without regulated growth. Our American model country has now shown what not to do, verse's how to do! There was a specific reason our ancestors built this country on certain by-laws and the foundation of God in order to preserve the life of this country. Study history and the facts are there, *"You remove God, then the time is only limited before the life of the body has no more purpose."*

There was a reason for tariffs and quotas within our country and a reason why our counter nations still have theirs in place. This reason goes back to the lesson in the Holy Bible of the manna provided to Moses and the people of Israel in the book of (Exodus 16). If we, as Americans will open our eyes and drop our pride to face the truth then we will begin to turn our negative economy into a positive workforce once again. But first we better be prepared for the tough times ahead to overcome our current issues at hand. There is only one way to overcome this and that is, "Face the truth!" By continuous neglect and greed our country will remain out of balance and hurt others in need. So, I pray to each individual in a position to serve, that you open your eyes to do what is right in the Lord's sight and for our children to have jobs and even an American life!

To put the world trade in laymen's terms, and develop a plan of action, let us address an analogy of free trade to simplify the overall goal. In addition, to keep it in perspective without boring you with how it can work, the obstacles and the end results, let's look at another idea or concept in a rough draft to possibly trigger someone into making the right steps. There is no doubt in my mind that we can develop a plan that can help our country and even help the overall body of all the parties involved. What happens to the body when a disease sets in one particular area? Can you see it spreading and even affecting other nations or parts of the body? The Lord has warned us of this and if we don't correct it, then the disease will only get worse before a major negative action takes place!

When you think of our country, imagine it like a large swimming pool. Prior to free trade, our pool was fed by internal pumping springs from within the pool. Other countries represent separate water hoses entering the pool and feeding the supply. Each hose supplied a specific need, but with the water valve in check to prevent overflow from within. Can you see where the internal springs can be cut off due to the expense of pumping them in compared to lower cost water coming from other countries?

Another important factor of balancing the water level within the pool is the supply and demand. Based on the evaporation rate of individual's consumption, there must be a check valve in place to properly monitor and adjust accordingly. Over time, with water being supplied in every direction, there will be no value left in the dollar at home without some type of restrictions and handle on the supply and demand.

Here is another idea the Lord has blessed me with that might help or trigger another solution. With our technology of today, why can we not develop a master program secure only for government officials in proper positions to monitor the supply and demand requirements within our country to maintain our jobs and our needed imports? For instance, let's call the program, "Operation Check Valve." Every supply house in this country is already on an inventory control basis with some form of existing program. So, how can we link these supplies and demands into a single <u>secure</u> pool to properly adjust each valve in order to not cut off our internal springs from within the pool? In addition, how do we overcome the lash back from the individual hose's supplying unlimited amounts of product to maintain a healthy relationship?

There is one part to never forget, when something has been able to run freely in the wild, then prepare for issues in order to regain control. This is where individuals cannot look at the money loss, but focus on life itself for love of their country and for their children! What is more important, life now, or your children's life of tomorrow? If we don't drop our pride and get a grip on life, then prepare for life to get a grip on you!

There is a way to develop a balanced program, not only for our economic future, but for our well being of tomorrow. The Lord teaches us in (Mathew 25) of using our talents for a specific purpose and if we neglect our talents, then it could be taken away. This does not only apply to a single individual, but to the single body with a purpose of a common goal in learning to work together for what they have in certain qualities or talents to move forward. If we don't use what we have in our strong points and learn to allow others to supply theirs with proper controls, then how can we honestly expect to maintain proper growth in the future? When you study the history in the Holy Bible, you will find a direct parallel in the purpose of the walls around a city compared to our modern day purpose of tariffs and quotas in world trade between countries. The walls for instance that King Nebuchadnezzar reconstructed in Babylon were for the protection of the people and control of what went out and came into the city. The gates were located in specific locations allowing passage in and out from different directions. In addition, the gates were closed at night for the people's protection.

This relates to our free trade and passage in this country by needing some form of controls or gates to maintain strength within this nation. Throughout history in the Word of God, look at what happened to a city when they dropped their walls in allowing free reign. Each one lost its direction and began to wonder in circles searching for survival. Personally, I am very thankful to live in a country with walls built by God and living in times where we follow laws with more understanding of there purpose to maintain life. The longer our government continues to bicker over these issues we will continue to see major money loss in stagnant behavior, lack of purpose to support our country, a deterioration of our jobs, and even our dollar value on a continuous decline. Like walls being torn down, everyone begins to go in every direction with a selfish purpose of survival overlooking the purpose of unity within a country to survive. There is a way for us to rebuild our walls by placing the wisdom of God and applying our history to the need of today to guide our future way!

Remember the engine analogy earlier? It is better to start a process while the engine still has life rather than sitting still and constantly talking about the problem. Along the way you learn to improve without over correcting the problem and shutting it down. The longer you talk the more money you lose and the harder it will be to correct the problem! It is far better to be alive than dead, than in the grave knowing we never tried! Or even worse, I would hate to know like Jesus warns in (Luke 16) that I had the resources right in hand but was too greedy to help others in this land!

Do you think Moses and the people of Israel knew what they had to face in their walk through the wilderness? There are so many lessons in this message for each of us to understand but the main message is one thing, believe in focusing on the Lord and He will provide the way! There is another great lesson that stands out when the people of Israel were at the front door of achieving their promised land. You can see how certain individuals always point out the negatives or tell you why something cannot be done and this very human nature is prevalent today in never making their step in faith.

In (Numbers 14) this same lesson is revealed in doubting what the Lord had instructed and the people could not recognize the existence of God with them through all the miracles and obstacles they had overcome. This lesson plainly reveals our human weakness in being blind to the facts and not wanting to face issues or giants in the land. But there comes a time like David and Goliath that you must step forward in belief and do what is right for the people in our sight! Like the plane in the air, how can it continue in flight without fuel, guidance, respect, and when things are just not working right? One thing to remember in life, **"It is not the obstacles in our course, but the goal in the end!"** Every obstacle has a solution and every goal has a reward! When you understand this in life then this is where you learn the art of moving forward! There is a reason each one of us goes through what we do in order to develop our true purpose and character to grow stronger in life. Don't ever look down upon your failures, but learn from them to be a better person in this world!

Do you think the people on the Mayflower worried more about their obstacles or their rewards? There comes a point when someone must stop and help the other man possibly being affected by a larger wake of pride or greed. It is easy to just drive on by and try to cover up the truth of your actions in how they may be affecting someone in your path. But the last thing anyone should ever want is to be left on an island all alone, being washed away by pride and with no resources to overcome their obstacles in life. Please don't allow your pride to ever think you can't stop to help someone in need that you may have washed ashore. Because I can assure you everyone when injured is gracious for a helping hand to pick themselves off of the rocks in life. We all do things we regret if honest with ourselves, and it is much better to face the truth here before it is too late. Because you never know when the truth may face you!

The ideas or thoughts mentioned previously are feasible and there is no doubt in my mind of how we all could benefit with proper dedication. Rather than boring you with the intricate details of the check valve idea, let's move on towards the ending, but the new beginning of another chapter in life. Sometimes in life it helps to be on the bottom to have a full perspective and view to really see the top. The object is to keep within the rules and experience voluntarily, verses involuntarily. This is what the Lord wanted in (Leviticus 23), by teaching us to remember our position in life and never to forget in pride where we have come from. If we don't stop ourselves and regain control to insure proper growth in life, we are only setting ourselves up for harder times ahead. This will not only affect the unfaithful, but even the faithful ones in life. There is no doubt our weather patterns are changing and even becoming more violent over a wider spectrum. One to two inch rains were considered a large rain several years ago and now areas are experiencing flash floods almost every time a front moves through. Tornadoes used to touch down on an individual basis within a storm but now there are multiple tornadoes popping up everywhere during this period. In addition, the sea levels are changing due to the increased melting of the arctic circle and you can see where the time period that scientist gave on the meltdown has been miscalculated due to changes in the environment. All of these natural events in life are going to continue and even increase due to the earth's cycle of life. We need to get a handle on the things we can control like mentioned previously, and prepare ourselves for the natural events in life. It sure makes matters worse if our home is not in order when a storm arrives and we can definitely rest in peace when we are prepared. There are two different preparations, one internally and the other externally. On the outside there is always work to be done, but the object is to be prepared to the best of our abilities for the days ahead. The inside takes daily nourishment and once you have received the key to life, through Jesus Christ, then you are in the ultimate safe room in Gods might. Check your survival kits to see if the true instructions are included because it would be sad if you only left a patch without the full instruction manual in the Word of God for your children or someone else who could seek shelter when you are not at home. Never allow your pride to forget the storms of the past to prepare for the ones in the future. Because when one storm may end, there is always another one in the horizon.

The Lord gave us in the book of Job a glimpse of the overall picture of how things work in this world. This message within this single life of Job was reduced from a picture larger than we can see. Think about something as large from East to West being reduced to a single body for us to try and even begin to understand or even comprehend. The Lord gave us this insight on how to live and be prepared in life for the storms ahead. We are taught how to serve, believe, have faith, and even treat those in mourning of sickness or loss of life. This book of Job is one of the toughest books to ever comprehend due to our limited minds and understanding of God's power and purpose in life. But to just stimulate the mind and try to look at this in something to relate, let us look at chapter 1 verse 6, between the Lord and Satan, as a Father and a son here on earth. The son once followed the father, and then as he matured, envy and pride began to set in due to not respecting or understanding his position in life. The father kicked him out of his peaceful and tranquil home of purity due to infection of sin. In verses six through twelve of chapter one, you can view this as a teenager who has rebelled but returned home still understanding his position requesting permission to go back out again, only to perform evil in order to test someone's faith. You can plainly see that the son had powers that interrupted the natural events or cycles of life and when you look at this child growing older with the power of evil spreading from one individual to the entire world, can you possibly see him beginning to grow arrogant in his power and being blinded by pride? As he grows stronger and matures in life, can you see him becoming jealous and wanting his father's position? During this time period, the father is observing the growth of evil constantly breaking the natural cycle of events, causing harm or destruction to what he has built and to his other children, which he loves from the heart. Then one day after all the brothers and sisters continuous cries from their hearts in prayer, he finally has enough and leaves his position to put a stop to this destruction once and for all!

There comes a point with every child who rebels in life that they must be stopped and when they won't listen, then they only grow into stronger rebellion trying to turn everyone in the family against the ruler of the house. The Lord has patience so far above our imagination or comprehension in His mercy and grace for each of us to learn and serve within His place! Can you relate a fraction of God's mercy to the mercy you give the one's in whom you love? What happens when they mature and don't understand their position? Can you see negative consequences of children who grow up in pride or greed with a parent in a position of power within a company? This is where we need to understand our position in life never treating others any different, and respect each individual for the person they are. There is a reason we experience things as we do, and sometimes we may experience something in order to test our faith to reveal God's glory. Think about it, how do you view your adversity or obstacles in life? Do you view them as something to learn from and grow stronger to be a better person? Or do you just go with the flow trying to stay afloat in life? There is a purpose behind every test in life and a purpose behind the laws of God to follow in order to not hurt others, or ourselves.

Throughout the entire Holy Bible you can see where the Lord provided leaders, judges, messengers, and even His direct works through the cycle of life in nature. When you look at the verses of Job 1:6 and Job 2:1, and think about this heavenly court recognizing certain positions in the Lord's presence, you can put this more in perspective for our understanding in thinking of it as the body of a church or any other body of proper organization. Think about the church for instance, from the pastor, to the deacons, to the elders, to the teachers, to the students, and to those who don't seek a position of leadership in front of others choosing to follow the ones who may lead. Everyone has a seat in the house of God and everyone is loved the same, being honored for their level of commitment in serving others in need. There is no jealousy of position in Heaven above, but respect for each individual soul in the love of God! Personally I'll be proud, no matter my position, to just be there in the presence of God!

Our Father, Lord above, created this world originally with a specific purpose of natural events and Satan through sin brings the birth pains of un-natural events trying to break the chain of love in God's life. There is a natural cycle of life in this creation, which we cannot comprehend fully, nor control! But it is up to each of us on an individual level to do our part based upon our talents in serving, preparing, and remaining faithful to God.

There is a song written by Ada R. Hebershon in 1907 that relates to this whole circle of life and warms my heart to hear the melody of the words from the very start. The name of the song is "Will the Circle Be Unbroken?" There is great joy in the victory of Jesus at the old rugged cross of knowing that God's circle of life is a chain that cannot be broken in love and knowing, without a doubt, that good will always overcome evil in this world! This is where we learn the art of two being one in God's Amazing Grace, teaching us how to live in love within this beautiful place!

It is very important to grow with our children, as God has been and will always be there all the way through this physical end! Don't forget to teach your children about the temptations of sin and only the temporary satisfactions that come to an end. We all have our moments in life that we all regret, but be thankful for every chance you may receive, never neglecting how to truly believe! Our sins in life always bring pains and even can cause tears like rain. We are to learn from our past and understand who we are to improve our future and build on a solid foundation of God being the ultimate college.

On a lighter note, but a serious note, don't forget to share with your children about the birds and the bees, to possibly prevent someone from being knocked to their knees. If our pride sets in and we don't prepare our children how to have respect for their bodies in treating it like a temple, then how will they ever know how to respect another for who they are in learning the sanctity of two being one. Warning your son or daughter about GI Joe in that Hummer or Barbie in that flashy new car will better prepare them for relationships ahead to possibly prevent a scar.

The Lord teaches us throughout the Holy Bible of the purpose of respecting time in a relationship and the consequences of lust. We are taught as adults from Abraham taking the Lord's promise into his own hands, to David falling to lust, and even Solomon, to how our sexual desires can cause us to lose more than our focus in our position of faith. By teaching our children how to overcome their sexual desires and to treat their bodies like that temple in walking away or taking a step back in the head of passion, will possibly save someone a lot of heartache in learning the purpose of control. If you could ask King Herod in the book of (Mark 6) about the affects of lust in having regrets, what do you think he would say? There are a lot of men and women who can relate with regret in wishing they would have walked away, cooling off to preserve their future day. Do you think King Herod would probably tell GI Joe to be careful or he could lose more than that Hummer? Or do you think he might tell Barbie to be ready to possibly trade in that flashy convertible for a new Minivan?

Spending time with our children and teaching them to build in time to understand the purpose of maturing will only lead to closer relationships and how to prepare for the winds of sin in this world. There is no question when children are brought up in respecting themselves, they will respect others. In every situation or sector in life, there comes a point that each individual must come together as one to be united with a purpose and single cause for our children of tomorrow. This is what the Lord instructs and teaches in the Word of God and our ancestors of this country followed this in order for us to be free! This does not only apply to Christians, but to every loving individual who wants the best for their children in their future life ahead. Life is a beautiful thing when we appreciate what we have been given and if we are not careful, our pride can cause us to neglect our purpose in teaching and serving others in need.

There is music in the air when you close your eyes and begin to see. In feeling the love of God through the blood of Jesus Christ in allowing us to be free! There is a letter to my daughter that the Lord placed on my heart and I would like to share it with you to hear the music of the Lord in whom it all starts. I'm sure every loving father or individual can relate in their love with their children or even their soul mate. Love is in the air when you listen and look at life in God's grace to respect what He has given to each of us in feeling comfort and safe and this is where you begin to hear the beauty in God's might.

* * *

Letter to Daughter

Dear Karlee,

You know I was thinking I need to teach you how to dance. Really! One day when you are (MUCH) older you will have someone to dance with, and you need to understand the purpose and how.

There is something very special when you are in the arms of someone who loves you and especially when you learn how to move together. The Lord teaches us how to dance in the Holy Bible when you open your eyes and ears to hear Him draw near. Think about it, the Lord teaches us how to become one and this is how you learn to move together and not apart.

Dancing in love is something very special and never to take for granted! It is not how fast you move, not how slow you dance. It is in the art of learning to surrender and move together as if it were your last dance.

You don't speak in the dance, you learn to hear the gentle whisper on your heart and this is where you learn to dance from the start. So close your eyes and imagine me there with you. You are in my arms and you hear me whisper, "I love you."

You don't have to have music to dance it is all in the art of romance. Love is something special and never think any less, because I know you will be beautiful as Cinderella in a dress.

You are very special to me and don't you ever think any less!! (To God All Glory, Amen)

I love you,
Dad

CHAPTER 10

Physical and Spiritual

*I*n the previous chapters we have read or addressed many different topics and issues in life. It all started with why we never quit, to having appreciation, to our roots in history, our inspiration, our differences, the importance of time, opening our minds in belief, and what to watch out for to maintain our perspective in life.

Throughout our adult life it is vital to understand our surroundings to the best of our knowledge, and our purpose to grow stronger in this physical and spiritual world. The Lord gave us the foundation of the rock in His work for us to build upon, but to never forget in whom gives life. There is <u>no other foundation</u> that is more true and precise with perfection than what has been given through Jesus Christ!

If we don't recognize our strong points and work on our weak points, then how do we honestly maintain proper strength? Or, if we don't analyze our surroundings, then how do we feel secure in our decisions to move forward and sustain life? It is vital to be aware of our surroundings and understand how to move in this world to not only live without being left behind or overlooking or understanding our position, but to prepare a path that has already been prepared for each of us, through Christ, to help our children of the future. Due to our human nature, it is very easy to become lazy and only think about oneself or those around you, but this is exactly what the other team of evil wants in causing us to feel that we can't make a difference in this world. Don't ever forget that all small things add up to big things and without the small things, there are no big things! Everyone has a place and a position that can help another achieve their goals in building a circle of life that is in constant motion adding value and strength. This is what the Lord set into place giving us the directions in whom to honor and how to help each other in growing on the right foundation.

Periodically, it is beneficial to create a mental picture of who you are to keep your life in balance. In addition, it is wise to take a snapshot on occasions to insure proper maturity is being reflected in all areas of your life. The more you pay attention to your personal picture and apply the Word of God you will begin to recognize depth in your words and actions beyond your imagination.

There is a never a stage in life to stop thinking and exercising your mind to grow or maintain your mental strength. It is very healthy to recall your joys in life and to learn from your mistakes to possibly share with someone else to help in their path or let's say, "Their game of life." Our bodies may become limited in our movements, but we can still exercise our minds in positive thoughts as we grow old. By doing this it will increase your chances of maintaining your mental health as you mature in life.

Briefly, describe a mental picture of yourself and what it would consist of in your mind. Think of the people around you and your environment as your backdrop in constant motion. Now think of yourself as the focal point in your picture. Can you see how your picture is moving, even when you stand still? When you look at yourself, are you pleased with what you see? What about your environment, does it need work? How does it make you feel? Can you see areas that make you happy and some that just aren't right? Are you satisfied with your picture of life? There is something very vital to realize in your mental picture with yourself in the center and that is, can you see how it is up to you to keep your life in order? No one in your backdrop can do it for you and it is solely up to you to learn and enhance your life to improve your environment within your personal self to possibly enhance or maintain the backdrop of someone else's picture in life. There is a time to focus on yourself to improve or grow stronger as you mature, and this is what the Lord teaches in the Holy Bible. When you think of the people in your backdrop of life, remember the commandment to treat others as thy self in love for one another, and if someone has done you wrong then pray for them to see the light of Jesus Christ.

In the book of Ephesians 4 and 5, the Lord tells us in His Word through the Holy Spirit to not allow anger to control you and to get rid of all evil behavior. By learning to be kind and forgiving one another in our life shows maturity in our Christian faith in understanding how God has forgiven you. As you mature in faith, you learn to leave things in the hands of God rather than taking them into your own hands. The Lord will prevail His justice in due time and if we take matters into our own hands, then we are going against the Will of God. The Lord will take care of all evil that you may see! So never wish or think of something wrong to another individual and always believe! Because you never know how the Lord may be working with the other person in your life to reveal God's glory in His mercy and His might!

When you look at your mental picture and only focus on yourself overlooking everything or everyone in your backdrop of life from which you can see, how short lived will your picture be? It is important to study your life at times and evaluate the hands that have guided your path in order to stay on track, or if needed, to get back on the right track of life with God guiding your path. Many individuals are being misled away from the Word of God in the Holy Bible in seeking their own distorted truth. There is only "One" truth in God our creator, giving us life in His mercy and grace to return home to Him through His only Son in saving us from the evil within this worldly place!

Not everyone travels the same distance in life or has the same desires, and when we learn to respect each person for their own picture rather than knocking someone down, then we learn how to connect in the overall single body through Jesus Christ. Our purpose is to unite and feel God's power to reveal His glory reflecting His light! There is nothing more uplifting or fulfilling in life than feeling the love within the hands of God above!

Some individuals in your backdrop of life may choose to live in the flatlands, and some may seek to climb mountains for different views or challenges ahead. If you notice someone in your life beginning to stumble or even fall, pick them up rather than just sitting back and not offering that helping hand in showing that you understand! There is depth in love within every picture in life.

Life is not something to take for granted and treat like a digitally enhanced picture! If you treat your environment like a computer and try to delete what you may not like in the picture, then you are forgetting how to live your Christian faith! There is art in a true picture with discipline of the human eye in understanding the natural true picture of life! In every back ground of an individual's life, we all wish we could treat it like that digital picture cleaning it up with the click of a button, but when we fail to understand the purpose of forgiveness in our Christian faith, then that negative in our background will never leave, when we only claim to believe! There is joy in understanding God's mercy in the hand of time, and when we learn to help others, acknowledging that we are not perfect, we then begin to feel God's glory through the Holy Spirit bringing our picture to life!

On a personal note, if I could zap my imperfections in my life, there would be a whole lot of clicking going on! It would sound like Shirley Temple in a tap dance with Sammy Davis, Jr.! Only outlasting their dance like the Energizer Bunny who keeps going and going and going... Now due to all my imperfections, I feel like a certified member of the Rat Pak in Vegas! But I am relieved to now have my understanding of true forgiveness and discovering my purpose in life.

If I would have just listened to Michael Landon in that Little House on the Prairie, or in Highway to Heaven, my return home might have been as welcome as that little town of Mayberry! I'm proud though for every imperfection in my life, in learning how to recognize and overcome my previous sins to possibly help someone on the wrong path as I have been! There is great joy in the fruits of the spirit in doing things right within the Lord's sight! He is the One who gives me the wisdom to learn from my past recalling people like Bob Hope or Bill Cosby who caused me to laugh! There is joy in the Holy Spirit of God when guiding your path! Life is a beautiful thing with God in your picture and keeping your life in perspective with Jesus Christ revealing the ultimate features!!!

Everyone, at times, searches for a perfect picture in life and some individuals seek perfection to the point of leading to obsessive compulsive behavior in their actions causing anxiety in their life. When you study the Holy Bible and open your eyes and ears to the Holy Spirit, you can find a point of peace that will allow you to relax and understand that there is no perfection through the human eye. Once you begin to understand this, then you can find your level of comfort in discovering your purpose in life and learn how to improve the areas that may need addressing. Many individuals get caught up in society or seeking perfection to the point it causes them to lose touch in life and they begin to constantly adjust themselves somehow on the outside due to something not being filled on the inside. There is nothing wrong with striving for perfection and this is what we are taught in (Ephesians 5), to imitate God living a life filled with love following the example of Jesus Christ. Unfortunately, in this life we are born with a sinful nature and cannot live a perfect life in our action and thoughts causing us to stumble or even fall.

Where many people have misunderstood the verse above is when they fail to look at the life of Christ in His walk and talk, verses having some wrinkles in His clothes or riding a donkey. It is not what you have on the outside, but what you have on the inside! Once your inside is right, then you respect life for what it is and not for what it is not! Our goal in life is ultimately that eternal day of joy and in this physical world we can experience pieces of it through the Holy Spirit giving us a major thirst for more! In the meantime, of our time allowed here, we are to maintain our surroundings within our individual picture of life and improve it internally and externally to the best of our God given talents to leave something positive for our children's future!

It is important to find your individual comfort zone and learn to respect someone else's for theirs. Everyone has a particular position in life they may seek or already may have, and it is our purpose to grow positively within it. For what purpose would it be to sit still when everything else in your backdrop or environment is in motion? The only way to balance you mentally and physically is spiritually, through Jesus Christ. Once you receive the Holy Spirit, you will enjoy the fruits of God opening your eyes and ears like never before! In the book of Romans 7 & 8, the apostle Paul tells us of life in the spirit and how allowing the Spirit to control your mind leads to a life of peace. This doesn't mean you still won't suffer or struggle with sin due to our human nature. But you will learn how to overcome your doubts or troubles in recognizing how the other team of evil is trying to distort your picture of life.

Visualize your personal picture again. Can you create a slide show of your ancestors, to your parents, to yourself, and to your children? Can you see how one comes to the front for a particular time period and then steps aside into the backdrop for another to take the center position, the Lord plainly tells us in the Holy Bible in Romans 8, of how everything works together for the purpose of good and this should reflect our lives with our children and others in our environment. Can you see the beauty of God's works in your personal slide show of life? Can you see the purpose to maintain a positive outlook and why it is important to acknowledge our past to improve the future? If you only exist within your picture with no purpose, then you are living in The Land of The Lost wandering in circles missing the comfort of God giving the eternal home through Christ. There is depth to your personal picture beyond your full comprehension, but it all begins with you maintaining control spiritually through the Son of God to build a strong home for our future!

In looking at your personal picture of life, what can you see that needs to be addressed? Don't ever allow yourself to become overwhelmed or just think it is too much because if you refer back to setting goals and putting them on paper, begin to devise a plan to improve any area of life! It is when you neglect to address an issue that begins to distort your picture and if you begin to think your picture doesn't need some attention, maybe you should look again! Because there is always something or someone that may need that helping hand in your backdrop of life.

It is important to know who you are and recognize your strengths and weaknesses within your personal picture. The Lord teaches us in the Holy Bible our weakness in order for us to grow stronger and to make us aware of how easily it is for our picture to become cloudy when not in focus. If you will recall the story earlier of the coach in the locker room prior to the game. What type of coach would he be if he only told you what you wanted to hear? Think about it, you make a decision to get yourself into shape and hire a personal trainer. Do you think the trainer would be doing their job if they only let you work what you wanted to address? In all growth there are pains and if everything is just lovely or like a bed of roses, where would you learn to push yourself to grow stronger? If your coach doesn't point out your weak points, then you are only fooling yourself and taking the easy way out!

It is very easy to conform to what you want to hear or what you may see in life and this is where you must look at yourself internally and externally to examine your readiness in life for the days ahead in order to set your mind in the direction of the proper headings in life! The only way to overcome the pressures of this world and learn to relax is learning how to keep your heart humble as a child in the Spirit of God! Keeping your heart humble is where you learn to exercise your heart with different emotions like a child's tender heart. You can witness a child being strong, being sad, being happy, and their emotion going from one extreme to the other based on what is in their path.

The object the Lord teaches throughout the Old Testament to the New Testament is learning how to control our emotions and do not allow them to control us. By listening to God's whisper on your heart and meditating in prayer, the Lord will reveal a deeper understanding based upon your level of maturity in faith.

Picture a young child sitting by their parent with their eyes full of love and trying to mimic their parent's moves. They understand their position and are trying to learn from the one they love. This is what the Lord wants and it takes our hearts as humble as that innocent child willing to listen and obey! As you grow and still keep the same heart of a child seeking our Father for direction, the Lord will be proud of His children as they mature. This relates directly with you as a parent with the child you love and how proud would you be if you witnessed your child helping their brothers and sisters in how to be humble in their position in life? Or how about your child helping those in need and teaching them how to truly succeed? Can you remember being a young child? Can you allow your mind to go there and feel the warmth on your heart when someone you loved or looked up to held you in their arms or showed that they were proud of you? There is someone in all of our lives that we reached out to as a young child at some point, and as we grow old we hold our emotions in trying to be strong. Everyone faces something in life that causes heartache and pains, but there comes a point to let them go and even shed tears like rain! When you learn to let it go, don't look to man for comfort, but look to God as your Father with His arms wide open waiting on you to come to Him through your belief in the life of Jesus Christ.

Do you know where you are in life with God? Do you see the purpose of life in Jesus Christ fulfilling the law to set us free? Can you feel the Holy Spirit in your heart and soul pushing you to make a step in life? Don't hold back or restrict God in your life and learn to surrender in understanding your position under the Lord! Are you happy with the person you are in your picture of life or are you struggling with your purpose and direction? Have you wandered off path or lacked understanding? Then turn to God in your ways and begin to pray! Once you make this step and finally let go, prepare to feel relief in the Spirit of God helping you through your day. Because the Lord is there just waiting for you to return to Him as a child to their father saying, "I am sorry and I love you!"

The moment you let go and make your step in faith, you will not want to participate in sin and your life will truly begin! You will discover purpose in this life to grow in positive ways helping others in your path, build something in love that will truly last! If you want something in your picture of life to improve in a positive way and you feel as if you are limited, then you are right! Because without God giving you life, wisdom, strength, direction, motivation, and purpose, you are helpless when only relying on human strength! Our strengths come from God and our weakness comes from our sinful nature, deriving from Satan. How many times have you thought about something positive and allowed negative thoughts to discourage you or restrict you? Do you know who lifts you up and who tears you down? It is so easy to look or take short cuts in life and consume only our human desires. This is what the Lord teaches us in the Holy Bible, to discipline ourselves to maintain our positive health and our future. Think about it, how many times have you thought of exercise and that is as far as you went? How many times have you thought of a diet but failed to reach your goals? In your mind, who wants to tear you down and who wants to lift you in the Holy Spirit? We all have different levels of fitness we seek and everyone feels revived after a nice walk or even some exercise!

Don't allow our sinful nature to make you feel weak or think you can't overcome anything in your picture of life! If you understand your position and seek the Lord for spiritual strength He will help you once you set your mind in belief! If you can't set your mind in believing with the help of God through Jesus Christ, that you can improve or overcome something in life, you then need to ask yourself, "Do I know how to believe?" In the book of Romans 10, we are told how to believe in our heart in confessing with our mouth that Jesus is Lord and Savior. Earlier from the very beginning, we are taught by Moses in Exodus 15, that the Lord is our strength and to believe in His power to help us overcome anything in life when seeking something positive within the Lord's will. Later, in the New Testament, we are told in 1 Corinthians, of the foolishness of God is wiser than men and the weakness of God is stronger than men. Paul, being guided by the Holy Spirit, tells us that, "Christ, the power of God and the wisdom of God, is our source of strength." When we believe we have faith, and with faith through belief, we are with God! In Galatians 5, we are told everything above in the battle of the spirits in our positives and negatives in life. The Holy Spirit will lift you and give you the strength and power to do what is right by God to face or improve anything in this physical life! If you honestly believe and want to make a positive difference in your life, the Lord will show you the way and give you guidance when you earnestly pray!

Picture yourself in a cave that is pitch dark all alone and cold inside. Can you feel the darkness in being alone? Now, you move through the cave feeling your way and calling for help as you silently pray. Then at a distance you hear some other people talking in the dark, debating on the way. You reach them and you feel some comfort in knowing someone else is with you but everyone is blind in the darkness searching every different way. People begin to argue in the darkness of who is right or wrong to lead the path and among all the immediate issues of being lost they overlook the purpose of being united together for comfort, strength, and even forgetting how to act. You begin to hurt inside with all the confusion being shown and again feel all alone in the dark. As the individuals argue, they become blinder focusing on who is right or who is wrong. While they argue, you begin to pull away and search for the way out of the dark cave. In your breath silently you still pray for guidance, deliverance and for everyone to focus on survival verses a constant rival. Then at a distance, you see a small fraction of light. You feel warmth immediately on your heart, and when you tell the others, they can't hear your message of survival because they are too worried in their fight of who is right!

The one's who listen, hear your call, and they decide to move forward to save their life, giving up the verbal fight. Then, as you regroup while the others still bicker, the others who joined you see the light in a distance beginning to flicker! Can you imagine the joy in seeing that light in the distance? Just because you see the light doesn't mean you won't have obstacles in your path! But what matters is learning to work together forming unity with order and respecting the position to follow each other along the way! Can you feel the importance in the pitch dark cave to work together in warning each other of obstacles in your path and helping each other after a stumble? Does it really matter in your survival of who leads the way when you are all seeking the same goal of freedom and equal rights taught by Jesus Christ to see another day?

Now, as you climb towards that flicker of light, learning to move together one step at a time, feeling your way, the unfortunate happens in you stumble causing you to fall back to where you began and hurt from your tumble! The fall wasn't the worst part, but it was those in line whom you helped and knew your heart, only turned their heads in your tumble from the very start.

Finally hitting the bottom from your fall, you pick yourself up once again to hear the ones still arguing over the path to take and who is the one to lead the way. So, as you get yourself back together, you look back up towards the light and call to those whom continue to fight. They can't see you nor can you see them, but a few feel their way to you leaving others behind being totally blind! Along the way back up you drop a rope as you climb for those who were blind and offended you verbally in your path, due to the love of God in being so kind! You do this in hope the others who are lost may find the rope and discover the way giving them hope to see another day.

If you honestly place yourself in this story, can you see where even if you stumble or fall, you must pick yourself back up again for your climb to begin? Just because you fall or may be hurt does this mean you ever quit? Absolutely not! There is no excuse, but only another excuse to not try again! Along this climb, you will discover the true meaning of a friend. As you climb toward that flicker of light, you begin to feel something beyond your might! Your spirit becomes lifted in your climb by something else blowing your mind! You then realize the power of prayer and staying focused on your goal reaching the light taking you to new levels in God's sight! The beautiful part is that little flicker of light you always felt on your heart in your belief is now becoming bright as you climb towards the light giving you more sight!

As you continue to focus on the light in your survival of life within the darkness of the cave, that little flicker begins to take shape making you tremble with joy! Because it is perfectly shaped as a cross that only grows as you climb in now knowing for a fact you are no longer lost! Now knowing the way without a doubt, you feel the love of God making your heart glow and you reach out to help others you don't even know! Because the last thing you ever want is for someone to not see the light and be left in that dark cave when there is a way to be saved to reach the eternal day!

Can you even begin to imagine the joy of your climb, sharing with others in your path and someone even being there to give you a hand to see you through? Would you say we have a story to tell and because He lives you can see tomorrow? Would you yell to others who are still blind in that cave of darkness and say, "I found the way! Please drop your pride of who is right or wrong. Open your heart to your Friend in Jesus and grab the rope beginning to feel your way through the darkness because the Roll is being called up yonder for that eternal day!

There is joy and power in the Holy Spirit of God and in Hebrews 4 we are told that the Word of God is alive and powerful cutting between our soul and spirit exposing our innermost thoughts and desires. Not only is the Word of God alive and powerful, but He is also holding us accountable!! There is only one way, being the right way through the light and belief of Jesus Christ! When you open your heart to receive Jesus Christ in true belief, you will begin to see that there is much, much more in life by learning the art of surrender in being free!

In the book of (Psalm 138), David gives thanks to the Lord for answered prayer which you can feel upon your heart and in (Psalm 139), David tells us how the Lord is all seeing, all knowing, all powerful, and everywhere present. God not only knows us being with us, He gives us the ultimate gift in allowing us to know Him through the Holy Spirit with Jesus Christ in our heart and soul! There is a very important factor in receiving the Lord, Jesus Christ, as your savior and that is the understanding of true repentance that many individuals neglect. We are taught in Nehemiah 9, how God puts no limit on the number of times we can receive this mercy, but we must come to Him with a repentant heart in order to receive it! In the book of Matthew 3, John the Baptist instructs to repent of our sins and turn to God! By making a180-degree change away from our sin to reveal a true repentant heart is how we understand true repentance in life.

Think about it, you have a child who has repeatedly disobeyed you and you finally address the situation properly to correct the issue. As your child listens to you and feels your heart, they even have tears in their eyes knowing they were wrong. Your child apologizes and gives you their word they won't do it again and returns to where they began.

In order to give yourself reassurance of the message getting across, you decide to observe in a distance your child to make sure they properly understood your instruction. As you observed would you note their actions to either commend or reprimand them in praise or discipline in proper timing? If your child acts a certain way in front of you minding your instruction but then acts another way against your will when out of your sight, would you describe this as a true repentant heart understanding your instruction? Now, reverse the roll of you being the parent and now you are the child under your Father God above. How do you see yourself in understanding and following God's instruction?

In the book of (Luke 13), the Lord Jesus calls for repentance and tells a story of a man planting a tree in his garden. This analogy of a Christian's life is critical to understand in repentance and producing positive behavior helping others in life. There is no limit to God's mercy, but if we continue the same sin over and over, are we giving proper respect to God, our Father? Absolutely not! If we don't learn from our sin and begin to produce positive results, then we could be cut down as the tree in the garden!

Sometimes we get clipped in life without recognizing how the Lord is trying to reveal that something isn't right. Often we face issues that could be prevented if we would only listen to the Word of God in His instruction. Without proper repentance, our sin will only continue to follow and even become worse in time! Think about it this way in your imagination. Now that you have climbed out of that cave in all that darkness by seeing the light, you discover a little spider crawling in your eyebrow. Immediately you swat it off in a distance due to your phobia of spiders! As the little spider flies through the air, you notice a single web still attached to your eyebrow and you grab the web in your hand. You try to break the web but you can't due to it is like something you have never seen. As you are stretching, trying to break the web, you notice the spider is on its way back! You begin to move faster in panic and finally you give up the web to address the spider in your face! This time the spider has grown with long legs and you finally swat it away again with its web still attached!

You cannot break the web and the spider is coming back again with vengeance for being swatted. Finally, just before that ticked off spider jumps back on with a vicious bite, you learn how to break the web in prayer asking for forgiveness and strength in God's might!

Our sins are like this spider and its web when you really think about it. We can only cover up our sins or push them away for so long before we must face them properly in repentance to break the chain of their web before they bite! If we continue to hide our sins or patch something that is not right, believe me, God will set you straight at some point in His timing and not ours!

In (Romans 3), Paul teaches us how we are all guilty under the eyes of God and in (Galatians 6), he tells us to pay close attention to our own works by not comparing ourselves with others. Each person in this life is fully accountable for their own actions and we are responsible for our own conduct. Within this lesson of (Galatians 6), we are told how we will harvest what we plant and this is vital to always remember for not only how we act in front of our children, in front of others in our life, but most importantly how we must answer to God when He opens that book of life!

When you make a decision in your direction of life, be sincere in your understanding the meaning, to not fall back in that cave of darkness and still be attached to your sins without true repentance from the heart. The last thing anyone should want is to be left in that pit of the cave or be cut down in life with no more chances to improve! Our sins do affect our children in more ways than we may ever know and the very important part of raising a child is teaching them how to pick themselves up again learning from mistakes in acceptance of consequences of wrong behavior. What are we teaching our children if we don't face our issues and handle them with maturity? Or what are we teaching if we feel above others in negative behavior and our children stumble or fall? Will they hide from their issues or face them to overcome them? Jesus teaches us a lesson of two brothers and their father in (Luke 15) that gives great wisdom in how to treat a lost son who returns home. Like the son in this story and the cave analogy, some people hit bottom before they open their eyes and begin to truly understand. By staying close to the Word of God in study and prayer, you can prevent many obstacles in your path of life and when you have faith you never lose hope! When you have Jesus in your heart, there is nothing in this world that can tear you apart, even after a fall from losing your balance! With Jesus you have God, and with God He will show you the way when you listen to the whisper on your heart giving you life to see another day!

In the book of (Acts 3), we are taught by Peter to repent of our sins and turn to God through Jesus Christ for our sins to be forgiven. He tells us of spiritual refreshment, after repentance from the heart, making our hearts sing with joy in forgiveness and understanding. There is no doubt that facing our weakness of sin hurts, but if we all don't purge ourselves in proper repentance, then the web of sin only grows stronger with Satan's grip of your life! There is no way to break that web without a humble heart in understanding in repentance through proper teaching and the receiving of Jesus Christ!

Think about a time in your life with someone you love and having issues in a fight causing emotional stress taking you away from what you two have as one. How did you feel once you both finally reconciled listening and understanding one another? Did you both make changes to improve the relationship? How did you feel after all the hurt was over and you two finally came back to one? How long did it last before you fell back in your own life and you had to come together again? In between the times above, did you fall into routines with little feelings or emotions in your relationship? Can you see a cycle in all of this above and the importance of keeping your relationship alive in different approaches with the one in whom you love and know? Relationships take willingness to give and learn how to grow!

People lose touch in routines and traditions in life unless we keep our perspective of how to keep love alive in our relationships. Jesus taught us this in how to be alive and how our weakness of following routines can cause us to lose touch in life. Think about it, how many times have you ever brushed your teeth and not thought anything of it? Have you ever had a time that you had to think hard over something of normal routine and wondering whether you did it or not? How many times have you wondered later in the day, "Did I even acknowledge the ones I love before I left for work?" Or how many times have you gone to church on Sunday and forgotten the message?

If we don't keep our eyes open in Christ, they can become blind to what is happening in the backdrop of our personal picture that continues to move in constant motion on the turntable of earth. When this happens, your life becomes a prison even when you are free and this is what Satan wants in your life, to restrict your vision causing you to have trouble in limiting your sight struggling to see! Think about it, how many people wake-up the same time everyday? How many people leave and arrive at work at the same exact time everyday? How many people sit in the same seat or park in the same spot everyday? How many people follow a specific routine every-day? What happens to the spark when something comes easily or in scheduled times? Can you see how life can be a prison even when you are free?

There is a time for routine and planning to achieve goals in life. But if we don't listen to the message of Jesus Christ and keep our eyes open in life, then how will we understand or keep our perspective in how to be free? Freedom requires discipline to maintain and when it becomes out of balance, prepare for consequences to come! We addressed this in the previous chapter of pride in how God taught us in the Old Testament in (Leviticus 23), how to keep our perspective in life by not allowing our routines to cause us to lose touch with what we have been given. Everyone begins to complain or miss something in life when they become complacent in their routines without searching how to grow, being guided by Jesus Christ and appreciating life! Everyday is a joy and we should strive to improve our lives for our children of tomorrow!

This is what we are taught in the Holy Bible and directly by Jesus Christ in how to keep our relationships alive and respect what we have because you never know when it could be taken away! The Lord plainly teaches us how to keep our relationship close with Him in belief and faith in repentance to keep our life in tune with the body having harmony in the spirit of God. Life is about obedience and growth with discipline to enjoy the fruits of our work from the garden God has given to each of us in this world! All our father wants is positive growth, keeping Him at the center of our lives for giving each of us life in His creation, and treating others as we want to be treated! What loving parent wouldn't want this for their child? It is vital to believe in His Son for eternal life, and to teach us how to be free in the Spirit of God within everything in this physical and spiritual world!

The book of (1 Peter), tells us about Holy living and how to apply the Word of God to our lives to grow in all directions. Not everyone lives the same as another and Jesus plainly taught us it was not about rules but following the heart in your love for God to grow closer in your walk of life. All the disciples had different personalities and characteristics, but the Lord taught how to serve one another to help your brother or sister in Christ grow in love. Just because someone may agree and disagree on a rule doesn't mean it is a sin, but if it causes another individual to possibly stumble, then it is a sin under God. The Lord plainly tells us in the Holy Bible that a true repentant heart and believer in God, through Jesus Christ, does not seek to perform evil in his or her life in hurting others. But they learn to grow in His Word and not wanting to break the laws of God to give them life in drawing closer in their walk with thee!

Like mentioned earlier, about routines in relationships, God wants us to understand and learn our weaknesses for us to find our strengths. When we repent and reconcile in our relationship with someone in whom we love, do we experience a joy feeling our life restored? How was a kiss or hug after a disagreement with someone you love in understanding what is most important in life? This feeling is what the Lord gives through Jesus Christ daily when we learn to repent of our sins giving us a vibrant thirst or hunger and passion to want more never letting go! With remorse and repentance, you will understand what and who is most important in life, causing you to want more in learning how to grow! When you get to this point in your spiritual understanding in feeling God's might, you need to remember something very important in maturity, and that is if you recall earlier, we compared goals in life to a child learning to walk as they grew, their steps became further apart.

Just because you feel our Father's hand in the Holy Spirit today doesn't mean you will feel His hand tomorrow. The Holy Spirit moves according to your heart in being humble and in tune with the Lord. In your spiritual maturity, the Lord holds our hands as we hold our child's hand learning to walk and at times to grow, we must stay focused in having faith knowing He is always with us even if we don't feel the presence. How would you ever learn how to grow stronger in your steps if someone continuously holds your hand and you could see them in your sight? In our walks, we learn to trust, knowing without a doubt, He will never turn His back on us, even if we fall, when we learn how to pick ourselves back up again in repentance learning from what went wrong and turning from our negative ways in life!

By staying close to the Lord in understanding His instruction to nourish ourselves daily spiritually, will help us to balance anything in life, even when evil is all around or if the daily pressures are getting to you in any way needing help. Life is limited and meaningless without purpose to grow in positive ways in every aspect of life. The Lord gives us true joy in spiritual refreshment with repentance from the heart and gives us purpose to grow within whom gives us life, seeing Jesus Christ! Keep God in focus of your picture of life and don't let it be distorted by anyone else thinking or claiming they have the way! Because all they have without God through Jesus Christ is limited vision, being distorted by the wrong message from the evil team in neglecting the truth!

Once you make your step in repentance, in understanding your position of not being the one who is in control, and confessing your sins to the Lord seeking forgiveness and guidance in your life, you will feel a load lifted that you can't explain in words of relief, and this is where you are set free from the bridle of Satan trying to hold you back in life! The first goal of Satan is to grab a hold of you and then spread to your family to destroy your home! Think about it, what builds a city, to a state, to a nation, and to the overall body of Christ in this world? Where does it all start? Remember, all big things come from small things, and all small things create big things! So do you see the spiritual war tactics to destroy the family first to spread the infection of sin to another picture in life?

The Lord puts great emphasis on the family in the Holy Bible to understand the importance of staying strong together as one body of believers and connected to the overall body of Christ. By keeping the Lord the head of your homes will protect you with the armor of God in your household keeping life in perspective as you grow from each generation to the next! There is great power in the Spirit of God when your life is in tune. Like the plane relation in the previous chapters of raising our children to move into the captains seat and us as the parent moving to the co-pilot position of the plane, we as adults need to understand our position in not being the one in control of the plane and move to the co-pilots seat for God to guide us in the Holy Spirit being our auto pilot in flight.

We all seek power in our human character wanting the fastest or most luxurious plane in life, but if we don't know who is in control of the true power in life, thinking we as humans can handle power on our own, then prepare for a very turbulent ride and a fatal landing in due time! The evil team wants you to think you are in control and can take anything on your self without help and this is where you must understand your position in order to properly land in respecting the purpose of self-discipline! Can you see the purpose of instruction in life on how to fly? Not only do we learn how to fly in the Word of God, we most importantly learn how to land!

There is no other navigation system by man that can hold up to what God has given in the skies above and in this land! You will find that man will fail you many times, but God is always there to guide you home when you listen to your heart in prayer to hear His gentle whisper in following the starts at night to give you future sight! When you move into the co-pilots seat and allow the Holy Spirit to guide your direction in letting go, there is a joy in being free that will take you to your knees! The only way to experience this joy is with God in the center of your life and repentance through the blood of Jesus to soar to new levels in maturity helping you mentally, physically, and most of all spiritually to be on the right foundation in order to grow and especially land!

The longer we hold out from God and don't apply the Holy Bible to our lives our fall which is inevitable in death will be like jumping from a plane high above the clouds with a parachute, but never pulling the cord due to our distractions in our fall. The other team of evil wants you to lose sight from your jump to forget what you have right in your grasp to save your life and learning to float in guidance of the Holy Spirit to carry you home. Don't lose sight in the distractions of this world and overlook the joys to life in the fruit of the Spirit of God! Because the longer we hold things in without repentance the worse our pressures become robbing us of our job in this temporary life and our picture becomes more distorted. Please don't do like I did and wait until it was almost too late in my fall before I surrendered to listen to God's call! Because now I am injured and it will take time to heal. But I know in my heart that God can rebuild me even better than before! Please draw closer to God and He will draw close to you teaching you how to be true! The Lord warns us of everything in the Holy Bible in order to recognize our weaknesses to keep our perspective and remain strong!

There is power in the spirit of God and He will lift you once you surrender to Him in giving you life like you have never known! All we have to do is return to Him bowing on our knees at the throne! Asking for another chance to live and be set free! At this point, please understand how to walk as that child being lead by God's right hard! Remember as you mature your steps may seem far, but this is where you learn faith in your belief standing on the rock of Jesus as your turning point in your life! In (Isaiah 3), we are told how sins are self-destructive and will bring destruction upon the lives of those who continue to live without proper repentance in opening their eyes and turning from their ways! In addition, Isaiah tells us the godly will all be well when right with God and us all will be restored in true faith! For your own study and questions on your salvation and deliverance, read and meditate on these four books:

Luke 6:43-49

Ezekiel 6:8-10

Matthew 21:30

Revelation 3:20

You will feel Jesus knocking on your door to insure proper understanding and belief. In (Revelations 3:1-3), we are told to wake up and strengthen what little remains and if we don't repent turning to God again to be prepared for what is to come like a thief in the night! So I ask you "Are you ready to live with purpose and direction in the love of Jesus Christ setting you free?" If so, bow down to your knees and cry out to the Lord for forgiveness and you will be restored! Being sincere in your heart, you will find relief the moment you finally let it go and return to your position of understanding that is in control from the very start! But never forget, this is only the beginning. Because what game in life have you ever seen that you could just step in and not perform within your position to play?

If you think you can just stand there and show up for meetings in practice without applying instruction and discipline to your life, then prepare to lose your game when you don't apply your heart every time you start! It is not what we have on the outside, but who we are with Jesus on the inside! It is very life threatening that we all drop our pride to listen and understand what the Lord is not only telling us in His Word, but also revealing in nature within His land! No one likes to be addressed when their heart or thinking might not be in the right place and this is where Christianity is put under such scrutiny in all directions from within the overall body to outside the overall body of Christ. As a true Christian, you allow Jesus to give justice and don't take it in your hands!

We as humans in this physical world, must understand and remember that we are not perfect in any way! In the book of James, read and study the message to apply to your life in finding true wisdom from God. It is full of God's power in how to live to receive glory in the Holy Spirit drawing you closer to God. There is always an area in your backdrop of your personal picture in life that needs work, or could just use some attention in your time learning to listen! Because when we work on one area, often we tend to lose focus on another and this allows a weak spot for the evil team's penetration! Always be open to help encourage in love to help or improve anything in your personal picture of life and especially to help those in your backdrop feel your love through Jesus Christ to grow together giving strength! Learn how to recognize your thoughts to insure proper thinking without something attempting to tear yourself or others down in this physical and spiritual world! When you feel something upon your heart, if it's positive, follow it! But if it is negative, turn from it in prayer for strength to overcome something wrong, for what is right under God! You will find that in your growth of the Holy Spirit, something only from God will uplift you to grow in love to new levels in life!

If your life is troubled or you feel lack of direction or purpose, listen to your heart and hear your instruction to move forward in life. If your life is broken in pieces or you are struggling to hold it together, quit your fight and turn it over to God through His Son Jesus Christ to feel the power of the Holy Spirit in trusting of His might! If you feel something is missing even in all of your success, then open your heart to Jesus and He will give you something money can't buy in eternal rest! The Lord is in every breath we take, when we open our eyes and ears to hear the message of life in love upon the heart!

Imagine yourself outside in the fall of the year with the trees turning colors and dropping their leaves. Can you imagine the beautiful colors from orange, to red, to green, to brown, to tan, to yellow, and even see squirrels running across the land? Now as you stand there all alone, you feel a gentle wind in the air blowing the leaves and even your hair. Can you feel the wind in the air and see the leaves falling to the ground while everything is quiet, not making a sound? You begin to feel the presence of life upon your heart enjoying what you see when the leaves are dropped in the wind from the trees. The longer you stand there feeling the gentle wind you drop to your knees in tears of relief when you hear a gentle whisper upon your heart for your new life to begin.

In this gentle whisper you feel as a child at heart in loving life for every part. Beginning to see colors like never before and hear the message within the wind. You learn how to repent and reconcile your life through the blood of Jesus to overcome your sin in learning the true meaning of a friend. When you watch the leaves in the wind, how do you feel? Or, do you even know where to begin? We begin in our heart and soul feeling life in our breath overcoming our fears of even death. This is done by opening our eyes to hear the message in the wind and where you learn to recognize His presence in feeling the breath of God to no end! May God have mercy and open our eyes to feel the love of Jesus Christ, Amen!

If we don't learn from our sins and return to the Lord, our lives are only going to become worse in being out of balance. What happens in life when out of balance? Can you see an adjustment needed to be realigned and return a better life? The Lord gave us instructions to build upon His foundation and enjoy life with self-discipline to grow our families in every aspect of life. With "God in your center, and you understanding your position of who is in control, will allow you to stand in faith in loving life through the Son of Man for appreciation within God's overall plan!

Life is about purpose and direction through obedience to reach higher levels, not only in this life, but the next! The Lord plainly teaches us this in the Holy Bible, but in order to truly succeed you must know the meaning in how to believe! Once you do this you will receive rewards in your heart that money can't buy and you learn the art of how to truly achieve!

In (Psalm 32), and in (Romans 4), we are told of the joy for those whose disobedience has been forgiven. There is joy for each individual with proper repentance through the love of Christ. When you read and apply the scriptures to your life, then you will grow strength with purpose to bring your world together. Always remember in your personal picture of life that, "Your world can't come together until you learn to bring yourself together!" Once you learn to let it go in repentance and turn your life back over to the Lord, you will begin to find balance in your life by understanding who is in control!

Great Joy

If you are struggling in your life in any sector, or you just want to grow stronger, search the Word of God and seek Him in prayer. Letting go in proper repentance, turning from your sins, you can find great joy in songs to the Lord giving Him praise. Upon receiving that joy of having a sincere heart you will sing along with many great bands like Casting Crowns and Mercy Me! Singing from your heart with tears saying "And Now My Life Song Sings", moving your soul in joy saying, "All Because Of Jesus I'm Alive" and "I Am Yours" no longer having a question of "Who Am I?" In feeling Jesus in your heart being your "Strong Tower" while teaching you to "Just Breathe" and knowing "God Is Watching Over You!" Asking the Lord to "Make Me Lord Jesus", and saying "I Believe", while "I Can Hear You in the Storm".

So please hear my prayer as I feel your promise to those under-going hurts knowing "God Heals Us When We Are Broken" within this land! There is no doubt of receiving relief and life with Jesus leaving you "In Wonder" of who you are! Giving you purpose and direction in the "Miracle of the Moment" saying "Right Here" is where my new life begins. "If I lose My Life and Surrender to You" saying "I Love You Lord" hearing your sweet, sweet sound in my ear, you will feel Gods hand in your life drawing you near!

CHAPTER 11

Commitment Levels

*W*hen you look and study history from the beginning of time to our current time of today, you can see the rise and fall of homes, to cities, and even nations when individuals lose their unity within the body to survive. In the previous chapters this has been mentioned on several occasions, but I now must emphasize the purpose of commitment to succeed in life!

By looking at the cycle of events in families, in churches, in business, and in leadership, you will find a common characteristic within every successful home or organization. Within every part of success you will witness unity and commitment in understanding each individual's position to build something strong for our children of tomorrow. Every time something in life falls, you can see someone who comes behind to rebuild or repair what has been injured in life. Within these individuals you will find love, and commitment to do whatever it takes to help restore or even grow what has already been built. Without commitment, there is little hope in anything to not only survive but last!

The Lord plainly reveals all of this in the Holy Bible, but due to our human nature of sin our picture becomes distorted in not looking at the overall picture in the Lord's commitment for His love to prevail in the end! Think about it like this to see the big picture, from the little picture in life that we are. When you give someone your word, do you give it to that person or to God? Let's go a little deeper, when you look upon someone how far do you see? Do you look for the love in Christ and then see the creator of man? Would you say your vision is being restricted or limited by man, if you can't see life in the breath of God in who gives us life?

There are three parts that are crucial to understand in keeping clarity within your picture of life. First part being God our Creator, second one human, and part three of Satan there are many workers who either guide with direction and purpose to give life or take away. It is crucial to understand our motives and other individual's motives for the life of the eternal picture in Jesus Christ! As a human being we must think about the positives and negatives in a decision to insure the longevity and right decisions to move forward in order to give life, not only in the present time but in our future! We all make wrong decisions at times, and this is where you must learn how to turn your negatives into positives to rebuild or maintain your balance in reconciling your wrongs in proper repentance.

With this being understood, lets go back to the question previously of when you give someone your word and commitment, do you only give it to that person or to God? The Lord, our God, is our Creator of all life, and if you give your word to someone then you are also giving it to God because in (Romans 13), the apostle Paul gives us instruction on authority and how love fulfills God's requirements. In addition, like Peter in (Mathew 26), we will be held accountable for breaking our word in commitment, and in (Matthew 5), Jesus teaches us about the law of God in how genuine faith guides you to live by God's law.

When you look at the three parts of man being God, human, and Satan in our sinful nature, think about your commitments on the level of depth in your mental picture. If you sincerely give your commitment to man and then intentionally break that vow for personal gain, would you consider this treating thy neighbor as thy self? In the book of (Deuteronomy 23), the Lord instructs us in making a vow to the Lord and being prompt in fulfilling whatever you promised him. If you make a promise and don't fulfill it, you will be guilty of sin, based on Verse 21, and Jesus confirmed this in the New Testament. With Christ in our hearts we are forgiven, but still accountable for all actions!

There is loyalty in commitment, and in (Hebrews 10), we are given knowledge of the truth in receiving Jesus Christ as our savior with understanding our sins there is no longer any sacrifice that will cover our sins. Because if you continue the sin using Christ as a crutch, then this is considered blasphemy against God!

Think about it like this in marriage or in any relationship. If you do something that hurts the one you love, then the both of you address it properly in reconciliation with forgiveness. Would you consider your forgiveness that you gave worthless if they continued the same action that hurt you to start with? The Lord plainly tells us to forgive in (Luke 17), if your brother sins and they repent. But if they continue the same sin then this is not proper repentance and you can relate this to our children and anyone in our lives who continues the same path in their heart either not understanding the Word of God or being right with God through the love of Jesus Christ!

There is a very important part to understanding in making a decision in self-confidence that we are taught in (James 4). In verse 14 we are asked, **"How do you know what life will be like tomorrow?"** Rather than committing to something in the future, James instructs us to say, **"If the Lord wills, we will do this or that."** This is where I went terribly wrong in my past by not properly thinking about my decisions and thinking I could overcome my sins on my own in attempting to make things right somewhere else in life!

When something isn't right in your picture of life, don't fall into thinking money will fix it or your works will overcome your sins without repentance in understanding how to get your life back on track with God. In your commitment think ahead to understand what you could face and live everyday honoring your oath in your word to others and most of all God above! Sometimes in life the unfortunate happens like Christopher Reeves and his wife Dana. But this doesn't change your oath, and reveals the character from the heart in understanding the commitment in love!

Why is it that certain species of animals understand the true meaning of commitment, but we as humans struggle to comprehend the sanctity in unity in serving one another? Throughout the Word of God this is taught and pointed out in our human nature to understand the meaning of loyalty. Why is it that when Bald Eagles mate, they are with that partner for life? Do you think maybe they weren't infected with sin causing them to lose focus? Or how about the characteristic of an elephant mourning a death in their herd and how they mature in life, have you ever looked at the pattern of life of an elephant with their memory and how the females spend time with blood relatives over several generations with the leader of the herd most likely having an even temper? The interesting pattern to this is how male elephants only travel with cows while nursing and then they move on to live alone or in herds up to seven members. Does the number seven mean anything to you? On average they travel in herds of three to five.

Another interesting part is how the males are generally peaceful, but sometimes goes mad during mating periods. Have you ever seen this characteristic in man? In addition to elephant behavior, if a male elephant causes too much trouble, his relatives drive him out of the herd hopefully to recover and return at a later date. Sometimes he becomes a rogue elephant and a dangerous outcast causing harm and attacking people or villages.

Can you possibly see the relation to our characteristics in life of how we mourn for our relatives in death or when they become lost in this world by not being able to handle their emotions inside? There is one other interesting part of an elephant's behavior that has been discussed, but to my knowledge never proven. It is when they sense their death they travel back to where their relatives passed away in graveyards to die with their herd. Do you think this has not been proven due to the cycle of man interrupting their natural patterns in life? To my knowledge this is only theory but the interesting part to all of this is the parallel to our life in our commitments in love and most of all how these animals being the Bald Eagle and the Elephant have a commitment in a pattern of life that parallels the instruction to humans in the Word of God in the Holy Bible.

The Lord plainly instructs us in how to live and maintain an even temper in the Holy Bible with the purpose to keep unity in life. In addition, the Lord stresses the importance of sanctity in relationships in being faithful to our family and in our actions in life. Can you see where we, as humans, being infected with sin, needed the book of instruction to guide our lives to control our emotions to remain in the herd? Not only did God give us instructions to live, He also tells us on several occasions of being buried with our families rather than being scattered across the land.

In (Ephesians 4), the Word of God teaches of unity within the body of Jesus Christ and the process of change may be slow. By trusting in God with commitment to grow in faith, you will find your life improving in your thoughts, attitudes and actions in every direction you turn. In addition, within this book, we are taught how to handle our angers without destroying relationships. This is like the rogue elephant in being separated from the herd. If we don't control our anger, this allows evil to set in and divide us from the love of Jesus Christ! You can see a parallel to the rogue elephant and the parable of the lost sheep or prodigal son taught by Jesus Christ in (Luke 15). Once they humble themselves and come to their senses, they are able to return to the herd with understanding the purpose of obedience!

In opening your eyes and ears with Jesus in your heart you will see things like never before! The commitment and admiration shown in Bald Eagles can soar relationships to high levels with a bird's eye view in knowing who created you! Commitments in life are no longer life threatening with God, through your belief in Jesus Christ! Don't allow your sinful nature to separate you from the herd in not understanding God's word! The evil team of Satan wants to destroy every marriage, family, and anything with unity of love! If you see something or feel something not right in love, address it before it grows out of control causing separation in the spirit of God! In (Ephesians 5) Paul instructs us on how to allow the Holy Spirit to guide our relationships in life and this is vital to follow.

There are different levels of commitment, but only one level of understanding. Meaning, in a commitment you are to do everything within your power to uphold your word and never lose sight of your oath with God in receiving Jesus Christ! Sometimes in life we all face things that go wrong, have problems, and even cause us to separate from a commitment. But this comes from a lack of understanding and how our sinful nature can misguide or infect someone in your path or even ourselves!

When you have God in your life through your commitment in belief of the life and resurrection of Jesus Christ, you begin to understand the level of commitment that the Son of God taught and showed each of us in how to live and even physically die in love for our next life to begin! Never did Jesus try to justify His innocence, nor his actions! Jesus taught us how to live in love and even sacrifice for the eternal future. We are taught how to build on the foundation of a rock in Jesus and how to forgive others who have hurt us in order to keep our relationship with God alive. When an individual understands loyalty in commitment, they will do whatever it takes to search for how to improve or repair something that may not be right or even broken! Ask yourself, "In your commitment of love in life, what are you willing to do to survive or repair something that is not right in your life?" There is only <u>one</u> place to turn for true help and guidance to correct something in life, that being the Word of God in the Holy Bible to receive your direction!

True commitment and loyalty does not give up in tough situations but they learn to evaluate how to regain strength and reclaim what was lost in love for life! Think about it, did Jesus give up in commitment did Peter or Paul give up in commitment? Did Abraham show loyalty and faith? Did Job show commitment in faith? Did our ancestors in American heritage show commitment? There is a time in this physical life that after every last effort has been made in love through Jesus Christ that the unfortunate happens in separating something wrong to eventually find something right! Or, even you can witness something built on the wrong foundation being tore down, only to rebuild on the right foundation of God to sustain life in our homes and relationships in the future!

Can you see this in the cycle of events in history not only in our relationships, in our homes, in our business in our nation for freedom, and even in the Word of God in the Holy Bible? Can you see where God has never left us and showed His commitment in love to restore His kingdom of glory? Often, when weak in faith or without understanding we leave Him or become lost in this world of sin! Life is full of joy in understanding the purpose with God's direction, but full of problems and issues when out of focus with God through Jesus Christ. If our country doesn't wake up and quit cannibalizing ourselves in lawsuits, suppressing the poor to feed the rich, constantly displaying negatives over positives, allowing our children to be misguided or run free without understanding the purpose in life with God at our door, then we are going to continue to deteriorate within our loss of direction! This breaks my heart to say, but it is the truth!!!

You can see this in our children wanting time with their parents, parents neglecting God in how to act treating others with no respect, people giving up in commitments and forgetting how to love in a relationship with sacrifice for the other! In addition, you can see how some leaders in positions to serve are neglecting their commitments to take care of the people and falling to someone else guiding their direction or their own selfish desires!

Did you know the same congress that formed the Declaration of Independence also formed the American Bible Society and voted to purchase 20,000 copies of scripture for the people of this nation? Or, did you know our first court justice, John Jay, stated "That when we select our national leaders if we are to preserve our nation, we must select Christians." Calvin Coolidge, our 30th president of the United States reaffirmed the truth when he wrote, "The foundations of our society and our government rest so much on the teachings of the Bible that it would be difficult to support them if faith in these teachings would cease to be practically universal in our country."

Our country is setting itself up for a hard lesson to come economically, agriculturally, and even in our way of life! It is only a matter of time unless we return to God and pray to be restored! The signs are everywhere in human behavior to natural disasters increasing around the world, and we must remain faithful in our relationships and especially in our relationship with God through the love of Jesus Christ! No matter what you face in life, never give up or lose hope! Because if you remain faithful and true, God will restore and deliver you!

We are taught this lesson in the book of Job and in the book of Daniel in the Holy Bible. The book of Job is on faith and understanding. The book of Daniel is not only on faith but warnings of what to expect when you backslide in faith. In both books of Job and Daniel, we neglect the message in not believing something like this can and will happen to every individual in life who keeps their faith and to those who lose their focus from God in true belief!

Imagine these two separate books like this to see the big picture in life. What happens to a large picture that is too detailed for our computer to download? Have you ever opened a picture or file on your computer that took time and high resolution to view? Could you see the picture or file when you only saw a single pixel of the picture? This is exactly what the Lord gave to us in the book of Job and Daniel in condensing the file to a single individual to see the big picture in life. But due to our restricted vision, we often don't comprehend or believe these stories of truth on Job and King Nebuchadnezzar never happened because they are so extreme over the life of one individual or let's say, single pixel!!

The Lord gave us something so large from East to West and condensed it for us to understand and view without only seeing a single piece of the puzzle! Follow the commitment and faith in Job and Daniel to understand the level of belief in all trials and tribulations to overcome anything in your path! Don't do as Nebuchadnezzar and allow what you know to be deceived by others or cause yourself to backslide in your belief! If so, then prepare to be humbled in some form in life or at the Day of Judgment! Don't wait, like I did, to use what you have in your grasp in the Word of God in the Holy Bible, no matter what you feel in life, never give up, live in love, enjoy the day, prepare for tomorrow and never lose hope! Learn how to balance your life daily and love everyday you are given to grow and mature in your cycle of life!

To understand the level of commitments in life let's look at it in the armed forces or military. We all have a commitment to our country as a citizen of the United States and some take their commitment to protect and preserve what our ancestors provided in the American Revolution to the U.S. Military. Based on the level of commitment an individual feels, he or she may choose to reach for higher levels of rank or Special Forces within the military. Upon their calling they feel a desire inside giving them a drive to seek new levels and there is a mandatory understanding of where they want to go before they ever move forward! Many people set out with a desire to seek a position and fail to succeed due to not fully understanding what is required in their commitment. This does not mean they are not committed to the cause, but they learn their position in where to serve.

There is great satisfaction in life when you learn your position and understand there is always someone greater and always someone on the rise! This is where you learn to become content and learn to grow in your position to either encourage those above you or uplift those coming behind you! There is no jealously but understanding who you are for the person God set you out to be! This is all part of our privilege in this country of being free! You can apply the understanding in the armed forces and America citizens to a business, to a home, and even to our church body. Think about it, what level of commitment does your pastor show in stepping up to his position? How about the elders and every other leader in your church? Don't they show another level of commitment by stepping up to their position? Or, how about the congregation in their position and the life they live? Can you see how all parties have commitment but each based on their calling moves to different levels? Each individual has a commitment to follow once they understand their instruction and without understanding how can someone expect to grow or have a relationship moving forward?

This is exactly what God gave to us in the Holy Bible with instruction to follow and giving each individual a mission of love with purpose to grow! Would you agree that with no direction or purpose in a commitment there is stagnant life just sitting still? What happens to a body of water without movement or encouragement to replenish what has been dried up or become stagnant? Everything has a purpose and direction to move forward and God reveals this in every sector of life!

Let's take this level of commitment to another level like the two mentioned earlier in the military and in the church. Can you see a level of commitment in being an American citizen in the United States of America? There is a relation to the congregation in the church, just as there is being an American in our commitment to serve. Each individual whether in the pews or waving to our military as they leave or return home has a commitment to honor those who protect our country in order to have the life we are provided! Like the individuals in the church body as an American, we have a choice to move to any position from the pew to the leadership or service in order to help each other maintain strength and God's honor in this land that He has provided to each of us today!

With purpose and direction there is strength and unity within the body of believers. There is the same need of commitments in our homes and relationships with others. Our commitments begin at home, in the importance of love within the family and grow to another sector in life. It is vital to teach and show our children true commitment in everything we do in order for them to have respect and understanding how sometimes we must go through the tough times to reach the good times! By not doing this it reveals our hearts level of commitment and teaches our children when times become tough how to give up! So I urge you to show your children how to be strong in every trial in life for their future commitments ahead!

Can you see why individuals are walking away from their responsibilities in life? Not only is there fault in individuals putting them into something they weren't ready for, they failed to understand the commitment in looking forward in life in order to maintain their perspective. The fault falls on what society is pushing, teaching, and mostly for what they are removing within their individual lives of God being in the center of life! It is very easy to fall into society who is pushing something on another and thinking this is okay because everyone is doing it. But, this is dead wrong!

Every individual has a personal commitment and responsibility for their own picture of life. It is our responsibility to understand our steps to insure our path for not only our neighbor but our children's future! Everywhere you turn someone is pointing a finger and blaming someone else for something that went wrong. It is time America wakes up and faces reality that there is no excuse not to correct something that may be in your picture of life! The longer we allow ourselves to sit around and wait for someone to make something better in our lives then we are only falling behind!

Everyone as a Christian and as a citizen has a responsibility to help one another in this country and have unity in love through Jesus Christ, to maintain and grow strength! The longer individuals neglect their responsibilities to properly serve in faith and as an American citizen the worse it will become! Americans truly need to open their eyes and refocus on the foundation of this country in not only helping others but praying to be restored in God's mercy! Our children, our economy and even many of our churches have lost their direction in understanding the purpose of commitment and causing separation within the body of Christ. Not only are our children hurting, now even adults are feeling the pain and loss of direction!

You can see America wandering in circles trying to patch or cover up issues in fighting the truth of accepting the Word of God. Due to pride, many won't do what is right in putting God in the center of their life! The Lord plainly tells us to never become tolerant of sin or prepare for consequences to follow. It is not our place to judge but to rid ourselves of wrong in order to build something that is right!

Think about it like this in understanding commitment and proper belief to understand the seriousness of following God's instruction. What happens when someone in the military violates the rules or the command? Are there any consequences or possible loss of rank? Isn't there even discharge in some cases? Just because they have reached or achieved position, does this give them a right to not follow the guidelines? Does this position of acceptance which is mutual in the individual receiving and the other party offering the position to the individual mean they now can just exist in their role expecting their rewards to always come? Please, don't fall into this lack of proper thinking that you don't have a commitment in every position to serve and grow without backsliding or losing your position in life!

Throughout life you can witness individuals who live their lives one way on Sunday, but another throughout the week. It is easy to claim something in belief but would you say with different actions from what they claim it shows their level of commitment? When individuals claim a position but don't uphold to it in their actions, how can they honestly expect their children to follow in their future or maintain their position within any organization or even under God for the child we all are? The Lord plainly teaches us about leadership in 1st Timothy and throughout the entire Holy Bible. It is sad when you see certain individuals holding on to a position but living another life which misguides our children. For the love of God, and our children, I pray that these individuals open their eyes to see what they are doing in misguiding and weakening the body of our homes, our churches, and even our nation! It may hurt to face something wrong but it sure feels better to confront it now rather when it is too late. Believe me!!!

Think about a person who claims a position or achieves a position in the Special Forces. How do you think every individual must act or follow instruction to maintain their position with the mission? Can you see a purpose of unity and being on the one accord? What do you think a team, moments before a mission, would say to someone not taking it seriously? What does anyone think following Christ would be any different? In the book of (Matthew 22), Jesus tells us the lesson that relates directly with this about a wedding feast being prepared and the guest refused to come. Further in the book of (Matthew 25), Jesus tells us how to be ready for His return and instructs us how to live until that day.

There is no difference in the principle of God's instruction in belief and following in our life compared to a vital mission of the armed forces to achieve a goal except for one is temporary while the other is eternal! Can you see the importance of maintaining your picture in life most of all spiritually and following your commitment in your belief to reach your goals? Both missions are life threatening but any other mission in life to whatever level it is, falls under the eternal mission of God's glory in overcoming all evil in this world! Within every mission statement and objective, there is a purpose to improve in love for our children of the future and to maintain positive growth!

Without love and commitment in life, what do we have left? There is a direct purpose and cycle of love in God's mercy that gives life, builds families, builds churches, builds relationships, builds businesses, and even builds nations! By individuals not understanding our foundations purpose in commitment in love from our ancestors and removing God from our picture, we can easily witness broken commitments in obligations, broken homes, and even a struggling nation! Our country needs to return to God and repent for all the evil being shown in our society! Asking in prayer for mercy and strength in God's grace to return our nation back to our foundation of God before it is too late! The Lord plainly shows us how to build and always stand in the Holy Bible when things are not right within God's sight! All of this begins in our homes and in our actions in love for life. There comes a point in every home someone must speak out in love for the family in Christ to correct and improve life!

Let's imagine this scenario not only in our homes but in anything properly built to open our eyes a little further. You are standing as a column supporting the different levels of flooring above you. At this particular point you are a single column with no help in support. The most important part to support the floors above you is your foundation from which you stand! Can you see the importance of an even or level balance for proper weight distribution? In addition, how important is the foundation when you plan unlimited levels of growth?

Now as you are standing firm on your foundation of a rock you don't worry about future growth. As time goes on in generations you stand strong while others learn to stand above you like the reflection of the rock from which you guide and stand. You know at some point, due to the cycle of life, that you must begin to look for someone with your strength from where you stand to step into place to carry on what you began. How would you feel in your position as that column holding up the other levels if the other person stepping in did not fully comprehend or discuss the rock from where they stand, giving you confidence that they understand the purpose and strength within our God given land? Would it hurt you inside when you knew your time couldn't carry the load anymore and you had to hand it over to someone in your home or business who didn't understand the purpose of love in giving strength to every level of life? Or, let's say someone does understand, but neglects the ones in who built the foundation of your home. Would you have concerns about your children's future generation of remembering how and from whom it all began?

It is so easy in life to only live in the moment and neglect our past and future! Every mother and father wants their children to never forget them and tell stories in future generations of where they have been. Not only to understand but also for laughs of joy in looking back to be remembered in life and never to be forgotten. There is never a point in life we shouldn't look back and learn how to grow but never trying to hide the truth. I'll never forget September 11, 2001, for several reasons. This is the year and month I began a commitment to build something to get away from my previous position and my shameful sin. I committed to make a difference not only helping others but attempting to build something for my family ahead. The day this journey began was September 11, 2001. My only problem was my lack of understanding how to build on the rock without sin being in my foundation from where it began. I never had a problem knowing how to stand, but I was mislead in thinking everything could be made right in time, moving forward without true repentance in turning away from sin.

That day America witnessed something life changing in our American culture and I also will never forget the pride I felt inside with everyone coming together flying flags, working in the recovery effort and even our government officials singing on the footsteps in Washington, D.C. Never in my life had I ever felt what I did that day and for those few days afterward with no planes in the sky and with everyone waving their flags in the air! It was so tragic for the families who lost loved ones, but prideful in the unity of the body in America for the first time I ever witnessed in my life! The part that broke my heart was how short lived the unity continued to last and how individuals began to separate seeking selfish desires overlooking the pains of the ones who lost their lives. Rather than looking to stay united, some individuals began to cannibalize the system that was in place to help those in need and virtually costing every taxpayer in some form or fashion.

There was a song that was written that only lasted about as long as the pride shown in America those first few days and it was sung by Daryll Worley titled *"Have You Forgotten."* This song says a lot in the message when you open your eyes and ears to what is taking place in this country. Our country took a major hit that day, not only lives lost but in our way of life changing from that point forward. It is so sad how something has to be either almost taken away or permanently removed before we open our eyes to what we have.

Our children will never know what it is like to walk into an airport not being looked upon as a possible suspect or threat and this hurts even though it is reality! What our children need to know is why this happened and to never forget why our country is built on God's foundation of love to give respect to authority and understand how our culture has changed. By doing this with our children, they will be better prepared for the winds of the world in knowing how to be safe, strong in life and understand how to rebuild when you stumble or fall!

God, our Father, wants the same thing every loving parent wants with their future generations of children. Each generation needs to make a commitment in life to remember where they have been and where they are going! This is exactly the message throughout the entire

Holy Bible of giving honor to God from which we stand and always to remember who created this land. The life of our country and the future freedom of our children, Americans can't allow God to be removed from our foundation and truly expect peace in true love for what has been given! Mark my words, ***"You remove God, then you remove life!"*** At some point in every home the family must learn to come together for strength in love and understand the purpose of a single direction not wavering on which way to go!

The Lord plainly gave us insight on our human weakness of becoming weak in our commitments throughout the entire Holy Bible. In the book of (Luke 22), the Lord, Jesus Christ, gives us instruction to remember He whom is the bread of life and to give thanks to God before we ever open our mouths to eat. With the life and blood of Jesus Christ, there is no other bread that gives life and no other foundation as solid as a rock! It is important to set aside time for family and friends at dinner to stay united in our relationships and in our homes. In addition, the Lord instructs us to set aside holidays to always celebrate and remember certain events in order for them not to be forgotten. I pray for not only my families sake, but for every other family in this world, to open their eyes and set aside time to remember God every individual who serves in this country and their families to not be forgotten! Never be ashamed of where we have been and always learn to stand in appreciation for finding the positives in every negative to insure proper growth!

When an individual fails to understand history and attempts to change or cover it up, then how can you ever remember or even know what to look out for and maintain strength in the future? Our ancestors made a commitment for our lives today in working to build something for our future and most importantly God taught us this commitment in His unfailing love through His only begotten Son, Jesus Christ. In the book of (John 3), we are taught God's promise for every believer in having eternal life and the fate of those who choose darkness over the light.

There is a proven cycle of events not only in the Holy Bible, in our homes but even in a business when someone steps in wanting to change the principle foundation from which it was built! When this happens within any organization, the unity within the body begins to lose direction and strength. Think about it like this as an individual person or even yourself. When you look at your life and see your struggles, failures, and successes, does it make you proud to see where you have been and what you have overcome? Or, do you try to cover up your post in neglecting what you learned? When a person of leadership can't discuss where they have been, then how can they honestly move forward?

There is great pride in working to grow and improve something in life that will give appreciation in not only our lives, but the lives of our children! It makes me proud to see where we have come from and even hurt for those in our past. I have respect for every individual who endured something to carry on the Word of God and to give us a better way of life! As a country, we have come a long way from where we have been and I pray that we get it together once again to move forward with direction and purpose! Rather than running ourselves in circles, trying to forget the past and not knowing where to stand, every American should have dignity in strength in who built this land!

One thing in life every individual will face at some point is change and this is normal in the cycle of growth. But in every change it is vital to understand the principle foundation to grow upon and never to remove something that is proven to work for something that isn't. In all growth there are principles that must be followed and continued in commitment to maintain strength in the future! This is like a tree in life when you really think about it. Can you even begin to understand the principles in the life of a tree compared to anything in our life that we choose to grow? There is a great lesson the Lord teaches us when we open our eyes and ears in understanding true strength in long term commitment.

Imaging a tree in life that is healthy and producing positive fruit reaching out to others. What happens if you attempt to transplant this tree to another location? Can you see its roots being broken and even a time period of the tree struggling to regain its strength in different soil from where it began? What happens in this process if you cut the tap root from the tree?

There is no difference in a tree having life and anything else we attempt to build! When you transplant a tree, it will suffer for a period and maybe even die without delicate nourishment and care given daily for it to overcome the shock. In this process, if you break the taproot or let's say "the principle foundation," then it is only a matter of time before the leaves begin to fall!

Our life is the same way of growing strength to produce fruit for our future generations. Rather than trying to transplant a tree of life that has eternal roots, we need to understand how to grow stronger in the foundation that we already have in place and this will teach our children how to properly grow! Our taproot is still in tact at this point, but by removing God from schools and other sectors in life, we are clipping away roots that help nourish the overall body of the eternal tree. It is time to rebuild these roots and nourish them daily in order to reconcile the life of the body of the tree! Due to our human nature many individuals seek something that grows fast and looks good. This is like comparing an oak tree to a pine tree and even to a Bradford pear tree.

When you look at the tree that has been standing for many years, do you ever wonder what it has been through? Do you give different levels of respect in the maturity of an oak tree to the maturity of a pine tree? Do you know why the oak is so much stronger than the pine? There is a direct lesson between these trees and our lives when you open your eyes and ears to the message being revealed. The oak tree is much stronger due to the purpose of time in growth and having many more roots that run in every direction giving it strength and nourishment to grow. Not only do these roots that branch out give it nourishment but they give it balance in the winds of this world by relying on the big things to the small things to sustain strength in the overall body of the tree! The life of an oak tree shows the purpose of growth in time and giving protection to others around who need to lean upon it in strong winds or storms. A pine tree may grow faster but what purpose does it teach in reaching out to give shade to others or even when the strong winds come they reveal their weakness by snapping in two.

Our society wants to be the beautiful oak tree but is neglecting the principles in our foundation that gives us strength causing us to settle for the Bradford pear! For instance, what purpose is a Bradford pear tree other than quick growth and to possibly either hide something you don't want to see or just to beautify a bare area? The Bradford produces no fruit and the first strong winds that come through can snap it in two!

When you build something in life, understand its purpose to achieve longevity like an oak tree! Our society pushes the Bradford pear and some settle with a pine. But before you decide to plant your feet in where you stand please evaluate the foundation to insure strength in your commitment of love, to give you the determination in your mission of Christ to sustain life for our children's future! In everything we do or even produce, it should be our objective to not cause separation within the different parts of the body of believers in Christ. Never in the Holy Bible does it teach us to separate ourselves under God, but only from sin! This doesn't mean to separate ourselves from other people who sin, but to help reflect the light of Jesus in the darkness of this world in caring for every lost soul!

This was originally taught in the Old Testament to the people of Israel and they were to go teach the Word of God to the world in their commitment to the Lord, but they failed to recognize the love of God in giving life to everyone who believes in the Lord's commitment to return His children in His mercy and grace. Over the years individuals allowed themselves to cause separation in the body and fell to the needs of their schedules causing distortion in their Christian behavior.

In (Philippians 2), we are taught an important message on how to grow as a Christian without complaining or arguing causing separation within the body of believers and in (Mark 7), there is another beautiful lesson taught in not falling into mans traditions or laws causing individuals to substitute the Word of God for human desires. Within every move in life, it is vital to understand your commitments of what you must face in order to achieve your goals!

Always seek God, being the creator and tree of life to receive the eternal rewards in protecting our children's future with the armor of God to give strength and the fruit of the spirit in our works being received as we stand in the winds of this world!

Many individuals today have fallen into exactly what Jesus taught against in the Word of God. On many occasions Jesus was criticized for eating with sinners, like in (Matthew 9), and even looked down upon by certain individuals who thought of themselves above others. Jesus taught in (Luke 7), a beautiful lesson on forgiveness of a woman who anointed His feet to another individual who overlooked the purpose of Christianity. It is very easy to fall to our human weakness of neglecting the purpose in our commitments with the Lord to separate ourselves if we are not careful.

Over the years of our society getting away from Jesus, it has caused many individuals to become lost within their Christian belief. In the past many individuals used the fear factor to influence people into a profession of faith and this has hurt the body of Christ by these individuals not only lacking understanding but even causing people to turn away from God. Think about it! How long does a commitment last that has been made on fear? Or, why would someone want to visit in your home if you talked down verses knowing how to look up? Many individuals fail to realize the message of God in only pointing out our weakness in order to grow stronger and understand our purpose of obedience in life. Why would someone want to attend a meeting if all they were told was how bad they were and they were going to hell? The Word of God warns us of where we will go if we don't properly believe in Jesus and repent of our sins. But many individuals fall to not either sharing the message of Christ in a positive manner or coming across as negative tearing someone down without picking them back up! The whole purpose in proper teaching or coaching is to share the negatives to understand the consequences and then reveal the rewards in God's glory of those who follow their commitment to Christ in reaching their goals.

The only way to properly reach someone who may be lost is by understanding the purpose of love, mercy, and forgiveness to allow the individual to open their heart to Christ. When this happens or takes place, you can witness the spirit of God moving within that individual convicting their heart and bringing tears of relief in understanding. It is our job to do the work and share with others how God, through the blood of Christ, has blessed our lives from our past to our current day. Don't become stuck in the middle causing you to face something in eternal persecution! Because there is much more to life than what you can see and it all is in how you understand the true art of being free!

Where so many individuals become lost in understanding Christianity occurs not only with non-believers, but even in the church body. Many individuals detour the name of Jesus due to caring more for public votes not wanting controversy or wanting their financial support and this is wrong! This is exactly what Joseph started to do in Matthew 1, in worrying about what people would think rather than standing for his love in Mary. Unlike Joseph, we may not have an angel come to us with instruction but this is given to us in the Holy Spirit convicting our hearts for what is right by God and not by man! There comes a point in every individual's life, to properly grow, that they must not worry about what others may think of them and do what is right by God in Heaven above!

Our society has fallen to tearing people down rather than picking them up and this is exactly what Satan wants in our lives! Ask yourself, "Had you rather look up or had you rather look down?" Don't fall short in your belief and commitment with the Lord through Jesus Christ. There is no other true way than with Jesus in following the Word of God in the Holy Bible!

As stated previously, there are different levels of commitments based on an individuals calling and you can plainly witness someone when in line with God's calling on their life in their works. Everyone has a purpose and a place within the body of Christ, but it is up to each individual to drop their personal desires and follow their heart in serving God's will! You will receive fulfillment beyond your imagination and begin to understand the purpose of God's instruction within this creation!!!

Many individuals overlook the art of balance which Jesus taught throughout His life, directly as God tried to get people to understand in the Old Testament. Christianity is serious as a special mission, but also as humbled as a child at heart. This is where many people become stuck in belief by not understanding how to be serious or mature when needed and how to live in freedom as a child laughing in the heart! This is done by learning how to emotionally adjust according to where they are. It is not about being fake, but real.

Christianity is about complete freedom and understanding the purpose of guidelines to stay within. This is where many people never make their complete step in faith or fail to understand how to live. Think about it, you have a child and take them to the park, first to build a playground and then to play in the park. Can you see the importance of instructing your children how to build and then how to stay within the park boundaries without getting lost or hurting others? Giving your child instruction and guidelines does not mean they can't have fun and enjoy life! It only means they abide by the rules put before them. There is a direct reason for structure and obedience in order to grow maturely in life. Not only as a child but also as an adult in understanding what Jesus taught in love to be truly free!

Based upon our level of commitment, it will guide the required discipline to live in understanding our position. But this never means to not learn how to train ourselves how to have mental balance to enjoy life and the fruit of the spirit of God! The Lord doesn't want us to be a robot, but learn to think properly without hurting others and living in love for life! This is exactly why we have the mental capability to choose, have free will, and learn to build upon His foundation. The Lord never intended for us to set ourselves apart, but learn how to bring others to unity in giving love within our picture of life. By showing and giving love will possibly witness to a non-believer in a way for them to draw closer to God, through Jesus Christ.

The Holy Spirit will convict and save an individual with their free will, but it is up to every Christian to provide the work and help those in need! Where many people overlook in heaven and in hell is there are different levels of rewards in heaven taught in Revelation

1 – 3, just like in hell there are different levels of eternal punishment that certain individuals will face! All of this is based on our level of commitment and following God's instruction. This is no different than the military reprimanding an officer who neglected their position, except for being everlasting. So, ask yourself in your belief, "Do you ever hurt that a friend doesn't know God?" It is very easy to only think of ourselves and neglect the spiritual needs of people around us in our picture of life.

Many individuals have turned away from church and ultimately God due to certain individuals characterizing others or feeling they are too far gone to receive help. We need to remind people that church is a place for fellowship and for individuals who don't think they are any better than someone for recognizing the sinner we all are since birth! There is great joy in the House of God who recognizes the Holy Spirit and learns to open their hearts directly to the Lord to feel His presence in their heart and soul.

Don't ever restrict God and feel He can't change someone or even yourself. There have been many lives in history like Paul in Acts 9, whose life made a complete turn and it is up to every true believer to encourage those seeking the life with God rather than tearing them down. Uplift everyone in your life and encourage those around you! But always remember we are all sinners under God and no one is any better than the next! Our lives should reflect the love for life in helping others whose faith may be new or weak and like the Word of God instructs in (Hebrews 11), allow your faith to guide your direction without being restricted by those teaching the wrong directions in life. Those individuals are only focused on the moment and allowing their picture to become out of focus in not believing in the eternal future!!!

In the book of (Malachi 3), the Lord was not only speaking to that generation but teaching us a vital lesson in returning to Him. Don't become blind to the facts of life and allow ourselves to become lost in this world! The Lord plainly tells us in this book of Malachi to put me to the test and try it if you want to receive a blessing! It is very easy to become weak when we see so much evil and people disrespecting others in life and I pray for us all to have strength to return ourselves back to the Lords foundation in which we stand. This all begins in our homes and then grows from there.

You will find, once you plant your feet in a true commitment with the Lord, Jesus Christ in your heart, that you will discover strength like you've never known. Study the wisdom in the scripture daily and build strength to stand in your commitments in life. Don't become down on yourself ever! Because we are all sinners and everyone has something in their closet of life in not wanting to be revealed in some form of faults. The important part is being able to recognize and admit to ourselves with the Lord in prayer that we understand where we have been in order to reconcile and move forward in life. Discover your weaknesses and then learn how to overcome in making something better for those in your current and future picture of life.

Why do you think Harvard University stated in their original Harvard Student Handbook in rule #1, "That students seeking entrance must know Latin and Greek so that they could study the scriptures?" There is great wisdom in the Word of God as stated in (Proverbs 2) that reaches levels beyond anything else in this entire world! As Malachi wrote with the Lord's instruction, "Put me to the test and try it."

James Madison, the primary author of the Constitution of the United States, said this, "We have staked the whole future of our new nation, not upon the power of government; far from it. We have staked the future of all our political constitutions upon the capacity of each of ourselves to govern ourselves according to the moral principles of the Ten Commandments."

There is a saying I once overheard that is very wise to under-stand in life. It was, "In life, if you don't stand for something, then you will fall for anything!" So I ask you for the life of our country and our children's future, to please focus on the Lord and pray for me as I pray for you! Everyone has something to be proud of no matter where you are in life! Rather than trying to transplant that tree in your life, learn to nourish it daily and give it proper time to grow under God in whom you know!!!

A Child to a Tree

We all start as a seed taking root from what is being sewn. As we begin to sprout, our foundation is the most important part in the longevity in the life of the tree. There is a purpose for daily nourishment to grow and love life from those who surround us in teaching us in whom they know!

As we mature, we stand in the shade leaning on those above and supporting us as we grow, giving us strength and protection in the winds of the world, in order to properly grow. The mature trees that surround us are to set an example in how to properly believe in the true art of being free! Giving us respect and honor in our foundation from where we stand and grow!

There are times the winds may become strong and there is always a tree taking the brunt of a storm. In times like this in these strong winds, this is where you learn to depend on those behind you to hold you up and give support within the family and even your friends.

No one knows which way the wind will blow and our leaves are like our souls in the wind. For everyday we look up to the sky and are constantly being pulled from end to end! There is only one way to truly balance in life, and this is under the cross of Jesus Christ! By understanding your roots within your foundation, this is how you know to stand and appreciate everyday God gives in His creation!

There will come a day when the old tree must fall to the new and all we can do is hope and pray that they never forget where we've been in giving honor and respect to those who stood in their path. Learning how to improve in understanding history, in order to carry on the Tree of Life with direction and purpose to properly stand!

Our children need and want to stand close in our lives as they grow. They need our protection and purpose to guide their future direction with our love and affection. In addition, they need the strength of a mature oak tree teaching them how to properly believe without ever letting them go! Plant your feet in your homes with God at the door to give your family strength when someone may become weak, our families need to know where to turn in the winds of this world to maintain their balance, and know without a doubt they can count on the family tree to uplift and encourage them in order to properly grow!

All of this strength is vital to teach in life and this I how you will be respected when you must step aside to those coming up beneath you. By giving your children the wisdom of God in the Holy Bible, will teach the ultimate goals in achieving and keeping their perspective in life. Not only will this carry on the strong foundation of the rock, it will allow our children to build something with purpose and direction in maintaining the proper foundation!

There is respect, honor, and liberty with God in our focus of life! So every time you look upon a tree ask yourself, "How solid is this tree in standing within the winds of being free and understanding the principles in the roots of the foundation in whom made it all happen in this beautiful nation of God's creation?" (To God All Glory, Amen)

CHAPTER 12

Press On

Throughout this entire book there have been many topics covered to share my divine understanding and wisdom that comes from, not man, to possibly help someone in many levels of life. The sole purpose of this book is to return our focus back to God and to open our eyes within our own individual lives with God, rather than someone misguiding us with wrong teachings in this land!

With God we have unity and true love that is unchanging in giving every individual purpose in their direction of life. As stated previously, it is up to each individual to do their part to gain control in their own personal picture. By the blessings of God, we are fortunate to have a country that offers so much opportunity and assistance when in need, but all of this isn't worth anything if you don't know how to properly believe!!!

What do we gain if we become lost in our game of life and lose focus of the eternal goals to truly succeed? How do we have unity within the body if everyone only focuses on the negative rather than accepting the truth and learning on an individual basis how to improve something in life? Our country over the years has become lazy and even now we are one of the most obese countries in the world! How does this make you feel? Are you proud or are you ready to do something to improve our standing in life? Everything begins with you and doesn't end without you!!!

The Lord plainly instructs us of not becoming lazy in the wisdom of Solomon in (Proverbs 12 & 13), and in (2 Thessalonians 3), Paul gives us instruction on laziness. Due to our human nature it is easy to give up or not help others when in need, but this is where everyone needs to come together and either uplift those below us or encourage those above us. There is great gratification in life when being knocked down and learning to pick your self back up to not fall the same way again!

For my entire life many individuals and even previous teachers have either discouraged me or told me something couldn't be done. This only added to my determination to only increase the feelings I've carried in my life and to prove something different! But now I must agree with those who once told me I would never amount to anything on my own. They were right!!! Because without a true understanding from the Word of God and now knowing who has given me the wisdom that I have inside, there is no way I could see the light in all the darkness of this world! Because I am not alone!!!

In my previous life Christ has always been with me since I first believed, but without understanding, I never could control the talents the Lord blessed me with in not respecting time, as I should have. Now I can tell you that not only do I have appreciation for life, but even a perspective of obedience in time! I fell not only to understanding the purpose of time, but even to what our society has shown in wanting everything before they were properly prepared to handle what they received. It is very easy to receive something when easily attainable, but this always has consequences at a later date! Our country on a large part has fallen to looking for that winning lottery ticket, an unearned handout, pushing something on someone with only caring about the sale or commission, that moment of temporary fame, and even sadly greed in suppressing the ones less fortunate.

My entire life I have always been proud to be an American and felt good about our nation giving equal opportunity to every level of life. There was a point in our country when there was true purpose and direction with much less corruption than what we have today. Not only in our personal lives, but also in our economy, we have faced moral downfall and a loss of being united in where we stand. This loss of direction and stagnant growth comes from removing our understanding of having God in the center of our life! By individuals being more concerned of votes or loss of business, they have turned away from God to avoid any additional struggles in their life and this is where they have it backwards and the other team distorts their personal picture of life!

If we are not careful and don't open our eyes, our country is heading towards a cycle in history that has already been proven when removing God and relying on man! This country is one of the most generous countries in all the world in helping others in need and this is something to be very proud of due to it is our purpose under God to serve others in every aspect of life. But there comes a time in every home that we can't take care of everyone else when we are hurting internally and causing worse possible troubles to come!

We are to always take care of our home, strengthen our family and treat thy neighbor as thyself! But not every neighbor will always agree and it is no ones right to force their will upon the other! We are to respect our neighbors for their own way of life and always stand on our foundation built from love in sacrifice! No true honorable neighbor wants to see their neighbor struggle or fall and they should respect and understand the purpose of regrouping your home to rebuild strength to help once again at a later date. When wounded you can only help someone for a period of time before you lose strength to sustain life!

It is time America Wakes Up and faces reality and comes together as one nation under God to find new strength to reconcile ourselves to who we are set out to be! Nothing in life is easy, and if it is, you better approach with caution! There is a cycle in life that every individual must learn how to focus on themselves to improve and regain strength to begin their climb all over again! This doesn't mean to cut others off but learn how to tighten down in areas where we have become wounded in order to strengthen our foundation of God's beautiful creation!

Every American citizen should be proud of what we have and for what we have come from in our past in order to improve the future! There is no better feeling of giving and helping others in need! But we are at a major fork in the road in our American culture that we need to come together in helping one another to return our countries focus back to God and work together for our children's future! Tell me what good is money without life? If we don't pull it together and refocus ourselves under God to do what is right by the people and for the people, then honestly, what do you see in the picture ahead?

In the book of (Jeremiah 29), the Lord plainly tells us if we look for Him wholeheartedly, we will find Him and this doesn't only apply to that point in time. For I am a living example of God restoring something broken when you wholeheartedly seek Him! Ask yourself, "What are you willing to do to improve something in life?" To improve any sector of life, this cannot be done without work mentally, physically, and spiritually! Don't lie down when times become tough! But turn to God and seek His wisdom in prayer from the heart to receive comfort like no one can properly explain! In the book of (Isaiah 40) the Lord, our Father, not only instructs us of His comfort but He tells us of those who trust in the Lord will find new strength to soar high like eagles in the sky! And there is a dear friend and brother in Christ that you will see in the near future who can tell this message along with many others better than I!!!

Another part to remember in work is the respect of time taken to achieve the rewards. Not all rewards come in this life and they are not always of any type of monetary means. But they come in someone just saying "Thank you" and most importantly knowing in your heart you've truly tried in this physical world only to receive your rewards in your eternal future ahead!

To my knowledge there is no other country that comes forth more in aid when someone is in need, this is important to remember when you are injured, because if you have nowhere to turn, then where do you go? There is only one place to go and this is to pray to God for help in order to give you strength to reorganize what has become lost in the life you know.

Think about it, if you have all the resources in your home in talent, in willingness, and even someone in the family with some financial means to help overcome a major issue, can't you see the purpose of pulling together to rebuild your home that has been neglected over the years? How would you feel inside if someone in the family did not contribute their strength in order to rebuild the roof that may be leaking?

This is like the fig tree that Jesus spoke of in not producing fruit and in (Matthew 25), where He discussed the parable of the loaned money. There is a direct cycle to those who use what they are given and to those who do nothing with what they have right before them! So again I ask you, "What can you do in your picture of life to help improve yourself or someone in your backdrop of life?"

It is time we overcome our differences, quit focusing on the negatives, and learn to move forward together as one body in our homes to build our nation! Rather than getting upset because someone isn't doing their part, then take on whatever you can to help that person and encourage them in love to possibly motivate them into seeing the light! Not everyone in life will see things as you do, but I can assure you the first time that other person has something removed in their comfort zone, they will humble themselves to receive what they can once they have had enough! Not only will they be happy to receive something they have lost, they will be more willing to do what it takes to work and achieve their goals at whatever the cost!

Our weakness in human nature is pointed out throughout the entire Holy Bible of how when we get knocked down we cry out for help making all kinds of promises and once we receive relief, how easy it is for us to fall right back where we've been before! Can you relate to this in any stage of your life? Have you ever suffered some sort of consequence like a failed relationship, continued struggles, or even prayed to God when you suffered pain with tears from your heart falling like rain, only to return to the same circumstance all over again?

There is a mindset you must reach and understand in order to maintain your commitment to not return to any negative in your life! This can't be done alone and there are many who would disagree because of lack of understanding in how to properly see the depth of love in giving strength in how to believe! I even fall to this limited vision without properly understanding the Word of God like mentioned in the very first chapter. I have always said, "my church was within," even before I had understanding and I was right! For the Lord plainly tells us upon the crucifixion and resurrection of Christ that we no longer had to seek Him in a special place within a temple, due to if we open our hearts to receive Him, He will dwell within us. But let me share where I was <u>wrong</u> in spiritual maturity in thinking I was so strong!

First off, I never understood where my strength and wisdom came from in my talents and now I know I am only a host with physical limitations being limited by man. I have always thanked and believed in God, but I never understood this fully before. My thoughts on church related to a previous governor who stated, "Church was a place for weak people," and this wasn't meant as a derogatory statement as it came across, I hope on his part, but as a statement of personal strength and belief within whom you know in your heart that saves or takes away! There is a point that every strong willed individual believes they can do it on their own and this is where I was so wrong!!!

There is power in numbers when united into one source and this is where I lacked understanding in the Word of God. To give a better illustration of this strength to someone who may think as I used to, let me challenge them to a game of Tug of War! The most important position in this game is the anchorman and every other position plays a roll in giving strength. To make the game a little more interesting, let's put it into reality by the pit in the middle is a deep dark hole with fire at the bottom! With this being reality, can you see the strength needed for support?

Someone you know may take this challenge and think they are strong enough on their own. But I guarantee every strong man has their weak days and can be taken to their knees! One on one the other individual may win physically, but when they are outnumbered they will fail! This is where I allowed myself to struggle in avoiding the church and fellowship. I allowed previous actions and teachings within the congregations to push me away from the church for what was being shown and knowing what was right in my heart. By myself staying out of church and not having a solid home or foundation, I eventually gave in to sin!

No one can stand alone in the winds of this world and honestly not expect to be swayed without something solid on which to latch on to! Even when fastened to the rock, you can still sway and this is where you must surround yourself with positive individuals who believe in you with love in their heart! Previously I mentioned that in a game each individual has a purpose to serve one another in order to reach the goal. So don't allow someone's vision to become limited like mine used to be in not understanding the art of being free!

It is very easy in life to allow something that is not right when we are only focused on the moment rather than holding true to the Word of God and honestly not properly thinking about our children's future! In times when we are hurt, burdened, or feeling weak, is when we are the most vulnerable to accepting anything to find hope and this is exactly what the other team of evil wants in order to hold you down in your worries or gain control of your life! *Think about it*, how many people have you witnessed taking advantage of someone below them or weaker in life? What about those who take advantage of someone not able to defend themselves? Do you remember the video footage of the elderly woman being robbed and hit physically by someone stronger than her? There is no difference in this video than someone in any weaker circumstance being taken advantage of! This happens in our homes, on our schools, in our courts, in our economy, in our health care, in our nursing homes, and the list can go on and on.

The negative side of our human character can be compared to an animal preying on an injured victim, and sadly it even goes as far as a vulture preying on the dead! It is very easy to take advantage of a situation that may seem okay at the time. But think ahead of the future in not only what you will have to answer for but is your decision going to help or hurt someone's future? If we only think of ourselves, then we are not working within the body to maintain life! Please don't do as I have in my past and drop your standards when you're weak but always remain true!!!

In (Ephesians 3) we are taught to not isolate ourselves from the church or other believers and how God's love will keep us strong! It is very important to find a genuine church home with sincere believers who uplift and encourage in understanding how to follow in serving through love with Jesus Christ and always reaching out to help others in need! There is POWER in the spirit of believers who align their hearts to focus on God through Jesus Christ, and to those who think they can win that game of Tug of War on their own, I pray for you when you are left all alone!

When our life is either blinded with sin or we lack proper understanding in the Word of God, our hearts can be hardened to not being receptive to receive what God has to offer in true joy, teaching us how to truly win! Unfortunately this happens even in the church body by others paying more attention to what or who is around rather than focusing on God to hear His message to grow and be uplifted in the spirit from this physical ground!

There is no neutral ground in this game of Tug of War! You are either on one side or the other as an adult. There is a direction being pulled but a stand of love on the rock with Jesus Christ being your anchor in your heart and knowing you are saved! By knowing this in your heart you have no fear and your vision becomes clearer! It is *vital* to understand how Satan works in this game of life by first tempting you physically and then tempting you mentally to pull on his team without ever recognizing what is truly happening in your life! This is where we are stronger in numbers fastened to the rock and can find comfort within the body of Christ in loving one another to build something not only for ourselves, but most importantly for our children's lives ahead. In (Ephesians 4 and 5) Paul gives us instruction to speak out in loving manners against wrong, for if we remain silent that could be interpreted as giving approval. Over the years this has been very difficult to balance. This is due to not controlling our human emotions and not placing matters in God's hand to seek guidance to properly address the matter. No one wants to be the addresser or the addressee, but at some point, if your family begins to suffer you must act in love to correct something that is not right!!!

The Lord puts great emphasis on the family in the Word of God and teaches us to be honest with each other without hiding the truth from one another out of love and with understanding. When someone is not honest in giving positive feedback or constructive criticism within the family, then the individual trying to grow or improve something in their picture of life begins to search other directions outside their homes and this can really hurt the love within the family!

Think about it like this, if you have someone you love in your heart, how would it make you feel if they had to go somewhere else to discuss something that could be solved at home with understanding in love for one another, verses talking with someone not even directly involved or even giving you a chance to listen? Why do you think there are so many talk shows and people being exploited in the public with matters that should not be on public display? Many individuals really need to **WAKE-UP** and face reality in how to grow positively within the family without tearing someone down or hurting them for life!

What do you think it teaches our children if they see their parents on public display spreading their wrongs without giving an understanding of what they learned on their own? Does this teach our children to look within the family and search every measure possible before searching outside? On a more serious note, by going on public display to be torn apart in not knowing how to positively grow, how will this teach our children not only to depend on the family, live in the family, but even how to grow stronger, if they are left all alone? Don't be fooled into thinking that you can go outside the Word of God and outside the family without affecting someone negatively in teaching them to seek someone else or something else without understanding how to be open in a relationship to positively grow or improve any aspect of life!

Examine your paths you take and always know your objective and direction! Just because something else is being shown or something might be easier in following others by taking the path of least resistance, does not necessarily mean it is a path of God in doing what is right! Follow God and not man in order to make it to the other eternal side! The Lord plainly instructs us to be obedient to authority, follow guidelines to maintain strength and to love in everything we do in order to be true! By following God and listening to your heart, He will guide you to do whatever needed to grow stronger in life with Jesus Christ!

It hurts deeply to not make everyone happy but there comes a point that every man or woman must step out on their own with God rather than following man to honestly know how to properly stand and grow! Many influential people are misguiding the public and I pray that these people see the light of Jesus Christ! When you become lost, it is like being in thick fog. It first begins to set in and you can still see, but the longer you travel in thinking you are on the right path, the worse it becomes and you begin to reach out to anyone who claims they have the way!

There is only one way, the instruction through the Word of God and Jesus Christ being your ultimate lighthouse to guide you through every storm! To those who are being misguided, "Snap out of it," and see the light! Our life is a test of our loyalty, service, and most of all, our faith, leading to our eternal life! Don't fall to misguided teachings in the fog of this world!

Please take the time to read the book of (2 Timothy) for encouragement in being faithful and how to act. In addition, be sure to read (2 Timothy 3 & 4) on dangers to avoid in life and how to recognize false teaching leading you away from the Word of God! This is more serious now than ever before and it is time to **WAKE UP**, clear the morning fog and return to the light of Jesus Christ! The Lord loves each and every soul on this earth, with sorrow for the ones who defy Him in following false doctrine! For the life of your children and mine, please strengthen your spiritual understanding and seek unity within the body to find new strength in the love of Jesus Christ!!!

Not only is our country suffering, but also the entire body is suffering from individual's loss of direction in moving forward together with unity and purpose! America needs to regroup or let's say, "Take a breath to accept the facts of what has happened since we began to remove God from where we stand." The proof is everywhere you turn in crime, people breaking their commitments, individuals not helping others in need and people running from the truth!

All of this begins in our homes in teaching our children responsibility, creativity, honor, loyalty, and how to sacrifice something now for something better at a later date! It is no one else's responsibility to abide and teach those in our picture of life how to have appreciation and grow maturely in life! Our teachers in public schools or in any other organization should not be held accountable for actions of a child who has not been properly taught at home unless they cross the line in respecting their position.

Every since we began to remove prayer in public schools in 1962 and remove reading Holy Bible in 1963, anyone who can't see the results of this are either blind to the facts or being stubborn in their hearts! Personally, I fully agree to never force anything upon anyone in religion, but on a moral basis you can't win a debate against the Word of God in how to treat all people who either believe or don't!!!

An individual's religion and belief is based upon their free will to accept, receive, and follow! Our position as a Christian should be to love and respect each person for who they are and always reflect our joy in the light of Christ in being totally free. We all must face things in life in order to grow and learn how to let it go! The test of an individual comes when humbled to reveal your true character, loyalty, understanding and faith in which you follow to guide your eternal future. *Think about it*, if someone tells you before hand that you are going to be tested tomorrow, is this a proper test? Everyone prepares for something when they know what is in their path, but the true test comes like the thief in the night! Our God, our Father in Heaven, has given us the book of instruction in how to live, act, and how to always be prepared for that obstacle in your path or that "Pop Quiz." With this said, I must ask are you prepared in your heart? Are you living right? Have you drifted in the fog of this world? Do you know without a doubt your life is right with Jesus Christ? We all fall short so don't let this discourage you! But allow it to motivate you to regain control and your balance in life for our children's future.

Everything begins in our homes where it should, on an individual level, and then spreads throughout the game of life. By removing the Ten Commandments in our public schools and other public facilities, we can plainly see the moral decay in not only our children but even in adults. The evidence is right before our face, and if we don't drop our pride, our differences, and learn to build in love with respect for each other, matters are only going to get worse in the fog of this world! Not only do we have past history of what happens when individuals or nations lose focus on God, but now we have current history in what happens in losing our direction or focus from our foundation! There comes a point we all must accept the truth before it ultimately faces you!!!

When this time occurs of handling the truth, it will be far greater than Tom Cruise and Jack Nicholson in *A Few Good Men*. I pray that we all come together to rebuild and restore the strength of God in our foundation of this beautiful nation. Our country and families have fallen into a world of compromise in not understanding the purpose of not allowing sin into our lives. Once the line is crossed, every other sin becomes easier in being lost.

The Lord plainly revealed this in what to avoid in the very beginning with Cain and Pharaoh in the books of Genesis and Exodus of the Holy Bible. This is so to understand in law, not to allow ourselves to be consumed with allowing something we know that is not right to continue in taking place and only growing worse or out of control at a later date. In the book of (2 Samuel 11), we are taught great wisdom on how continued sin makes us insensitive to it and how covering it up only leads to more sin. Can you see this anywhere in our society today in how matters are only getting worse instead of getting better? Even those who may not believe as I do or you do can't deny the facts or the wisdom of God. You can plainly see how individuals don't know whom to believe or follow and are taking the wrong attitude of the phrase in the movie *Gone with the Wind* in saying "Frankly my dear, I don't give a damn!"

It is time every individual rebukes this attitude and begins to work together for the American life of our children's future. Never before has there been a nation, in my eyes, more blessed by the Lord than the United States of America, other than the Nation of Israel. When you look at Israel today, they are steadily struggling with their heritage and trying to encourage those who have moved away to return to try to maintain their culture, If we don't **WAKE UP** and see what is before us, America will follow the same path in inner struggles of not understanding how to follow the instruction of God in compromising our children's future. The Lord does not want this for any one. He wants unity within the body with love to give strength in our purpose to live.

Allowing compromise on standards of living that you know are not right in your heart will affect your future generations and even your way of life! Most importantly, when someone does this, what is it teaching our children when we give on the principles to truly succeed in life. There must be a point of no compromise in order to properly sustain a future. What is it going to take to see the light and move forward? It is very wise to catch yourself in your loss of balance before having to grab hold of what ever is near due to your internal fear of a fall and listen to God's call.

Over the years I used to think Rambo would have been a good match for the Terminator, but now I see Mr. Universe losing his Terminal Velocity in falling to compromise. Maybe it would do him good to watch the Last Samari to regain some respect for the principles in life. Due to the Terminator now losing strength, I'm feeling confident in allowing Rambo to not ever waste his time as a Veteran. I think I could even handle this match myself. But there is one major advantage I have and that is I did not understand before,

God is in my corner of life and giving me wisdom to step back when the Terminator says, "I'll be back." Talk about moving out of a ring, I would move faster than the Six Million Dollar Man and then support him like the true fan.

Our ancestors placed the moral conduct of God in public facilities to point out our foundation, proper teaching, social obligations, and as a reminder that everyone is accountable for their actions. They did not force the Christian belief of Jesus Christ on others for understanding the purpose of free will, but they did set God's principles in place for our foundation to maintain strength and growth. By individuals removing the Word of God and guiding others away from the Holy Bible, they are largely doing this for financial gain in claiming they know the proper way to succeed. This is very sad and so wrong. If you truly read the principles, every successful person is teaching and writing they all derive and parallel the Word of God in the Holy Bible. I don't know about you, but I not only can tell a difference in something generic verses something original, I can feel the difference. Personally, there is nothing wrong with something generic with proper understanding to insure the same outcome or goals are achieved, but if the ingredients are changed to satisfy another taste, beware of the possible side effects or the lack of results.

When individuals allow themselves to search the world rather than the Word of God, you will witness the same cycles of rotation over and over in trying to maintain balance that can't be eternally fastened for life without Jesus Christ. With this taking place individuals don't know how to properly stand or pick themselves back up if they stumble or fall without the roots of love giving security and support to move forward. Compromising away from principles or standards will eventually cause someone to totally lose their perspective and possibly even cause them to forget who they are. Don't fall short in life and settle for something you feel in your heart is not right. For example, imagine this scenario to see the depth of understanding. Let's say your neighbor lives a certain way and his standards in the way they keep their home are not the same as yours. Now you have been invited for dinner at your neighbor's house and you accept their invitation. Before you arrive at that dinner date, have you mentally prepared to relax or adapt to their way of life to enjoy the night? Or do you expect them to change their home in order to better suit you? On the other side of the coin with the dinner host, do you feel it necessary to totally change the way you act or your standards that you follow within your home? Why should it be any different with guests in your home verses with your family in your normal way of life? If we act one way for some people but differently for others, what is this showing and teaching our children in how to be themselves in maintaining their future?

By giving in on standards or principles, it can be dangerous if we don't properly teach our children where to stand and how to handle compromise. For instance, it is okay to adjust the thermostat, but it doesn't make sense to turn it off or on in order to control the room temperature, when we can simply adjust it without completely disconnecting the power source to the A/C. Think about this analogy for depth of understanding. What is happening in America is beginning in our homes and causing us to work like a cooling system with no refrigerant or Freon in the lines. When families have God in focus, the compressor is productive and feeding the output in their emotions with the spirit of God giving purpose to live. If the country has no walls or ways to contain the air in life within a room, then the air just blows out with no controlled environment. This causes the homes or individual compressors to run constantly trying to maintain with no balance or direction in room temperature. All rooms must be balanced and controlled to have comfort in our way of life! If all we do is constantly adjust the thermostat and don't give the compressor a chance to rest instead of running constantly, then would you agree the compressor may age before it's time? Can you see the importance of a balanced environment with some sort of controls, rather than just blasting hot air?

It is important to teach our children how to negotiate a compromise without giving in on a standard principle that has proven itself over and over again in how to maintain strength in life. We all can adjust or adapt, but we cannot separate ourselves from the true power source that gives us freedom in equal rights to protect our children's future. Not everyone will agree with our Christian belief and this is their right as an "American". But for the most part, even the ones who don't believe still seek the same principle foundation in love for their children to have a positive future without hurting others in life. Everyone has a right to speak freely according to the Constitution of the United States and just because you are a Christian believing in Jesus Christ does not mean you cannot speak on your belief. If someone can speak freely without God, then it is only fair to allow someone to speak freely with God. We just have to learn from our history in how to respect each other without forcing someone's will on others. This is how we all learn to live with our neighbors and enjoy that dinner when we are invited.

Here is another analogy to think about. If your home has some major issues that need to be addressed, how do you honestly expect to get along or enjoy yourself during this dinner invitation, especially when you and your neighbors don't even see eye to eye? Can you see the importance of first getting your home in order before you entertain guests? If we entertain guests in our homes and cover up the issues that are causing major problems, are we truly treating thy neighbor as thy self? Absolutely not! I have fallen to this wrong thinking also in failing to understand how some problem that is deeply covered or rooted can affect our neighbors when they may be depending on us. For the love of God, and the strength of our nation, every American citizen needs to come together without worrying about who is right or wrong in order to regain strength in doing whatever we can to help or serve others in protecting our children's future. We need to strive to keep world peace but never force our will upon others.

Imagine this scenario within your home. You have a child and he or she creates a debt that they can't pay. You receive a phone call saying, "Your child has gone past due and either you help or they lose their home." What would you do if you had the means to help? There is a time our children must learn responsibility and face consequences. But there is a time to lift that burden in order for them to go to work and repay what they can in the future. If we hold our children down while our pantry is full, we are not setting a good example. Is this how you want someone to treat you? Can you see how America is one big family? We have people right here at home who need our help.

Let's reverse the roll and now you are elderly. How would you feel if no one in your family helped you when you were in need? Would you hurt if your pantry was empty and you were hungry while your children are eating anything they want? There comes a point in survival that we must do our part within our homes to work and help others in need to truly help in the art of how to succeed. Just because someone in your family creates a debt does not mean we are not to help if we are able to when they are honestly trying to work their way out of their circumstance in life. If we don't help our children or our parents supplying their needs, we will see division coming into the picture of life. If someone is trying, help. But if they are not, then they must learn the hard way. But this doesn't mean to ever give up.

On a larger scale, we can see this nation as our home and if we don't work in doing our part within the unity of the body then are we doing our part as an American citizen? Without a doubt you can say our parents have created a debt, but does this mean we are not liable for their past mistakes? Absolutely not! Our country needs to pull together and do whatever we are able to do to rebuild our infrastructure for our children's future. It would break my heart to know that I left this physical place without using my God given talents or gifts God gives in Matthew 25, to not only do my part as a man of God, a husband, a father, a friend and as an American citizen. What point is it to hold on to something that isn't worth a flip in the dirt when we are gone that could have done something to help not only my children's future, but also yours?

When we look at our total economic picture in the United States of America, we can see the same thing in our national debt to our household debt in those individuals whose debt load increased due to inflated equities and credit being given so freely. *Think about it*, you can see this in how it was only a matter of time before it hit our homes. By our credit lines increasing in free trade is the same as an open credit line on a personal credit card. The credit giver was more concerned with their sale or what they could make in profits verses looking at the dangers of our human nature in not understanding how to properly manage ourselves without God guiding the direction in the respect of discipline and obedience. At some point in debt we begin to border things that we never would have done unless under extreme pressure to survive. This is when we become vulnerable to sin.

It is very easy to look upon what someone else may have and want it so badly that we lose sight of our own dollar value earned. This not only happened in our homes with easy credit given but it has happened also between our nations in our "American dollar losing value to the foreign currency. Now, causing our foreign nations to wish they just had their value back in return. This can be corrected. But first we must come together as one nation under God with liberty and justice for all. Can you now see the importance of the Tenth Commandment, "Thou shall not covet." For if we covet something or someone we can lose sight of what we have.

There is no difference in the principle of personal debt to national debt. If we don't fix the problem, it will only get worse requiring more money to cover up the issue. Then it is only a matter of time before people get hurt or left out. We can correct this if we face the facts and build back on our foundation to restore our beautiful nation. Every individual in the United States of America needs to dig into ourselves to find whatever talent we may have to help rebuild this country back to where it stands. Sometimes we first must discover what it is that is holding us back before we can see forward. If we are truly honest with ourselves, we know what is holding us back, but we first must swallow our pride to accept the facts.

There is so much opportunity in our country and it is as easy as opening our eyes to read the classifieds. It amazes me at how we can open any classified section of a local paper and find employment opportunities looking for individuals who are willing to work with integrity and offering incentives upon acceptance. What is wrong with this picture when all we hear is how our jobless rate is increasing or how a town is shrinking?

Unfortunately, I believe Ed McMann can explain this better than I. There is no excuse for this, other than our pride and laziness restricting our life. So what if I have to flip burgers or even clean toilets to start over or even to begin. Our problem in America is our pride and how people have lost respect for the dollar earned over something given easily. It is amazing how the value of the dollar would begin to increase with more respect in appreciation for what has been earned. You can see how winning lottery ticket might not come and I know for a fact there are some who wish it never did.

All things aside, if everyone would drop their pride and bite the bullet, we could pull through these hard times and find new strength with a purpose needed for our children's future. We all need to quit looking in every different direction that is being misguided or distorted without God in the picture. If you want direction and purpose, then listen to what God is telling me to tell you. Pick up that ax head in (2 Kings 6) reattach it to the handle to make progress with God guiding the way.

Our country will only become worse if we don't listen to the truth. Remember, the poem on the husband who wouldn't listen and sent that temporary rose? Can you see the message not only to an individual but also to the overall body of Christ and even to our nation? Somebody better **WAKE UP**, and quit patching things with money without working and start beginning to listen. I am here to tell you a patch will not work if you are only covering up something not right by God. You want strength? Find God! He never has left us, but we have left Him. It is not too late to reconcile and find new strength. We must find unity, overlook our differences, drop our pride, reconcile with repentance, go to work with purpose, and love and joy of everyday we are given. All of this begins on an individual level and then spreading like wild fire with a direction to overcome our suppression.

You want to see an instant turn around in our country? Well, here's how. Quit focusing on the negatives before you and find the positives in everyday. You say this can't be done? Well, I'm here looking at a brick wall under restriction and can state, "You are wrong." If our media would learn to balance positives with some negatives in every broadcast verses their unbalanced focus on negatives, eventually you would see an immediate impact on our American attitude spreading like wild fire. So I ask all of you media executives, "Who do you care more for your life or your children's future?" You wonder why you struggle for the ratings. It is right here in plain sight. Think about it, how does the crowd react when all they see is their team being knocked to their knees? How positive and uplifting is the emotion of a winning team? Not only a winning team, how about a team who is consistent in making effort to strive in every positive way? Can you see the respect of fans and players who understand that not every game can be won? Sometimes we must lose to win.

If all the fans hear is constant fighting and others pointing fingers, then can you see how some who bought their season tickets would give up their seat and walk away? **WAKE UP** America! Get it back together and enjoy your game of life like never before. Work smart, be proud of your work, and do your best with what you have for your children's future.

You want to see our jobs return to the United States, well, quit looking at the government leaders and allow them to do their job while you do yours in working harder than ever before to regain our reputation as hard workers who are willing to do what we need to succeed. We have the talents and we can do this all together for our children's future in regaining our American standing on God's foundation.

Every job has a purpose to fit all the different sectors in life and just because someone may choose to work on an assembly line doesn't mean they can't be as content as someone who went through education to reach a level of success. This doesn't mean anyone is any different but we all choose our positions in life and are given the opportunity in this free country to move up based on our sacrifice. If you can't see this or understand this, don't look at me but look to God and ask yourself, "Am I truly being honest within my heart or am I not wanting to let go or accept something that may be hurting or helping other people?" And, for those of you on top, ask yourself the same question before Cousin Eddie pulls up at your door to teach you a valuable lesson.

Please don't let this get you angry with me because I can assure you I understand many positions. I have been on top and I have been on bottom. But never have I lost my faith in God, through Jesus Christ, and there is no doubt in my heart that we all can improve if we return to the cross of our foundation. Everywhere you look you can find something in your personal picture of life that can be worked on or even just in needing time to listen. Seek God for your direction and purpose by first understanding your position in being content in your heart. Then move to other areas to help people in need. Because if our home is not right, then who are we to instruct or help someone else in need? This is why I could never speak freely before and only gave bits and pieces to someone in need. I thank God for my forgiveness unlike the movie "*Unforgiven*" with Clint Eastwood, because I am excited to be an American being free.

If our country wants to truly return to unity with purpose, it is going to take God being in the center of our lives. For those who disagree, I'll pray for you and I will even help you in finding your direction and purpose in life. There is nothing worse than just existing with no belief, without direction to reach goals. And whether we seek the same goal or not, I'm sure those who don't seek God still want a good life for their children's future.

Be prepared for a time period to rebuild new strength. It will not happen overnight like the movie Grease, or the song Grease Lighting. We must be prepared to face obstacles in our path. Sometimes matters can become worse, before they get better. But with God guiding your direction, you will face challenges like a true athlete in understanding how to grow. It takes work with commitment to achieve goals and when you feel you are not making progress, pray to God for guidance in His strength. Associate yourself with other positive believers in order to overcome your hurdles.

The other team wants you to give up or fall weak in life to tear you down and to feel there is no hope. Well, I'm here to tell you, **"There Is Hope No Matter Your Circumstance in Life!"** Don't fall weak to the easy way out or to some false hope in man, but allow God to teach you how to stand. Look ahead to the future of children in what is best for them and not yourself. With God, you can do anything when working within His will and committing yourself to do whatever it takes to help improve anything in this land.

When someone in your family or even your neighbor needs help, let go of what is holding you back in the name of Jesus and serve those in need to improve our overall picture of life. If someone has a debt and you are able to pay, help them to get out from under their burden to lift their spirit in helping others by sharing God's blessings while serving others. Our children's future depends on the direction we go and I pray for your children and mine that their life or world is better than what we have now. Don't scare your children by revealing or showing things that aren't right without teaching them where you went wrong in order for them to properly grow strong.

We are told and taught in (Nehemiah 8), to not feel sad or burdened by God's law but to live in joy within it. We all have our days of feeling weak or our failures tend to take us down when not obeying God's word, but this is where we should be very happy with praise of thankfulness for having God's mercy and grace. Not only should we feel God's joy in the Holy Spirit from the heart in His love and mercy, we should be proud for the recognition of how to correct and improve our lives in God's sight. Imagine how sad it would be if we did not have the Word of God in His book of instruction and no knowledge of how to return to Him through His only Son, Jesus Christ. This would be a reason for extreme sorrow, but instead the Lord has loved each of us so much that He not only gave us His instruction in the Holy Bible, He provided a way back home through being born again, with Jesus Christ.

The first emotion or character trait of facing sin is in remorse once we drop our pride. Then repentance with God will begin to give you new strength. There is great healing with a repentant heart as we are taught in (Hosea 14), lifting a weight when you have been held down and this will begin your road of reform in staying close to God with Jesus Christ in your heart.

The Lord doesn't want us to be unhappy, feel depressed, or to feel burdened. He has never moved, changed, or will change His way. All He wants is for each of us to respect, honor, and be lifted in the Holy Spirit of God. In the Spirit of God, we receive many fruits of joy. If you ever begin to feel burdened or your vision becomes distorted, then rationalize your thoughts and seek wisdom to find strength in earnest prayer. The other team of evil wants you to feel like this world is all there is and wear you down causing you to lose any hope in your life. Don't fall into this and allow the false teaching being guided by evil spirits to infect your thinking. Always be on guard to keep on track in God's will, through Christ.

There is great comfort and joy in the heart with Jesus, knowing you are not only forgiven, but also saved. Everyone when truly honest has encountered wrong or evil thoughts what are never mentioned or expressed. Unlike some individuals who allow these evil thoughts to control their actions and words. This is where the Word of God teaches us how to control and remain obedient to do what is right in God's eyes and show His love for others.

When you really think about it, we are no different than animals, except the Lord gave us the thought process to retain and rationalize our thoughts to control our words and actions. Not only did He give us this thought process, He gave us the capability to build based upon the gifts He provides. Take a person who was raised in the wild of a wilderness, with no guidance or education verses someone with proper guidance and rules to follow. Can you see a difference and the reason behind education to build upon, starting with the Word of God as our foundation?

This may seem out there, but if you are honest with yourself, you can see the truth. We all build upon what we are taught and shown. This is where I am thankful for the love of God for teaching and giving the proper way to live and think. There is great joy in God's knowledge and understanding how to live our lives with Him guiding the way.

When you learn to rationalize your thoughts in proper control through love with Jesus Christ, you will keep your body and mind in tune with God allowing you to hear and see like never before. You will feel soft music on your heart in caring for others before you part. When you learn the art of belief in God through His Son, Jesus Christ, you will find the music you hear and see will open doors when you pray from your knees.

Don't ever feel sorrow or depressed because the Lord God Almighty wants you to feel His joy and receive peace in your rest. The Lord is our shepherd and will comfort you when in doubt. So draw close to Him and He will draw close to you in giving you strength to do your best in life above all the rest.

In (Nehemiah 3), we are taught how to teach and build by making others feel needed. This is such a valuable lesson to apply, not only in our homes, in our schools, in our work, but in everything we do. All of this begins in our homes to not only teach our children, but to protect our children's future. Within this chapter of (Nehemiah 3), not only were we taught the importance of our foundation at home, but also we are taught to work together for a purpose in life to grow stronger in the arms of God.

On a large part, many individuals have forgotten how to follow Christ within the overall body and this has created a weakness in the walls of not only our homes, but in our nation. In John 1, there is a vital part that is being overlooked in society causing us to follow Jesus for our own purposes rather than properly following His instruction on how to remain strong. In every task we seek, it is vital to insure whose glory we truly are after.

This is where I was wrong in my previous life in not properly understanding that what really matters is not being the best wanting recognition, but putting myself behind others to help them achieve their goals. We all fall at times to wanting recognition, but we should really ask ourselves, "Is our recognition for God or for man," to keep our perspective in life? Sometimes we must step back and allow someone else to step forward to properly serve and grow. This message started in Genesis and ends in Revelation in how we are to encourage within our Christian faith with God guiding the way.

Our life has a beginning and a physical end that everyone will eventually face. The Lord gives us instruction and places dots in our path to connect before we face our death due to our impurities of sin. It is our job to follow His instructions, focus on the day and look toward tomorrow as we pray. With Jesus in our hearts and God making the way, there is glory in our works without sorrow of what we could face tomorrow.

God gave us the beginning and the end with parts in the middle within the Holy Bible to this physical side. The Lord tells us how to live, worship, and look forward with understanding in life. In addition, the Word of God tells us the history of truth in what to expect when we get out of balance without God in the center of our lives and most importantly it tells us the eternal future. But here is where the Holy Bible has been neglected or overlooked.

The Word of God has never stopped with miracles, lessons or even in the works of God. Only man stopped the divine stories in the Works of God. Meaning, ever since Jesus Christ setting us free did not mean the end was near, but this was only the beginning of true life through the blood of Jesus Christ. Throughout the generations God has touched many lives like those in the Holy Bible. But by man not noting for record the divine stories of God, man fails to recognize the Lord's works in today's chapter of time in between Genesis and Revelation in the Holy Bible. Humans by nature of sin have lost or become complacent in God by certain organizations protecting the Word of God without adding and preserving God's works in today.

This creates a stagnant attitude and disbelief in people sitting around waiting, becoming impatient and even believers, to fall behind for not keeping the Word of God alive. God is life and the Holy Bible is alive and powerful teaching us life. What happens when you stop working on something or paying attention to it? Would you say you could possibly fail to maintain it over time? What happens when you overlook it and think it is complete, needing nothing else to grow? We don't know the dates or time of the exact pinpointed beginning or the coming end to this physical life for our eternal life to begin and it is our purpose to have faith and believe with no doubts. Does it really matter about dates or time for exact proof? Absolutely Not! What matters is your belief and faith in knowing who created life and who gives life.

Think about the Holy Bible like this: being a business idea in creation, then growth and giving instruction. In any business you know what you must do to succeed and you set goals in time. There comes a point you must pass your company to another generation, but does this mean your business stops. Absolutely Not!

You know at some point there is an end but a new beginning to eternal life. But does this mean you don't work daily to grow and build on the foundation already given following instruction? Absolutely Not! You are to build and grow on a daily basis adding to what has been given, not trying to take away from your foundation to start all over again. This is what Satan wants you to do in distorting your picture and losing belief. He wants you to start over again on something that will not last without God in the picture!

In (Isaiah 66), we are given a promise from God that will never waiver as an individual or a nation when you properly believe. God plainly asks us, **"Why would I give birth to something and not deliver it?"** This is not only a promise from God but also a major piece of wisdom to apply to our lives. If you make a promise, keep the promise. And before you ever begin something, think of how you will see it through. Don't fall weak and give up. If you believe in your heart the Lord will help you find the wisdom everyday you begin to start. All we have to do is what the Lord instructs us to in (Hosea 14), in coming back to God to receive our deliverance and find our purpose and quit living like (Hosea 12).

In addition to God's promise, we are taught in (1 Peter 3), how He is being patient for our sake. He doesn't want anyone to be destroyed, but wants everyone to repent. I pray for every individual in the world and our nation, to reconcile and begin to move forward in positive ways. There is great relief once the burden is lifted and we face our sins to begin to grow all over again. It is time that we all **WAKE UP** and come together to remember our roots of our foundation to rebuild our homes in this beautiful nation.

Every American citizen needs to do their part in helping however they can for us to strengthen anything within our picture of life even if it is just voting to keep the right ones in office to the wrong ones out of office, to insure our longevity of life.

This is not only something written for this time period, but for the future time ahead in our children's grandchildren to come. We must never forget where we have been to learn how to stay strong with God throughout understanding to the best of my human comprehension until now. My entire life I have attended different churches, approached many pastors and even spoke with individuals searching for answers. One thing I've learned in all the years I have been seeking for deeper understanding of what I felt inside could not have been taught by man. Man has limitations to understanding just as I did. But when you search the Word of God daily and meditate throughout your day, the Lord will reveal deeper understanding based upon your level of maturity. The object is to be open as a young loving child watching their parent graciously weave something together. If you are not open and only read with your door closed, then you can witness a picture in your life, while the Lord is trying to knock on your door. The longer you go the harder the knock.

Picture a young child sitting beside their father with their eyes full of love and trying to mimic their moves in love. This is what the Lord wants and it takes our hearts as humble as an innocent child willing to listen and obey. When you learn this, the Lord will protect you and guide you. As you grow and still keep the same heart of the child seeking Him, the Lord will be proud of His child and one day pick him up in His arms to feel His might as He holds us in love and compassion. The object is to live your whole life as a child under the Lord who matures to help teach their younger brothers and sisters how to be humble and understand their position. As I speak to you now, I have tears of joy because I feel the Lord's arms around me giving me comfort and security knowing He is in my heart. The Lord will fill you inside to a point it will overflow to the outside and surround you like words can never describe. There is power and glory in the Word of God, through Jesus Christ, beyond our comprehension.

I pray that you will open your heart as that child you are and begin to listen.

It breaks my heart to see so many people distorting the Holy Bible and not following the right direction. There is no other way than through Jesus Christ to reach God our Father in Heaven above. Many have begun to follow people of influence who are trying to lead others down a path of thinking everything is great in this world without recognizing sin or hell in the end. Many people have taken the good out of the Bible and left the bad to conform to what the world wants to hear and this is what I fear. If an individual claims that he is a Christian without recognizing Jesus Christ, then he is a false teacher or witness to the Truth of God. You must be able to speak your belief without holding back in worrying about other individual's thoughts. If you can't state who you are with Christ, then who do you really think you are? Don't neglect your purpose or become tolerant of allowing sin in your life, because this will only lead you to be hurt by words or actions that will affect the heart like a knife.

There is nothing worse than someone who is one way to this person and another way to the next. The Lord wants us to be consistent and true in our words and actions to every individual no matter their position. In (Revelations 3), the Lord tells us that individuals whom are neither hot nor cold will be spit out of His mouth.

The Lord plainly tells us how to act so why do so many people neglect the facts? The Lord is our shepherd and we are His children of the herd. Our position is to follow and free the Lords presence in His joy caring for every other individual as a loving brother and sister with no envy, but love in compassion for each other.

In the book of (Hebrews 13), we are given a better closing than what I can give in any form or fashion and in (Psalm 19), we are taught of how the law of the Lord is perfect, converting the soul with rejoicing the heart. May my life be living proof to you of God's glory and how someone lost can be restored with God in their heart guiding the way.

Don't ever feel down or you have no purpose to move forward in life. Many teachers and past people of influence have made predictions on the end of time and they were wrong in doing this. Because even Jesus said in (Matthew 24), **"that day and hour knoweth no man, nor the angels of Heaven."** God doesn't want us to live in fear, but treat everyday like it was our last. Because He knows our human character of becoming complacent and not being the best we can be on a daily basis. So what if it is tomorrow or thousands of years ahead as long as our hearts are right with God through Jesus Christ, there should be no worry, but only concern for every other lost soul in this world.

As I began to study the book of Revelation, I had these words placed on my heart, **"What has been said, has already been said and there will be no more."** In other words, enjoy life within your time and don't focus on the end. Focus on the new beginning knowing there is no end. All we can do is be watchful and be prepared in our hearts. The Lord has already given His direction and our destiny in His Word. There is mystery in time that has already been predetermined by God our Father in Heaven above. No man will ever know the time in which the Lord will show. Keep your hearts humble and close to the truth, for the Lord has given His Word and our future in the book of Revelation. When you become weak or may have doubts, go to the Lord in prayer to seek strength for your days ahead. No one is perfect and we all stumble and fall, but with Christ in our hearts we will be saved and spared at the end. So don't ever lose hope no matter the wait, but be thankful for everyday you receive to give glory to God helping those in need. Make the most of what you have and learn to appreciate life in every giving way.

Don't forget we are at a fork in the road in this country and we need to come together as one in repentance to find new strength with direction for our children's future. On numerous occasions throughout the Holy Bible, God showed His mercy when the people turned back to Him. In (Genesis 18), we need to recall a valuable lesson of pleading for our nation to be spared and begin to rebuild with purpose for children's future. How heart breaking it would be if we knew we could have done something when we did not. One way or the other, we are going to face in time, a title to a song sung by Otis Redding called "Change Is Gonna Come."

There is one other final lesson to share before we move to another chapter in life. In (Genesis 19), Lot's wife did not understand the importance of turning from sin. We are to learn from it and move forward without dwelling on the past. If all we do is look backwards, it will hinder our steps in moving forward. For the Lord Jesus is our shepherd and only He can deliver us from all evil in God's mercy and grace. All this is said out of love, not only for my family, but also for yours. And it is all to God's glory, in Jesus name I pray, Amen.

If you recall in the very first chapter of the book, I stated that my wife and I were sitting in our vehicle looking out over Pickwick Lake below the dam while everything was at peace. The Holy Spirit placed on my heart these words exactly out of nowhere when we were talking. I said, "You have something to give me that I lost so long ago." That was just over eight years go and this anniversary will be eight years and I'll be forty years old this December. Last week I received the answer to my statement above. I always thought it was family learning how to love again and give love to others in an affectionate way. That was only the physical part of what she had to give me that I lost so long ago. We both had something to give each other and even spread to others, but I know now the final answer to what I lost so long ago.

My heart has always believed and cried out in prayer since a young child being pushed aside or left alone. The Lord has heard my prayers and always been by my side even without my recognition until now. Here's the beautiful part of what she gave to me and from what I lost so long ago. The day of my self-surrender in Forrest City, Arkansas, I called prior to arrival on several occasions to confirm what I could bring and asked what to wear. Every time I spoke with someone I asked if I could bring my Bible and every time I was told "No" very rudely. The time had come for my arrival and I can never express the feeling of that walk across the parking lot. The day was cloudy and with a very light drizzle, more like a gentle mist. Everything was still, even the wind, and my wife and I walked into the foyer of the prison fighting back the tears.

As I stood there in our final goodbyes, I asked the officer once again at the front desk, "Can I bring my in bible with me?" She rudely said, NO! Then my wife and I stood there for our final goodbye hug having no clue of what lay ahead except for the fact that they told us there was no room at the camp and I was going to the medium prison to stay in the hole until they had a bed come open at the camp. In my heart I never worried or was I scared but I hurt for the love I had for my wife and children in having to leave them.

The moment arrived and another man came out front and told me, "It was time." I turned and asked one more time, "Can I please bring my bible with me?" He said, "yes", that will be fine!" The lady at the front desk spoke out against it, but the officer with me overruled her. My wife immediately ran out to her truck to get my bible to bring it to me. She came back in the entrance with her bible, mine was at home. But hers, with her name on the front cover was in her hand. *"This is where my wife gave me what I lost so long ago!"* She gave me back the "Word of God" which I had lost in my life, but have now found. My house has been restored and my prayers have been answered from that young child crying from the heart wanting a family and direction in my life. I have always been true in belief, but never before understood as I do now.

She gave me what I lost so long ago. And now is only the beginning of God's plan coming together for everything I've gone through in life. My life has been restored and the blessings exceed the cup that runneth over.

I can never begin to say thank you to my wife for her belief and strength, for she is a courageous woman. But I now know it was all part of God's plan to reveal His glory in my life ahead. The Lord's hand has always been with me but I never understood how to see it properly until now with my understanding from the Word of God and for the wisdom He not only gave, but still gives. Now my life-song sings glory from the heart.

My wife and I said our final goodbye and I never can give words for the pain in my heart in watching her walk back across that parking lot. It broke my heart as I can still see it now, as it was yesterday. We both were under the impression of me being taken to the hole at the medium security prison when we parted and my wife said she said a prayer in her truck with tears pleading from her heart for me to not go there. Little did she know at the time that the Lord answered her prayer immediately? While I was changing in that cold room, a man walked in and said you have five minutes to get changed and I'll carry you to an open bed at the camp. I moved very quickly and when he came back he asked me, "What was taking me so long?" I told him, "I was waiting on him, he wasn't waiting on me." Anyway, he carried me directly to the camp and all I had on was a jump suit and my wife's Bible in my hand. When a person walks in, everyone always stares at the new guy, but I walked in with my head up and with God's word in my hand for everyone to see in whom I believed.

There is <u>no fear</u> with God in your heart, and you can learn how to love like never before. Once you face the facts and accept the Truth in surrendering your heart to the Lord, He will then set you free in your understanding of how to believe. The time has come for this chapter in my life to end and for my new life to begin. To my wife, "<u>Thank you</u>." For giving me back what I lost so long ago, and I wonder what the Lord was thinking when "God Made You". I am sorry for what you have had to go through in all of this, but "I Cross My Heart" and promise to give to make all your dreams come true. Because you are like one of "The Seven Spanish Angels", and "Have I told You Lately That I Love You"?

And to my children, "He's My Son and She's My Cinderella", I promise to be honest and true. To teach and show love in everything I do. In life never quit, but learn how to overcome your wrongs to make things right. And this can be done with God guiding the way through your belief in Jesus Christ to give you the ultimate sight. Always know there is "A Glorious Day" and "Where Your Heart Belongs". Because "You're Not Alone", and "Stay Strong".

It is time to "Return to the River" in knowing my sins are now forgiven on the bottom of the "Ocean Floor". I know on my heart God will "Watch Over Me" because "You Raise Me Up To More Than I Can Be". It is "My Will: to serve the best I can and "All for the Glory of You" to "Tell Me the Story Again". Because "I Was Made to Love You and Be Loved By You".

"Here We Go", "Love Is Here" and "I Will Sing of Your Mercy" in my reflection of now being "Washed By The Water". "Even Though the Journey is long to The Mountain of God", "I'll Praise You More", and I ask you God, to "Speak To Me" and "Show Me Your Glory" for "I Am Yours And You Are Mine". In Jesus name I write and may these songs touch you as they have touched me.

To every other individual in life, I pray you understand this game of life and you hold on to that ball of life in Jesus Christ with all your might. Don't ever let someone take it from you and become lost as I did in my past. Always keep Jesus within sight and never take your eye off of the ball to feel the spirit of God's call. Listen to our Father in Heaven and allow your heart to be filled in serving the Lord's will. Never give up what you carry inside when times get out of balance and even when time may seem faint.

For the Lord is right beside you and with you, even when you can't see in all the darkness of this world, so no matter what you face, seek God and He will deliver you from this place.

All To God's Glory, In Jesus Name, I Pray. Amen.

* * *

My Prayer

Dear Almighty Father in Heaven above,

I seek you again today feeling your love. Lord I ask you to please give me understanding and wisdom in my task. Lord please bless me as I go forward in providing my needs, to reveal your glory and tell my life story. Reveal your works within my life most of all for your glory. Lord I ask you to hear my prayers and give me words as I pray for there are no words for what I feel in my heart in where it all starts. Lord I know you know my heart and I pray for strength to face what I have in my path, I can only do so much with my limitations. This is where I ask for your help because I can't do this without you. I thank you Lord for sending your Son, Jesus Christ, and for the beauty in your perfection within your creation. There is nothing more gracious then looking at the moves and patterns from big to small and I thank you Lord for allowing me to witness it all. You are my true Father, and I am honored to feel your presence in my life in hearing your call. Please Lord help me mature into the man you want me to be as I surrender my life to you in order to be set free. Please Lord forgive me of my sins and wrong thoughts. Lord I ask you to show me the way throughout my day.

In Jesus' Name, Amen

Closing

*O*kay, I must admit it is hard to stop something once you start, and I now know what Solomon meant in (Proverbs 1) in writing, **"Fear of the Lord is the foundation of true knowledge, but fools despise wisdom and discipline."** King Solomon teaches us great wisdom of God in Proverbs, Ecclesiastes, and Songs of Solomon in the Holy Bible. I pray that we all return to our roots of God, and take the time daily to study His Word. I urge you to read the book of Proverbs and apply it to your life, and learn where true wisdom comes from. Knowledge is one thing, but the wisdom of God will open doors for you like never before!!!

Now in my final closing, I would like to share with you how the love of God, in Jesus Christ, not only motivates people to reach higher levels, but even motivates animals when we teach and show love in our words and actions. This is a true short story that I hope touches your heart, as it will always touch mine and my families even when it is time for me to part. May God bless you and your family as He has blessed mine!!! Here's the final closing, before the new beginning of my life ahead.

My Dog Tram

Once there was a black lab named Tram. He was raised and originally trained with professional trainers. In his young years he was trained with discipline with little if any love in security of a solid home.

After reaching certain levels of awards at a young age, the trainers cast him out due to feeling he did not have what it took to be a champion retriever. Tram was passed from kennel to kennel with no love or affection, and no stability of a home.

When he was just over (3) years old, we purchased him to replace another black lab we lost named Tucker. Upon leaving the trainers home in our truck with the carrier in the back, the friend and trainer who located Tram for us through his contacts asked, "Don't you want to load him in the carrier you have in the back of your truck?" My wife and I both said "No thank you", and let him ride in the back seat of the truck in my son's lap. You wouldn't believe the smile on my son's face and you could feel the love between them both. Tram just laid there so delicately in my son's arms, like he knew he was finally home.

We went on to give Tram a home and I began working with him by expressing love and joy when he completed something before him. At night, I would work with him in the back yard to train him in two different ways of sight and smell, while I rewarded him with love in my arms for his reward.

Once Tram was ready, we sent him to a friend, who was a trainer to pursue the ultimate titles offered to hunting retrievers. After a season or two of going to the trainer's home and returning back to our home, Tram began to come alive in his performance due to knowing he was always coming home and received love.

The time had come to enter him into the Grande Championship which was a several day event. He did well, but eventually came to a test he failed. It was disappointing, but it did not change anything in our love or belief that he could be that champion we believed! Even when the first trainers or home cast him out in saying, "He did not have what it takes, and he would never be!" We loved Tram, and we would never give up our belief in him.

We continued to press on with more practice, and Tram becoming more comfortable going back and forth between our home and the trainers. Then Tram really came alive once he had no doubt of his security in a home, and knowing the one's who loved him would always be there for him! The time came again to re-enter the Grande Championship all over again. This time was different because Tram excelled beyond others disbeliefs and went on to capture that Grande Title because of the love and security he felt at home!

Not only did tram win this title once, but he is now a two time Grande Champion joining other retrievers in the 500 point hall of fame for hunting retrievers. He wasn't the most graceful dog or the best, but one thing Tram had above all the rest was his heart filled with love in wanting to please those around him, to feel the love in return. It wasn't the ribbons, the trophies, or all the other awards that made him happy. It was the love and security he received in a solid home giving him strength in his heart to do his part!!!

Tram is a true champion not only in the field, but at home with the family! And, all of this is only said to show and prove in never counting out anything with the power of love given through Jesus Christ in encouraging someone to reach all levels in life. Love has powers that go beyond mankind!!!

Personally, I don't know if I'll ever achieve the awards in this life like Tram did through love in reaching his goals before him. But I know beyond a doubt, there are far greater rewards in Heaven that will be there when I go home, and these same rewards are not only for me, but every other believer in Christ serving within Gods' will!!!

One thing though, I can relate first hand with the motivation and strength given through the security of a solid home full of love within the family! My home was broken and scattered as a child like Trams, and when the Lord brought my wife and I together in that blind date my eye's began to see all over again! I am honored to be a part of her family, and to learn the true meaning of never giving up when you stumble and fall. And to teach and give my children the home they deserve. With this I'm already a champion with now allowing God to control my life, but there is still much work to be done! To not only restore God in my family, but I pray to possibly help yours in some way!

Tram's time is almost up, and now mine is just beginning. I will always miss Tram once he's gone, but I'll always remember him for what he has shown to everyone in what is possible when we give love and forgiveness from the heart which Jesus teaches to each of us in the Holy Bible!

Sleep well in the arms of God! And may your days ahead be blessed in the love of Jesus Christ, guiding the way to reach the eternal rewards to receive peace in your rest! May these songs reach you as they reached me in this final word to "America" the sweet land of liberty feeling the "Healing Rain" in knowing "His Name Is Jesus" the author of liberty and justice for all! (In Jesus Name, Amen....)

Quick Order Form

Email: books@BalancedLifePublications.com

www.BalancedLifePublications.com

PLEASE NOTE: Credit cards accepted through the website with a PayPal buy link. http://www.BalancedLifePublications.com

Postal orders pay by check made out to: Balanced Life Publications, P.O. Box 166, Aberdeen, MS 39730

Please send more FREE information about:

☐ Other Books   ☐ Speaking and Seminars

_____

_____

Please send me:

Quantity: _____ *Special Delivery* books @ $24.00 ea $ _____ add $5 shipping and handling for 1 or 2 books. Please contact us for additional shipping charges. Quantity book sales available on special request. Contact us at books@balancedlifepublications.com for more information on our publications.

Name: _____

Address: _____

City/State/Zip: _____

_____

Phone: (   ) _____

Email: _____

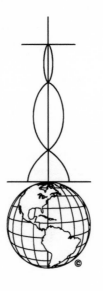

www.SpecialDeliveryBook.com

CPSIA information can be obtained at www.ICGtesting.com
Printed in the USA
LVOW060055020512

279915LV00001B/137/P